DATE DUE

Soc
Glc

Social Movements and
Global Social Change

Social Movements and Global Social Change

The Rising Tide

Robert K. Schaeffer

ROWMAN & LITTLEFIELD
Lanham • Boulder • New York • Toronto • Plymouth, UK

Published by Rowman & Littlefield
4501 Forbes Boulevard, Suite 200, Lanham, Maryland 20706
www.rowman.com

10 Thornbury Road, Plymouth PL6 7PP, United Kingdom

British Library Cataloguing in Publication Information Available

Library of Congress Cataloging-in-Publication Data
Schaeffer, Robert K.
Social movements and global social change : the rising tide / Robert K. Schaeffer.
pages cm
Includes index.
ISBN 978-1-4422-1489-7 (cloth : alk. paper) — ISBN 978-1-4422-1490-3 (pbk. : alk. paper) — ISBN 978-1-4422-1491-0 (electronic) 1. Social movements. 2. Social change. 3. Equality. 4. Globalization—Social aspects. I. Title.
HM881.S33 2014
303.48'4—dc23
2013047155

♾ ™ The paper used in this publication meets the minimum requirements of American National Standard for Information Sciences Permanence of Paper for Printed Library Materials, ANSI/NISO Z39.48-1992.

Printed in the United States of America

Let us realize that the arc of the moral universe is long, but it bends toward justice.
—Martin Luther King Jr.

Contents

Acknowledgments

This book grew out of a long political engagement with my partner Torry Dickinson, a community activist and educator, a collaboration with my colleague L. Frank Weyher, and the encouragement of Sarah Stanton, who asked me to submit a book proposal to Rowman and Littlefield. It drew on my experience growing up in Berkeley during the 1950s, 1960s, and 1970s, where I witnessed or participated in the free speech, civil rights, black power, antiwar, countercultural, youth, feminist, gay, and disabled movements. I took part in nonviolent protests and went to jail. During the 1970s, I worked for community, environmental, and democratic socialist movements and studied politics and sociology from a global, environmental, and world-system perspective at UC Santa Cruz and SUNY Binghamton. During the 1980s, I worked for Friends of the Earth, where I organized a union, and Greenpeace. I took my first academic job at San Jose State in 1990 and my second at Kansas State in 2000, and I have written a number of books about global social change and social movements. This book draws on my political experience in social movements and my research as a scholar. It owes a debt to the women and men who worked for change and shaped my life. Let me thank Claudia Carr, Nancy Chodorow, Torry Dickinson, Metta Spencer, Angela Gennino, Marianne Massenberg, Rainelle Burton, Jim Mellen, James Weinstein, Giovanni Arrighi, Immanuel Wallerstein, Marcus Rediker, Benedict Anderson, William Friedland, John Judis, Tom Turner, David Brower, Andre Carothers, and Joseph Rotblat. Let me also thank the graduate students in my classes on social movements, who challenged my ideas and gave me the opportunity to advance and reconsider them.

Chapter One

Social Movements and Global Social Change

Social movements have changed the world. During the past two hundred years, social movements overthrew monarchies, won independence from colonial empires, and founded republics in postcolonial states. They established "republics"—constitutional governments based on popular sovereignty—first in the United States and then in a majority of countries around the world. In some new republics, political factions established dictatorships and one-party regimes that denied people their rights and inflicted cruelties on them. In recent years, however, social movements fought successfully to overthrow many dictatorships and democratize a majority of the republics. Social movements also fought to expand citizenship in the republics. At first, only a small minority of the people in the republics could exercise suffrage and claim their rights as citizens. But social movements soon demanded that citizenship and suffrage be extended to others, and today a majority of residents in the republics claim citizenship.

These three developments—the rise of the republics, the democratization of the republics, and the expansion of citizenship in the republics—had important consequences. The demise of dynastic states brought an end to the ferocious rivalry for control of colonial empires that erupted in successive world wars. The fall of dictators brought an end to the dirty wars, gulags, and routine violence that regimes inflicted on subject populations. The expansion of citizenship curbed the violence of private, nonstate actors and restrained the violence deployed by state officials in the republics.

Although these developments were important achievements, global social change has been partial and incomplete. Dynastic rulers still cling to their thrones, dictatorships in many republics retain their grip on power, and citizenship has *nowhere* been granted to *all* the residents of *any* republic. The expansion of *liberty* has been accompanied by persistent *inequality*.

When thinking about social change, it is important to keep in mind *both* developments—growing liberty and persistent inequality—at the same time. To understand why social change resulted in these two contradictory developments, it is necessary to examine not only how social movements advanced and assisted social change but also how they obstructed, delayed, and compromised the meaning of social change.

STATES IN 1800

In 1800, most of the states in the interstate system were governed by dynastic monarchies. The kings and queens who ruled these states claimed their power as an inheritance and relied for their authority on the "divine right of kings." The United States was the only country in the world that identified itself as a "republic." This new republic differed from dynastic states in two respects. In a republic, the government derived its authority from the "people," not from "God," and was based on "popular sovereignty," not the "divine right" of kings. Moreover, the people used their sovereign authority to create a binding set of contractual agreements that defined relations between the people and the government. As a result, they created constitutional government based on popular sovereignty in the republic. By contrast, the rulers of dynastic states accepted no binding legal restrictions on their authority. Governments in dynastic states provided to their subjects only the privileges that kings and queens might allow.

During the next two hundred years, the idea of creating constitutional government based on popular sovereignty in a republic spread around the world. The subsequent rise of the republics was accompanied by the fall of dynastic states. Today, a vast majority of the 193 states that belong to the United Nations call themselves republics.[1] Only a handful of dynastic monarchies remain. The rise of the republics transformed the character of the capitalist interstate system from one dominated by dynastic states to one based on nation-state republics.

When republics were first established in the Americas, Europe, Africa, and Asia, military leaders and political parties frequently seized power and established dictatorships. They abrogated constitutions, dissolved legislatures, manipulated elections, looted public treasuries, and arrested, tortured, and murdered their opponents. But social movements in the republics eventually forced dictators from power and (re)established constitutional government based on popular sovereignty in a majority of the republics by the end of the twentieth century. Of course, dictators remain in power in many states, including China, the world's largest republic.[2] The democratization of the republics transformed the political character of republican governments around the world.[3]

When they first created republican government, the founders gave popular sovereignty to the "people." But the elite group of merchants, planters, landlords, industrialists, and professionals who organized constitutional government insisted that citizenship and suffrage be given to only a small group of people like themselves. In the United States, the elite "1 percent" who created constitutional government granted citizenship to adult, white, Protestant men with property, who made up only "10 percent" of the population. They then divided the vast majority—the "90 percent"—of people into two subordinate groups—"denizens" and "subjects"—who were assigned a different legal and social status.

People assigned to the "denizen" population—adult men without property, immigrants, women, and children—were given some rights but were denied citizenship, suffrage, or both. Although members of these groups have sometimes been described as "second-class" citizens, like passengers riding in coach on a train, they included immigrants, who were *residents* but not citizens, so it would be inappropriate to describe them as second-class *citizens*. Instead, they might be identified as "denizens," as residents with some but not all of the rights extended to citizens.

Of course, many people possessed few if any rights in the new republic. Convicts, sailors, indentured servants, and slaves were under the direct control of public officials or private authorities, the adult white men whose "liberty" consisted in part of dominion over others. The people who were placed under the control of public officials and private authorities might be identified as "subjects."

Because the men who designed constitutional government divided people into three groups, with a minority of citizens on top and a majority of denizens and subjects arranged below, the social structure of the new republic resembled a three-tiered pyramid. Of course, denizens and subjects objected to their subordinate status and fought to claim citizenship and suffrage in the

United States and in other republics. Their efforts slowly expanded citizen-ries within the republics. By 1920, a majority of the people living in the United States could claim citizenship and suffrage. Although the expansion of citizenship and suffrage inverted the pyramid and changed the *shape* of society in the republic, it did not change the social *structure* of inequality, which remained intact. Today, a large minority of residents in the republics remain as denizens (children and immigrants) and subjects (convicts, or-phans, and people with some mental disabilities or contagious diseases). Still, the expansion of citizenries within the republics transformed social and political life for people in republics around the world.[4]

These three developments—the rise of the republics, the democratization of the republics, and the expansion of citizenries within the republics—also contributed to a decline of violence among states and a reduction of violence by state officials and nonstate actors.

Why did these important global changes occur?

They occurred because diverse social movements struggled to create con-stitutional governments in colonial and postcolonial settings, because social movements fought to democratize the republics, and because social move-ments labored to expand citizenship within the republics.[5] Of course, they were not always or everywhere successful. Indeed, their work is far from done. Still, their collective efforts to change society have transformed the interstate system and the social contours and political practices of individual states around the world.

THE RISE AND DEMOCRATIZATION OF THE REPUBLICS

People living two hundred years ago would find it difficult to imagine that these changes could occur. At the time, constitutional government based on popular sovereignty was a novel and fragile political innovation.[6] In 1800, it had existed for only a few years in the United States, "a marginal republic perched on the edge of a vast continent on the fringes of the European commercial system."[7] In France, Napoleon Bonaparte had abruptly terminat-ed the Second Republic in 1799 and installed a dictatorship in its place. In Haiti, rebellious slaves successively defeated indigenous armies led by white planters and mulattoes and invading armies from Great Britain, Spain, and France and, in 1804, established a republic. But a foreign embargo and indigenous dictatorship prevented the nascent state from recovering from the brutal twelve-year war and consigned the postcolonial state to political isolation and economic penury.[8]

Despite these inauspicious beginnings, social movements subsequently fought to create republics around the world, first in the Americas during the nineteenth century, then in Europe during the first half of the twentieth century, and then, after World War II, across Africa and Asia. Today, a vast majority of the 193-plus states in the world identify themselves as republics.[9] Significantly, diverse political movements—capitalist, socialist, Islamic—all adhere to the principle of constitutional government, though they qualify it by describing their state as the "Republic of Korea" (capitalist), the "Socialist Republic of Vietnam" (socialist), and the "Islamic Republic of Pakistan" (Islamic).

Of course, the struggle to overthrow dynastic states and colonial empires around the world was a difficult and protracted process. Moreover, the rise of the republics was marred or compromised by three troublesome developments. First, some of the new republics, like their dynastic peers, conquered and colonized other people, engaging in "imperialist" behavior that compromised their stated commitment to popular sovereignty and the "rights of man." Second, dictators seized power in many republics, made subjects of their citizens, and prevented them from exercising popular sovereignty in any meaningful way. Third, great powers and indigenous groups partitioned postcolonial states or seceded from republican states and founded separate states of their own, a development that typically led to conflict within and between divided states and successor republics.[10]

After World War II, the two most powerful republics—the United States and the Union of Soviet Socialist Republics—together created the United Nations and other institutions to curb imperialism, prevent war, and promote decolonization, developments that contributed to the demise of dynastic states and the rise of republics in their place. Then, starting in the 1970s, the fall of dictators in capitalist countries in southern Europe, across Latin America, and in East Asia and the collapse of communist regimes in eastern Europe and the Soviet Union led to the widespread democratization of the republics, a process still under way in North Africa and the Middle East.[11] Unfortunately, the division and subdivision of states as a result of partition and secession accelerated during the past twenty years, most recently in Sudan.[12] In 2011, South Sudan seceded from Sudan and became an independent republic. But fighting has erupted between the two countries and between ethnic groups in South Sudan, where "heavily armed militias . . . are

6 *Chapter 1*

now marching on villages and towns with impunity, sometimes with genocidal intent. 'We will kill everyone,' the representative of one ethnic militia vowed. 'We are tired of them.'"[13]

Of course, imperialism, dictatorship, and the conflicts associated with partition are still problems in many republics. Nonetheless, the spread and democratization of the republics has transformed the interstate system from one dominated by dynastic empires and their colonial empires to one dominated by sovereign and increasingly democratic republics.

THE EXPANSION OF CITIZENSHIP

The rise and democratization of the republics was accompanied by the expansion of citizenship within the republics. Initially, the architects, the men who designed constitutional government, reserved citizenship—the right to exercise popular sovereignty and to vote, bear arms, represent oneself in court, acquire and dispose of property, and make contracts—to a *minority* of

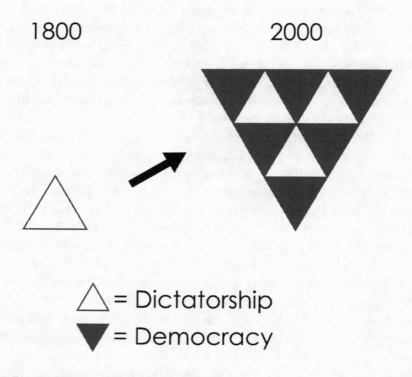

The Rise and Democratization of the Republics

residents in the republic. In the United States, they awarded citizenship only to adult, white, Protestant men with property, both as a matter of principle and of practice. In *principle*, they argued that citizenship should be restricted to responsible actors, to men capable of making rational political decisions without constraint (property ownership was thought to free men from coercion by landlords or employers). In *practice*, they believed that "liberty" for citizens was based, in part, on their dominion over others, the liberty to exercise their authority over wives, children, employees, servants, and slaves. So from the outset, the architects extended the rights associated with citizenship only to a minority of residents and denied some or all of these rights to a majority of people, who were divided into two large groups.

The architects gave some rights to "denizens," a group composed of women, children, and immigrants. People in this group were not allowed to vote, though they could sometimes inherit and dispose of property. Male children and immigrants might eventually become citizens when they reached their majority or if they naturalized. But authorities denied virtually all of the rights and opportunities associated with citizenship to "subjects." They made indentured servants, convicts, orphans, slaves, and people whom they viewed as threats to public health (people with mental disabilities or contagious diseases) or public safety (Native Americans, political dissidents, Japanese Americans) the subjects of state authorities. They also allowed *private* citizens the legal authority to control the denizens and subjects in their charge. By delegating state authority to nonstate actors, the architects gave husbands, fathers, employers, ship captains, and slave owners the right to assault, abuse, and even kill their wards without fear of legal consequence.

By dividing the populace and assigning groups different sets of rights, the architects created a pyramid-shaped, three-tiered social hierarchy. A minority of citizens sat on top of the pyramid. Denizens occupied the middle tier, and subjects formed the base of the pyramid. Together, denizen and subject populations made up a majority of residents in the early republics. [14]

During the next two hundred years, groups of denizens and subjects fought to claim citizenship. In the United States, for example, adult white men without property claimed citizenship in the early nineteenth century. Adult black men acquired citizenship in the mid-nineteenth century, and adult women, white and black, won citizenship in the early twentieth century, at least in the North. These successive expansions made citizenship available to a majority of people living in the republic. Over time and around the world, citizenship expanded in the republics, and today a majority of people in a majority of the republics count themselves as citizens. This was a significant achievement. Still, it is important to recognize that large groups of people (chiefly minors and immigrants) are still treated as denizens, and a large number of people (convicts, orphans, illegal aliens, and people with mental disabilities or contagious diseases) remain the subjects of state authority. The acquisition of liberty and equality by a majority of people in the republics has been accompanied by persistent and durable subordination and inequality for a minority of people.[15]

The rise of the republics resulted in the demise of dynastic states and their colonial empires, a development that transformed the interstate system. The expansion of citizenship within the republics reshaped the social contours of countries around the world. Still, the rise and democratization of the republics did not eliminate dynastic states (Saudi Arabia) or bring an end to dictatorships in the republics (China). Moreover, the expansion of citizenship did not eliminate denizen and subject populations in either residual dynastic states or in democratic republics (the United States, France).

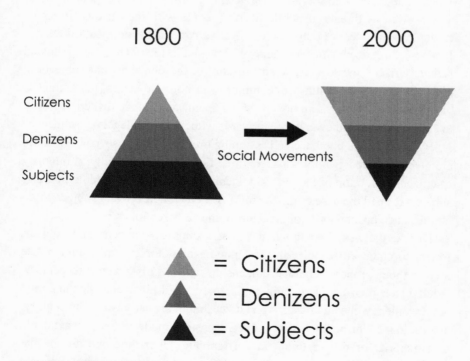

Social Change and Social Movements

Why has liberty and equality advanced? Why has subordination and inequality endured? The argument here is that social movements have been responsible for *both* developments. To understand the totality of global social change, it is necessary to examine the role that social movements have played in both advancing and retarding change. Social change during the past two hundred years has been the product of a multisided struggle among different types of social movements.

SOCIAL MOVEMENTS

The architects of constitutional government in the republics invited citizens to exercise popular sovereignty in the new republics. They also invited people in dynastic states to create republics in which they might exercise popular sovereignty and claim "the rights of man." In the republics, citizens organized political parties and social movements to claim the opportunities provided by institutions in the state and civil society. Of course, the architects did not extend this invitation to denizens and subjects, whom they regarded as incapable of responsibly exercising popular sovereignty. Nevertheless, denizens and subjects in the republics and in dynastic states and their colonies fought to claim the rights and opportunities associated with citizenship, even though they were not invited or permitted to do so.

Early on, three *types* of social movements emerged: aspiring, altruistic, and restrictionist. These three types of movements have defined the field of social movements around the world during the past two hundred years. Like the "ideal types" used by Max Weber and Emile Durkheim, these types identify movements that mark the boundaries or corners of the field. As a practical matter, particular social movements have often combined features from different types of movements and drawn participants from different corners of the field. Moreover, different types of social movements have often changed their character or location on the field over time. Many aspiring movements have adopted restrictionist positions once they became citizens or acquired state power.

Aspiring Movements

Denizens and subjects have frequently organized aspiring movements in response to the inequalities imposed on them by state officials and private authorities. They have fought to create republics in dynastic states and colo-

Altruistic   Restrictionist

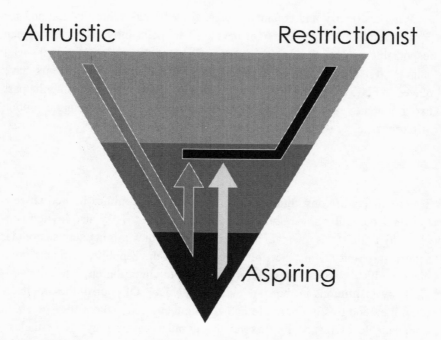

Aspiring

Types of Social Movements

nial empires, struggled to democratize republics, and demanded that citizenship be expanded to include subaltern groups. Historically, *status*-based "nationalist" movements such as Sinn Fein and the Indian National Congress and *class*-based "socialist" movements such as the Bolsheviks and the Chinese Communist Party fought to create republics, while Solidarity in Poland and the African National Congress in South Africa struggled to democratize them. In the United States, slaves, workers, feminists, and civil rights activists fought to expand citizenship and participate as equals in civil society and in state institutions. The upward thrust of aspiring movements has propelled social change around the world. Aspiring movements sometimes acted alone, but they were sometimes assisted by altruistic movements. In altruistic movements, people from higher-status categories (citizens and denizens) assisted subordinate groups (denizens and subjects).

Altruistic Movements

Citizens and denizens have often assisted subordinate groups who lacked the legal standing, political capacity, or economic resources they needed to act effectively on their own behalf. It may be difficult for subaltern groups (denizens or subjects) to organize politically without triggering a response by state officials and private surrogates who have been authorized to use violence to defend the social hierarchy. Historically, the altruistic movements from "above," which collaborated with people from "below," included male citizens who supported women's suffrage, female denizens who participated in movements to abolish the slave trade and slavery, and citizens who organized on behalf of incarcerated prisoners and death-row inmates, battered women, and trafficked children. They have included "relief" organizations such as the Red Cross, Oxfam, and Doctors without Borders; legal aid groups such as the American Civil Liberties Union and the National Association for the Advancement of Colored People; and resource-mobilizing, philanthropic organizations such as the Rockefeller, Gates, and Soros Foundations.

Although altruistic movements have been motivated by an aversion to injustice, they have also been motivated by self-interest, which has complicated their relations with subaltern groups and aspiring social movements. In recent years, some scholars have excluded altruistic movements from the study of social movements, arguing that their privileged status makes it difficult or impossible for them to appreciate the lived experience or "standpoint" of less-privileged groups or to meaningfully assist them. Many scholars assume that people in social movements act rationally in their own self-interest. If they act on behalf of others, they may be doing so either because they are acting against their own self-interest, which is irrational, or because they are really acting in their own self-interest but are doing so covertly, which is dishonest. Either way, many scholars often treat altruistic movements, which they describe as "conscience constituents," as unreliable social actors or as ineffective agents of real social change.

But altruistic movements should be included in the study of social movements both because they have, for better or worse, collaborated with aspiring movements and because they have contributed to significant social change.

Restrictionist Movements

Social change has also been shaped by restrictionist movements that opposed the creation of constitutional government, imposed dictatorship and resisted democratization in the republics, fought to prevent the extension of citizenship to denizens and subjects, and worked to preserve social *in*equality as a political principle and social practice. Their collective efforts have changed the direction, slowed the pace, and compromised the meaning of social change. Their work has ensured that the structure of social inequality remains *intact*. They have frequently used the authority given them by the state to engage in collective or individual violence against subordinate groups, or they have assumed their authority without official license, engaging in extralegal or vigilante violence to defend social hierarchy and inequality.

Historically, restrictionist movements have included the Sons of Liberty, the Ku Klux Klan, and the Tea Party; prohibitionists and Mothers against Drunk Driving; fascists, the Taliban, and the Catholic Church; Fox News and the Heritage Foundation; and the National Association of Manufacturers and sometimes the American Federation of Labor.

For the most part, sociologists have excluded restrictionist movements, what Sidney Tarrow called "the ugly movements," from the study of social movements.[16] By defining social movements as "antiauthoritarian" challengers, scholars have excluded "pro-authoritarian" or restrictionist movements from the field, largely because they seek to preserve authority, defend inequality, and deny power to denizens and subjects. But restrictionist movements should be included because they have shaped the pace, direction, and meaning of social change. Also note that when aspiring movements acquired citizenship, they often adopted restrictionist views and prevented others (children, immigrants, orphans, and convicts) from acquiring comparable rights.

ACTORS AND ACTIVITIES

Participants in aspiring, altruistic, and restrictionist movements created bureaucratic organizations that enabled them to conduct strikes, stage protests, and wage war with their opponents on an ongoing basis. They also acted alone, as individuals, or as participants in informal social networks to engage in a wide range of activities—filing lawsuits, conducting hunger strikes, setting themselves on fire, migrating, and rioting—to express their anger and their determination to make social change. By focusing on the activities or "repertoires" of formal social movement *organizations*, many scholars have downplayed the contribution to change that disorganized actors and social networks have made. But there is little doubt that people alone or in social networks have contributed to real social change. For instance, the 1958 lawsuit filed by Richard and Mildred Loving, an interracial couple who were arrested in Virginia for violating the state's law against interracial marriage ("The Racial Integrity Act"), eventually persuaded the US Supreme Court to strike down restrictionist laws in sixteen states and allow interracial couples to marry.[17] The individuals who filed lawsuits that led to Supreme Court decisions in the *Dred Scott* case, *Plessy v. Ferguson*, *Brown v. Board of Education*, and *Roe v. Wade* contributed to social change and persuaded other people to participate in abolitionist, civil rights, and pro-choice and pro-life movements and organizations.

Individual protesters have often ignited significant social change. In India, Anna Hazare conducted a hunger strike in 2011 to force the government to adopt anticorruption legislation. In Tunisia, Mohamed Bouazizi, a street vendor, set himself on fire to protest his mistreatment by police. His suicidal protest in December 2010 ignited widespread antigovernment protests that led to the fall of the dictatorship and to elections for a democratic government. During the late nineteenth and early twentieth centuries, individual anarchists who believed that dramatic acts of violence would incite widespread revolt assassinated the czar of Russia (1881), the president of France (1894), the empress of Austria (1898), the king of Italy (1900), the president of the United States (1902), and the archduke of Austria-Hungary (1914).[18] Although these assassinations did not immediately trigger revolt, the archduke's murder led to World War I, which contributed to revolutions in Ireland and Russia.

People who belong to social networks have also contributed to social change. Long before Facebook, people have encouraged their friends, relatives, and associates to engage in activities that resulted in change. The fifteen Buddhist monks who in 2012 set fire to themselves to protest the Chinese regime's policies in Tibet and died as a result might have belonged to a social network that adopted suicide as a form of protest.[19] People in social networks have also used desertion and migration as a form of protest. Slaves in the US South escaped their captors and fled, individually and in groups, to the North and to freedom. Sailors deserted ships. Indentured servants, Benjamin Franklin among them, deserted their masters and struck out on their own. Although scholars have not treated flight or migration as one of the "repertoires" of social movements, deserters, fugitives, and political refugees have contributed to social change. The flight of slaves contested the slave owners' authority over fugitive slaves in the North and contributed to North-South conflict and, eventually, civil war. The exodus of dissidents from East Germany in 1989 led to the collapse of the communist regime. Demographers now treat migration less as the product of individual choice and more as the product of political and economic decisions made collectively by members of informal social networks. In light of this, desertion, flight, and migration should be seen as repertoires that social networks used to make change.

Of course, it may be difficult to distinguish between actions by individuals and members of social networks. What should we make of the "107 Tunisians [who] tried to kill themselves by self-immolation in the first six months after [Mohamed] Bouazizi's death"?[20] Were these the actions of individuals acting alone, like the anarchist assassins? Or were they members of social networks that encouraged this practice, like the Buddhist monks? We don't yet know. This book is designed to encourage students and scholars to ask these kinds of questions and discover possible answers. The book provides a framework to help people begin that process and determine the origins of social movements that advanced, assisted, and resisted social change.

People sometimes took action as individuals and as members of informal social networks because they could make forceful demands for change without exposing themselves to the risks associated with joining formal organizations. Remember that it was often illegal for denizens and subjects to join formal organizations or engage in public protest. If they did, state and private authorities could identify, arrest, or assault them. During the Great Mutinies of 1797, striking British sailors purposely avoided creating a union or other formal organization because they wanted to prevent participants from being identified as mutineers by the authorities and then immediately hanged.[21] To avoid retribution, denizens and subjects have often refused to join formal organizations and have instead engaged in protests—mutiny, riot, migration—that provided them with a degree of anonymity and protection from assault. The people who recently joined the protests in public squares across North Africa avoided joining dissident *organizations* because to do so might invite a visit from the regime's secret police. Instead, they joined mass rallies and riots because the crowd allowed them to participate anonymously and because it provided some protection from violent assault by state police and private thugs.

It is important to appreciate how individuals, social networks, and formal organizations have employed a wide range of activities—lawsuits, hunger strikes, self-immolations, assassinations, mutinies, riots, desertions, marches, demonstrations, and armed rebellion—to express their anger, publicize their demands, recruit others to their cause, and persuade or force public and private authorities to make social change.[22]

MOVEMENT GOALS

During the past two hundred years, diverse types and kinds of social movements have engaged in a wide range of activities to secure "liberty, equality, and fraternity," at least for themselves. Scholars have paid more attention to the first two goals—liberty and equality—than to fraternity, or the solidarity provided by real or fictive communities. They have neglected struggles for community because they viewed these efforts as nonpolitical or reactionary. After all, many movements resist social change because they think it will undermine the solidarity that their community provides. But they should be included for two reasons. First, movements built communities to protect themselves from the rapid social change associated with capitalist development on a world scale. In this context, community building was a *response* to social change. Second, they built communities to create the social networks that could provide them with the human and economic resources they needed to survive. These *non*political social networks could then be mobilized to press for social and *political* change. In this sense, community building *advanced* social change. For example, the communities provided by the Catholic Church have been mobilized by aspiring movements (the United Farm Workers), altruistic movements (Catholic Charities), and restrictionist movements (anti-abortion, anti-contraception, anti–gay marriage groups). African American churches provided sanctuary (in both the literal and figurative sense) to participants in the early civil rights movement and provided the *private* resources that parishioners needed to sustain *public* protests.

The political scientist Robert Putnam famously argued that participation in private, apolitical bowling leagues contributed to participation in public, *political* activities and organizations. Still, it is important to take a broad view of the diverse goals that different types of social movements have adopted around the world.

SOCIAL CHANGE *AND* SOCIAL MOVEMENTS

The approach advanced here has several distinctive features. First, it starts with social change. It identifies a significant set of global social changes—the spread and democratization of republics in the interstate system and the expansion of citizenries within them—and argues that social movements have been collectively responsible for making change. Starting with social change invites scholars and students to identify the social movements that shaped change, analyze their activities in relation to other movements, and examine the role they collectively played in advancing and/or retarding change. This strategy differs from the approach taken by many scholars, who start by examining a particular movement and then try to determine what change might have resulted from its activities or repertoires, an empirical task that has proved difficult. As Sidney Tarrow admitted, it has not been "particularly fruitful [for scholars] to examine the outcomes of single social movements on their own."[23] By starting with social change, it is easier then to determine how social movements contributed to change.

Second, this approach takes a very broad view of social change and social movements, examining global social change and social movements during the past two hundred years. It invites scholars and students to examine different types of movements (aspiring, altruistic, and restrictionist) that took diverse forms (individuals, social networks, formal organizations, and political parties), engaged in a wide range of activities (lawsuits and petitions, riot and migration, protest and insurrection), adopted a variety of goals (liberty, equality, and solidarity), and created political institutions to realize them (constitutional government based on popular sovereignty in a republic).

Moreover, this perspective invites scholars and students from different disciplines—history, sociology, political science, economics, women's studies, and ethnic studies—to contribute to a comprehensive understanding of global social change and social movements around the world. By and large, scholars regard their colleagues in other disciplines as strangers, aliens, or foreigners. They need to introduce themselves to one another's work and treat one another as friends and collaborators.

The ideas advanced here are not proprietary. I do not intend to patent and protect the ideas outlined here but instead offer them as "open-source code" that might help scholars and students to develop their own research applications and use their investigations to test and rebut the theories and arguments made here.

Third, this approach provides an optimistic view of social movements and social change. The rise and democratization of the republics and the expansion of citizenship has been a positive development. Still, these developments have been accompanied by persistent and durable inequalities. As a result, it suggests that scholars and students take an optimistic view about global social change, a perspective that is tempered by a realistic appreciation of its limits.

The next chapter examines the emergence of constitutional government based on popular sovereignty in the United States, the first republic of the modern era. Chapter 3 looks at the rise of the republics, the decline of dynastic empires and their colonies, and the creation of a new, republican interstate system after World War II. Chapter 4 examines two problems that have plagued the republics since their inception: dictatorship and division. Chapter 5 looks at the successive waves of democratization around the world during the postwar period, a process that continues today in North Africa and the Middle East. Chapter 6 looks at the expansion of citizenship during the nineteenth and early twentieth centuries. Although some groups ascended into the citizenry, other groups, who were seen as threats to public safety or public health, were driven downward into denizen and subject populations. Chapter 7 examines the trajectory of these "descendants" and the "remainders," groups of people who remained in the assigned places throughout this period. These two chapters explore the complex character of social change in the United States. Chapter 8 looks at efforts by the civil rights, youth, feminist, and homosexual movements to expand citizenship during the postwar period and at recent efforts to extend citizenship to immigrants.

Chapter 9 examines the relation between social movements and global social change. Chapter 10 examines aspiring social movements and some of the problems they have encountered. Altruistic movements are examined in chapter 11 and restrictionist movements in chapter 12. The book concludes with a critical discussion of social movement theories and suggests how the framework advanced in this book might contribute both to academic research and to social change.

Chapter Two

The New Republic

In 1776, white settlers in thirteen of the British colonies in North America fought to establish an independent state where they could practice constitutional government based on popular sovereignty for "the people," a term they used to describe themselves. Although many "people"—men and women without property, indentured servants, slaves, and Native Americans—also fought for liberty, they did not immediately win their freedom. "The only 'people' who mattered in public affairs [after the revolution] were mainly taxpayers, freeholders, and Christians of a particular Protestant persuasion," George Billias observed.[1] The ruling-class architects of change then invited the citizens of the new state to exercise popular sovereignty through representative institutions. By calling the new state a republic, the architects laid claim to a classical institution from antiquity, which gave their project legitimacy and at the same time introduced a novel form of government that they believed would, in future, replace the dynastic state as the basic political institution of the capitalist interstate system. In short, they championed an institution from the *past* to shape a new political *future*.

Why did the architects fight to create constitutional government based on popular sovereignty in an independent republic? They did so to address economic and political problems created by the earlier emergence of a capitalist world-economy and a capitalist interstate system based on dynastic European states.

Capitalists and state officials in Europe discouraged the ascent of capitalists in their colonies, which were tasked with providing resources to European states. The adult male merchants, manufacturers, financiers, and landowners who employed workers, servants, and tenants, who possessed slaves, and who kept women and children in the American colonies viewed this as a problem. As a solution, they demanded the creation of an independent state that could provide them with the resources and protection they needed to improve their place within the capitalist world-economy.

Although dynastic states in Europe sometimes provided domestic ruling classes with access to state institutions and parliaments, they prevented their subjects in the colonies from accessing political power in European home-lands. As a result, the ruling classes in the American colonies argued that their political status was not commensurate with their economic power and that they were deprived of political rights given to their economic peers in European homelands. Moreover, the rulers of dynastic states could deprive their colonial subjects of their life, liberty, and property without cause. The ruling classes in the American colonies complained that their weak political status made them vulnerable, as subjects, to arbitrary authority, and this made it difficult for them to defend their economic status.

To remedy these problems, the architects wanted to create a state that would *contractually* guarantee their access to its political institutions (consti-tutional government), recognize their right as citizens, not subjects, to exer-cise political power through the state (popular sovereignty), and provide legal mechanisms to arbitrate disputes and prevent authorities from depriving them of their liberty or property without cause or legal recourse (the rule of law). In short, they advanced constitutional government based on popular sovereignty and the rule of law in an independent republic to address the economic and political problems associated with being the colonial subjects of a dynastic state in the capitalist world-economy.

The men who designed constitutional government moved toward these goals in stages. At a series of congresses, conventions, and conclaves, the architects negotiated a series of contractual agreements that created a basic operating system for the new republic—think of the Declaration of Indepen-dence as Republic 1.0, the first state constitutions as 2.1, 2.2 . . . 2.13, the Articles of Confederation as 3.0, the Constitution as 4.0, the Federalist Papers as 4.5, and the Bill of Rights and other constitutional amendments as 5.1, 5.2, and so on.[2] By designing a *proprietary* operating system, they slowly created a sovereign state, provided citizens with secure access to power, and defined their rights in relation to the state and one another.

The architects who designed this new operating system distrusted "fac-tion" and feared the "multitude." They worried that citizens might band together around their own special or separate interests as members of the ruling class, take power, and use the state against other members of the ruling class. They also feared that the masses, the majority of people who were not admitted to these conclaves, might capture the state and use it to deprive the ruling-class minority of its political authority and economic power.

To prevent a "faction" from seizing state power, the architects *divided government* into separate branches and created firewalls between them so that a faction trying to hack into the system would be able to seize one part without compromising the integrity or security of the whole system.

To prevent the "multitude" from seizing power, the architects *divided civil society*. They reserved citizenship for a minority (adult, white, Protestant men of property), denied citizenship to the majority of residents, and divided them into denizen and subject populations, each with their own divisions and subdivisions. Moreover, the architects *armed* this privileged citizenry and gave state militias and nonstate actors the authority to use violence against denizens and subjects, in public and private settings, to protect the state and the citizen minority from the multitude.

As a result, the architects created a civil society in which citizens were invited to exercise popular sovereignty through political parties and social movements. In France, the architects extended this invitation more broadly and encouraged not only citizens but also denizens and subjects to organize social movements to claim "the rights of man."

To appreciate these developments, it is important to describe the economic and political context in which the republics first emerged.

THE RISE OF THE CAPITALIST WORLD-ECONOMY AND THE INTERSTATE SYSTEM

During the long sixteenth century (1450–1650), capitalists and state officials in western Europe created a capitalist world-economy in Europe and the Americas.[3] Capitalists located in western European states organized a global division of labor that allowed them to obtain a disproportionate share of the wealth produced by the slaves, Indians, sharecroppers, yeoman farmers, and wage workers who produced commodities in the near periphery in eastern and southern Europe and in the periphery in the Americas.[4] This structural inequality, which resulted in "the concentration of advantages in one zone of the world-system [the core] and the concentration of negative effects in the [periphery]," became a characteristic feature of the capitalist world-economy that subsequently incorporated the rest of the world. [5]

As the gains and losses from this new economic environment became apparent to its participants—wealth and power for some, penury and slavery for most—capitalists struggled to achieve two political goals. First, they fought to capture states that would serve their economic interests. Second, they struggled to prevent capitalists in *other* states from capturing the emerging world-economy and imposing the rule of a single state over the world-economy, which would have transformed it into a world empire monopolized by a single political entity, like Rome or China.

In the Netherlands and England, aristocrats and merchant capitalists joined forces and collaborated to capture *existing* dynastic states. [6] They then demanded that states provide them with economic protection and subsidies that would help them compete in the world-economy, raise armies and navies to capture colonies and protect them from economic and political rivals, create efficient bureaucracies that could mobilize public economic resources without imposing burdensome costs on them in the form of either corruption or taxes, provide political mechanisms to settle disputes among different ruling-class factions, which had separate interests, and create a "balance of interests among owner-producers such that a working [coalition] . . . [formed] the stable underpinnings of such a state." [7]

When they captured state power, the new ruling-class coalition did not destroy the dynastic political institutions and state structures of "feudal" states. Instead, they kept dynastic institutions intact and made only minor modifications to political relations. They extended power to people based not only on "privilege" (the aristocracy) but also on "merit" (the bourgeoisie), and they directed states' structures to provide public resources (subsidies, armies, bureaucracies, revenues, parliaments, and courts) to private entities. Essentially, capitalist classes sought state power so that they could obtain public resources—subsidies, armies, bureaucracies, parliaments—that private wealth alone could not provide. *Private* entrepreneurs used state power to leverage vast amounts of *public* wealth and power.

They were content to borrow dynastic states because "old" institutions provided political legitimacy to a "new" group of stakeholders (the aristocratic-bourgeois alliance) and because these institutions promoted *in*equality as a political and economic principle, which helped them rationalize the rule of the few over the many.

The ruling-class coalitions that captured state power in the Netherlands and England persuaded state officials to act more effectively on their behalf than ruling classes in Spain, Portugal, and France. In these latter states, dynastic bankruptcies crippled domestic ruling classes. For example, the Spanish government repudiated its debts in 1557, 1575, 1596, 1607, 1627, and 1647.[8] Bankruptcy ruined capitalist monetary institutions and undermined their ability to finance trade. Eventually, state officials found it impossible to borrow the money they needed to raise armies, fight wars, and protect the economic interests of indigenous ruling classes. Entrepreneurial classes also found it difficult to enlist the state on their behalf because other factions of the ruling class—conservative aristocratic landlords, a Catholic clergy that pushed the Inquisition to the top of the state's political agenda, and "a parasitical court bureaucracy"—demanded that the state serve their parochial interests first.[9] As a result, "Spain did not erect . . . the kind of state machinery which would allow the dominant classes in Spain to profit from the creation of a European world-economy, despite the central geographical position of Spain in the world-economy in the sixteenth century."[10] Because entrepreneurial classes in Spain, Portugal, and France were unable to persuade the state to serve their interests, they were subsequently assigned subordinate economic roles in the world-economy.

As the world-economy expanded, the capitalist classes that shaped economic development struggled to capture states that could serve their economic interests. They also fought to prevent the world-economy from being captured by a single state and transformed into a world empire.

During the long sixteenth century, Spain used bullion from its American colonies to finance its efforts to create an empire that might monopolize the world-economy. But costly military expenses bankrupted Spain in 1557. Dutch armies subsequently defeated Spanish forces in the Netherlands in 1575, and English ships destroyed the Spanish Armada in 1588. By the end of the century, Spanish efforts to monopolize the world-economy collapsed.[11]

In 1648, competing states in Europe agreed to recognize one another as sovereign or independent states in the Peace of Westphalia.[12] This treaty was significant because it created an interstate system that counted multiple dynastic states in Europe as its members. Henceforth, the capitalist world-economy would be controlled by *many* states, not just *one*. Although Napoleon, Hitler, and Tōjō subsequently tried to capture the world-economy and create empires to rule over it, other states successfully combined to defeat them and restore balance to the system.

Since 1648, the constituent members of the interstate system combined in different ways to prevent individual states and factions or groups of states from acquiring too much economic or political power in the system. Political scientists have argued that states combined in different ways to maintain a political balance of power in the world because it ensured that the world-economy was controlled by *many* states.

Some states—the Netherlands, Great Britain, and the United States—achieved a hegemonic or superpower status in the interstate system. But their dominance was temporary, and they did not attempt to change the *multi*state character of the capitalist interstate system or create a global empire.

According to Immanuel Wallerstein, the creation of a capitalist world-economy and a capitalist interstate system composed of multiple dynastic states were the two "central institutional achievements of historical capitalism" in the early modern period. [13] There would soon be a *third* institutional innovation. The creation in 1776 of constitutional government based on popular sovereignty in a republic was an innovation that eventually transformed the political and social *character* of capitalist states in the interstate system from one based on dynastic states to one based on nation-state republics.

DOUBLE TROUBLE: COLONIAL SUBJECTS IN DYNASTIC STATES

The creation of a capitalist world-economy and a dynastic interstate system were significant economic and political achievements. But they created problems both for ruling classes in dynastic states in Europe and for ruling classes in their overseas colonies.

When ruling classes in Europe captured dynastic states, they kept dynastic legal systems intact. This meant that their *rights* as subjects of dynastic rulers were based on traditional and customary *privileges* granted by the king and could be revoked. As a result, ruling-class subjects were vulnerable to arbitrary authority, which might deprive them of their life, liberty, or property. This was a problem for individual subjects of the king, even wealthy ones, both in Europe and in the colonies, because they had no real legal recourse if dynastic rulers took action against them.

Still, while ruling classes were the subjects of kings in Europe, they fought to obtain access to state power though parliaments, which they used to promote their collective and individual interests. [14] But in the colonies, the king's subjects were denied access to the levers of power and representative institutions in dynastic states. Ruling classes in the American colonies of dynastic states were therefore *doubly* disadvantaged: they were *subjects* of the king and also *subjects* of political institutions in dynastic European states. In the Declaration of Independence, ruling classes in America objected to being both the subjects of the king *and* the subjects of Parliament.[15]

Political philosophers such as Jean-Jacques Rousseau and John Locke suggested a set of solutions to these problems. First, they recommended that elites create a new "social contract" with a made-to-order, not a hand-me-down, state, a "republic" that would serve their particular needs, what they called "the common good of the people."[16] Second, they argued that political authority be derived from the "popular sovereignty" of the people, which was made up of free citizens, not from the divine right of kings. As Gordon S. Wood observed, the word "subject is derived from the Latin words, *sub* and *jacio*, and means one who is under the power of another; but a citizen is a unit of a mass of free people, who, collectively, possess sovereignty."[17] Third, Rousseau argued that the people should be given *contractual*, legal protection of their rights as citizens of the republic *and* guaranteed access to state power through representative institutions. "Rousseau identified republican government with the rule of law, under the sovereignty of the people, when they act to serve the common good," Sellers explained.[18] Essentially, a new relation between the people and the state should be based on a set of constitutional agreements, voluntarily made.[19]

The idea of creating contractual or constitutional government based on popular sovereignty in an independent republic took root first in the colonies of America. It did so in part because settler merchants and planters in the British colonies had come to rely on formal contractual agreements to regulate and define their economic relations. As the geographical space of the world-economy grew, it became increasingly difficult for participants to rely on informal, oral agreements to conduct business. Participants increasingly relied on formal, written, and binding contractual agreements to conduct business and secure their respective rights and property, in good times and in bad. They preferred written contracts that could be tested and enforced by the courts, which provided a mechanism for the resolution of disputes between parties. As Gordon Wood observed, "In the increasingly commercialized eighteenth century, contracts became much more voluntary, explicit, and consensual, much less declaratory of previously existing rights and duties and much more the consequence of conscious acts of will . . . contracts came to be thought of as positive bargains deliberately and freely entered into between two parties who were presumed to be equal but not entirely trustful of one another. Such formal written contracts made sense in the emerging commercial world."[20]

The growing role of contractual agreements to define *economic* relations gave rise to the idea that contracts might also be used to define *political* relations. Moreover, the British decision to *charter* the new colonies allowed American settlers to draw up constitutions and practice parliamentary politics. This provided the settlers with contractual templates that they subsequently adopted for their own collective use.[21]

CONSTITUTIONAL GOVERNMENT: A NEW POLITICAL OPERATING SYSTEM

In 1776, an alliance of white settlers, planters, merchants, farmers, and artisans in the American colonies announced their determination to withdraw from the British Empire and establish an independent republic in the thirteen colonies. The coalition that met in Philadelphia included free traders and smugglers who objected to the British navigation acts and the restrictions they imposed on American trade, land grabbers who coveted lands possessed by American Indians and foreign empires outside the colonies and objected to the territorial limits set by the British on the colonies, tax evaders who objected to taxes imposed on them by the British to pay for their collective defense, slaveholders who objected to British efforts to restrict or abolish the slave trade, and settlers who supported increased immigration and the rapid naturalization of new immigrants and objected to British restrictions on both. They wanted a government that would lay claim to lands west and south of the Appalachians, treat with Indians, open trade with other countries, encourage the rapid immigration and naturalization of foreign workers, provide aid to domestic industry, and protect them from predatory dynastic states in Europe, which possessed adjacent lands in North America.[22]

Although the settlers struck for independence, they might instead have demanded representation in Parliament, like the Irish later achieved, or the creation of an indigenous parliament, where they could practice a limited form of self-government in a wider commonwealth, as English settlers in Canada and Australia later achieved. But they decided not to settle for anything less than independence, and the British government was not yet ready to grant political concessions to colonial subjects.

In the Declaration of Independence, the settlers made two sorts of complaints. First, they argued that the king had denied them access to state power by depriving them of representative institutions in the colonies and in England, for example, by rejecting colonial laws and dissolving colonial legislatures. Second, they argued that the king visited "repeated injuries" on his subjects by quartering troops, imposing taxes, restricting trade, depriving people of their rights without benefit of trial, impressing sailors, and setting "the merciless Indian Savages" on them. In short, they objected both to being subjects of the king and to being the colonial subjects of Parliament. Because the king had broken the implicit social contract that bound him to his colonial subjects—the king "has abdicated Government here, by declaring us out of his protection and waging war against us"—the settlers declared the existing social contract null and void.[23] As Richard Brown observed, the king "had broken the contract that made men subjects. They were therefore free to create a new allegiance."[24]

The architects of the new republic created a new social contract in stages. George Billias has persuasively argued that the "complete expression of American constitutionalism derives not from a single document but rather from a collection of six texts written between 1776 and 1791" that together formed "a kind of 'supertext.'"[25] Using a more contemporary vernacular, the architects created different versions of a proprietary "operating system" that was collectively owned by the ruling class, by "the people." The Declaration of Independence (1.0) created an independent republic; the first state constitutions (2.0, 2.1, 2.2 . . . 2.13) provided contractual government with applications specific to each state; the Articles of Confederation (3.0), a clunky attempt at federalism, created a framework that was subsequently reengineered in the Constitution (4.0), which consolidated federal powers and also divided them into separate branches; the Federalist Papers (4.5) provided arguments for adopting the Constitution; and the Bill of Rights (5.1, 5.2, 5.3, etc.) protected individual rights from attack either by "factions" or by the "multitude."[26]

The architects who designed and introduced the new versions of this operating system hoped to create a new social contract that expressed their "collective will," as Rousseau suggested, and establish a durable "will and testament," a legacy for their heirs. Although contractual government was the product of voluntary agreement by its architects, their heirs and assigns were *not* given the opportunity to subscribe to the agreement—they could only amend it, and then only on terms provided for in the will.[27] As one participant observed, "Let us remember that we form a government for millions [of people] not *yet* in existence."[28] In *The Rights of Man*, Tom Paine objected to the last-will-and-testament character of the new operating system, insisting "that the authority of one generation should not be considered binding on its successors," but his objection fell on deaf ears.[29]

The architects labored for fifteen years to construct an effective and durable operating system for constitutional government. The task was difficult because the architects harbored two great fears: they distrusted one another and they feared everyone else. So they took extraordinary measures to design a system of government that would protect themselves from one another, what they called "faction," and shield themselves from "the multitude," which they feared might impose a "tyranny of the majority."

Eventually, they divided *government* to prevent a faction of their own from seizing power, and they divided *civil society* to prevent the multitude from imposing their will on the citizen minority.

Against Faction

The architects recognized that the ruling-class citizens of the new republic were a diverse group. They consisted of merchants, planters, farmers, and artisans, each with separate interests. Although they shared a common identity as men of property—the eighteenth-century term used to describe the people who would later be called "capitalists"—and agreed to make common cause, the architects worried that they might easily divide into "factions," which James Madison warned was a "dangerous vice."[30] Madison described a faction as "a number of citizens . . . who are united and actuated by some common impulse or passion, or of interest, adversed [*sic*] to the rights of other citizens, or to the permanent and aggregate interests of the community."[31]

The architects distrusted one another and "the natural lust of power so inherent in man," and they worried that their peers might band together around a particular political passion or economic interest, create a faction, and attempt to capture the state and establish a monopoly of political power.[32] This mistrust grew out of their experience with the monopolization of religious authority by the Church of England, which prevented not only Catholics and Jews from practicing their faiths but also other Protestant denominations; the monopolization of economic power by the English East India Company and other chartered companies, which monopolized trade with the colonies and restricted the growth of private enterprises in the

American colonies; and the monopolization of political power by the ruling classes in England, which excluded men of property in the colonies from representation in Parliament. Like Adam Smith, who opposed monopoly and advocated free trade and competition, the architects of constitutional government in the American colonies were determined to prevent religious, economic, or political *factions* from monopolizing power.

To prevent factions from monopolizing power, the architects *divided* government and assigned separate powers to different branches. By dividing government and establishing a system of "checks and balances" on would-be factions, "so that no one or few individuals can subvert the republican purposes for which all governments exist," they sought to prevent any one faction from monopolizing power.[33] James Madison argued that checks and balances "harnessed the ambition of one official to counteract the ambition in another."[34]

So they first divided power between the federal government and the states, which were themselves divided into thirteen parts. They then divided power in the federal government (and in the states) into executive, judicial, and legislative branches, which they subdivided again into two parts: House and Senate.[35] By dividing power, they created a series of firewalls to prevent the spread of flames ignited by passionate factions. As George Washington explained, there were "combustibles in every State, which a spark might set fire to."[36] As fire marshals, the architects labored to prevent the fires ignited by faction from spreading. They further insulated the branches of government from faction by creating indirect elections for president and for senators and directing that judges be appointed, not elected, to lifetime office.

The architects' determination to prevent factions from monopolizing power had ironic consequences. By insisting that the state not be permitted to establish one particular Protestant faction or denomination as an official religion, they created a *secular* state that was indifferent to *all* religions, a development that has caused consternation among the faithful to this day. They were men of faith who distrusted men of other faiths.

By dividing power in the state, the architects created a government that mirrored the capitalist interstate system, where no one faction or state could monopolize political power and establish an empire over the world-economy. The result in both cases was the creation of a balance-of-power politics.

Against Majority Rule

The architects distrusted one another, but they *feared* the multitude. They worried that a political, economic, or cultural majority might capture power and use the state to attack the rights and power of the citizen minority. By "minority" they did not mean ethnic minority groups, which is how people use the term today. They used "minority" to describe *themselves*, the 1 to 10 percent of the population with economic wealth and power. They feared what Madison called "the intemperance of the multitude," the great majority of people *without* property.[37] They worried that a majority of debtors might demand easy money or the cancellation of debts, which would ruin the minority who extended credit; that adult white mechanics and soldiers without property might swamp them at the polls; that abolitionists might try to abolish the slave trade and then slavery itself; and that a majority of states in the North might close the Mississippi to navigation by people in the South or prevent slave states from expanding to new territories in the West.[38] Madison worried that the intemperate multitude might "rage for paper money, for the abolition of debts, for an equal division of property or for any other improper and wicked project."[39] His peer, George Clinton, from New York, warned that "the people when wearied with their distresses, will in a moment of frenzy, be guilty of the most imprudent and desperate measures . . . [and] vibrate from one extreme to another. The effects of this disposition are what I wish to guard against."[40]

For Madison, the problem was that "in a republican government the majority however composed ultimately give the law. Wherever therefore an agreement or common passion unites a majority, what is to restrain them from unjust violations of the rights and interests of the minority, or of individuals[?]"[41] And William Manning argued that the Constitution was "made like a fiddle, with but few strings, but so the ruling Majority could play any tune upon it they please."[42]

To protect themselves from the multitude, the architects designed constitutional government to prevent capture by a majority that might try to play its own tune. So they divided *civil society* and restricted the franchise to protect the citizen *minority* from the noncitizen *majority*. For good measure, they also armed the citizen minority and authorized them to use force, if necessary, in public and private settings, to defend their authority and preserve the state.

Although many people today think that the architects wrote the Bill of Rights to protect individuals from *government*, they advanced them to protect the citizen *minority* from the noncitizen *majority*. As James Winthrop argued, "the sober and industrious part of the community should be defended from the rapacity and violence of the vicious and the idle. A bill of rights, therefore, ought . . . to secure the minority against the usurpation and tyranny of the majority. . . . It is therefore as necessary to defend an individual against the majority as against the king in a monarchy."[43]

To further protect minority from majority, the architects took steps on behalf of the slave-owning minority by counting slave property as three-fifths of a white man to bolster their representation in elections. This gave them disproportionate weight in Congress and in the Electoral College, "with the consequence that most American presidents until the Civil War were southerners and slaveholders."[44] They adopted rules in Congress that allowed individuals to delay or prevent passage of laws by legislative majorities through the use of the filibuster and imposed "gag rules" so that majorities could not even discuss antislavery petitions submitted to Congress.[45] They decided that supermajorities would be required to adopt important legislation, such as treaties, or to amend the Constitution, which required approval by a two-thirds majority of both houses of Congress *and*, for good measure, also the approval of legislatures in three-quarters of all the states.[46] "The process of changing the Constitution was so cumbersome and required such broad [majorities] . . . that it was substantially inaccessible and extremely difficult to change," Brown observed.[47] The fact that the US operating system is difficult to amend is one reason why contemporary states have abandoned interest in the US Constitution, which "appears to be losing its appeal as a model for constitutional drafters elsewhere," according to a new study by David S. Law and Mila Versteeg.[48]

The architects devised a whole series of mechanisms to obstruct the majority in *government*. Equally important, they divided *civil society* to keep the multitude at bay.

Although the architects argued that "We, the People" had inalienable rights, they divided "the people" in civil society into three broad groups: *citizens*, *denizens*, and *subjects*.

Citizens could exercise popular sovereignty and enjoy all the rights and duties set out by constitutional government. But the architects counted as citizens only a minority of people in the new republic. They restricted the franchise, defined citizenship narrowly, and reserved for themselves the right to define who might be admitted to this august group of self-selected citizens.

They allowed states to decide who might obtain suffrage and citizenship, a decision that allowed some states to take extremely restrictive views.

At the same time, the architects divided the majority into two broad groups: *denizens*, sometimes called "second-class" citizens, who possessed some of these rights but not all of them; and *subjects*, who were denied all of these rights and who were subject to military, civil, and private authority. They then subdivided these groups and assigned a different social and legal status to different groups. So denizens consisted of men without property or without a Protestant faith, women, children, and immigrants. Subjects consisted of convicts, sailors, slaves, and servants, each with a somewhat different social and legal relation to the state.[49] By dividing the majority of people into denizens and subjects and subdividing them again by age, race and/or ethnicity, place of birth, religious affiliation, economic means, and so on, the architects made it extremely difficult for the members of separate and differentiated groups to "obtain the suffrage and then betray the interests of the people," as Madison put it.[50]

To protect themselves from "the rapacity and violence of the vicious and the idle" majority, the architects armed the citizen minority and authorized it to use collective and individual force against denizens and subjects in public and private settings. The architects did *not* insist that the state establish a monopoly of force, which the sociologist Max Weber later argued was a characteristic feature of the modern state. The modern state, according to Weber, was the "human community that (successfully) claims the *monopoly of the legitimate use of physical force* within a given territory" (italics in the original).[51] Instead of asking the state to monopolize force, the architects deputized citizens and allowed them to use force to maintain public order and keep denizens and subjects in their place. They could raise mobs against immigrants and malefactors, beat wives, children, and servants, flog convicts, sailors, and slaves, and murder American Indians on their own initiative, without the prior approval of state authorities.[52] Because prosecutors, judges, and juries were selected from the citizen minority, they defended the use of violence by nonstate actors and allowed them to inflict grievous harm on denizens and subjects with legal impunity. By allowing the citizen minority to bear arms and deploy violence, the architects created a powerful force of nonstate actors in civil society who took it upon themselves to use physical force in public schools, workshops, and private homes.

Most governments have been reluctant to arm their citizens, for obvious reasons, and have tried to monopolize the legitimate use of physical force, as

Weber suggested. Still, dynastic and republican states permitted nonstate actors to use violence in many public and private settings (schools, jails, the military, homes) until very recently. Weber failed to appreciate the diverse kinds of legitimate force used by nonstate actors and substantially overestimated the state's ability to monopolize it, even today.

Why did the architects delegate or subcontract the authority to use violence to citizens in the new republic? They did so in part because they did not want the state to have the authority to deploy violence and "quarter troops among us" and in part because they believed that citizens should assume responsibility for disciplining workers and family members and be given a free hand, as it were, to "correct" them. As a result, deputized male citizens embraced this responsibility with enthusiasm and have defended their right to bear arms and use force in public and private settings since the revolution. Recent efforts to promote "concealed carry" and "stand your ground" laws are the contemporary expressions of this tradition.

THE NEW REPUBLIC AND THEORIES OF THE STATE

When the architects created constitutional government based on popular sovereignty in a republic, they designed it to be a durable, proprietary operating system for the ruling classes in the United States. In debates about theories of the state, sociologists have argued that the relation between ruling classes and the state can be characterized in different ways. Ralph Miliband argues that the capitalist state was an "instrument" of the ruling class.[53] Others, like Nicos Poulantzas, argue that the state was "relatively autonomous" from the ruling class. Fred Block goes further, arguing that "capitalists do not directly control the state, for the state is under the direction of 'state managers.'"[54] Claus Offe suggests that the state was "independent of any systematic capitalist-class control, either direct or structural, but that the state bureaucracy represents capitalists' interests anyway, because it depends on capital accumulation for its continued existence."[55] And Theda Skocpol goes even further: "No existing neo-Marxist approach affords sufficient weight to state and party organizations as *independent* determinants of political conflicts and outcomes."[56]

The perspective here is a little different. Historically, the relation between ruling classes and the state in the republic has been both instrumental *and* relatively autonomous. In the United States, the ruling classes created constitutional government as a proprietary operating system to guarantee their access to the state, which provided them with vast public resources that they could not afford or obtain on their own. The result was a very "instrumental" relation between ruling classes and the state. But they worried that a faction might monopolize state power and feared that a majority might seize state power, which would obstruct their access to the state and public resources. So they divided both the state and civil society to prevent the state from being captured and used by a faction or by the majority as their instrument. The result was the creation of a state that was "relatively autonomous" from any particular ruling class faction and from a popular majority. [57]

As a result of these two developments—the creation of a proprietary state designed to serve the collective interests of the ruling class and the division of the state to prevent it from being captured by faction or by the multitude— the architects created a state that was simultaneously an "instrument" of the ruling class as a *whole*, but also "relatively autonomous" from any single faction and the multitude. As Nicos Poulantzas argued, after Marx, the "State can only truly serve the ruling class insofar as it is relatively autonomous from the diverse factions of this class, precisely in order to be able to organize the hegemony of the *whole* of this class" (italics added). [58]

The architects exhibited a high degree of class consciousness when they designed the state, but they created a hands-free operating system that could function *without* a high degree of *collective* class consciousness or intervention by their ruling-class *successors*. In fact, the architects did not trust their successors to exhibit the same kind of camaraderie and collective will that the founders possessed. That is why they designed a system that required their successors only to pursue their separate interests.

Of course, the architects did not always succeed. As Charles Bright observed, "When the Democratic Party collapsed [during and after the Civil War] as a national competitor . . . the Republicans were able to secure unchallenged control over the federal apparatus." [59] They then used their monopoly as a faction "to execute their partisan program unchecked by other arguments," passing the Morrill Tariff, the Homestead Act, and the Immigration Act, creating a national banking system and providing federal lands for railroad construction. [60]

But by and large, the architects prevented ruling-class factions from monopolizing state power. This would prove more difficult in other republics, where dictatorships established states that were not simply "relatively autonomous" from the ruling classes but often "extremely autonomous" from ruling classes and the masses. In fact, the states that have come closest to

Skocpol's description of state organizations as "independent" of ruling classes have been *dictatorships*. Dictatorships often blocked access to the state by other classes so that they could increase their own autonomy. But this was difficult to do, as we shall see.

Nor did the architects always succeed in preventing majorities in the republics from seizing state power. Still, when the masses took power, as nationalist and social movements did in the nineteenth and twentieth centuries, they typically *adopted* the republic operating system designed by the architects and deployed it, in an "instrumental way," on behalf of the new ruling class to accumulate capital, provide collective and individual wealth for its members, and promote economic development.

Of course, contemporary sociologists who analyze the state have drawn not only from Karl Marx but also from the theories of Max Weber. Following Weber, they argued that the state could be understood as an ideal type and that each state possessed many of the same universal features. So, for example, Weber argues that one key feature that all modern states possess is their "monopoly on the legitimate use of physical force," and another characteristic is that the bureaucracy or "state apparatus" is a single-minded and rational organization.[61]

Although these assumptions are useful conceptual tools, they do not accurately depict the history of *states* in the interstate system. If a single state had captured the capitalist world-economy and created a political empire, one might be able to talk about the state as having a single, universal form. Instead, the modern world-system was characterized by a *single* world-economy with multiple *states*, which took *different* forms. For example, states in the core were "strong," while states in the periphery were "weak." Moreover, the dynastic states that first emerged differed in important respects from the republics that arose in the Americas. If one starts with a conception of a single, universal state, it is difficult to appreciate the difference between dynastic states and republics or explain how the spread of the republics resulted in the creation of a state that eventually became a kind of universal model or "ideal type," to use Weber's language.

Moreover, contrary to what Weber argued, states in the interstate system did not possess a monopoly on the legitimate use of force. Weber did not consider the legitimate use of force by nonstate actors, who deployed violence against intimates and strangers without fear or sanction by the state. If one assumes that the state early on possessed a monopoly of force, one cannot explain how or why some states first subcontracted violence to nonstate actors and then attempted to monopolize it, a process that is still incomplete, even today.

Finally, Weber assumed that state bureaucracies were single-minded and rational organizations. But in the republics, the architects purposely *divided* government into separate and competing bureaucracies so that they could not act with a single-minded purpose at the behest of a faction or the multitude. Indeed, even in single-party states, where rulers insist that bureaucracies conform to the party line and act with a singular purpose, intramural conflict within and between bureaucracies makes this extremely difficult to achieve. The Chinese Cultural Revolution demonstrated how hard it was for Mao Zedong to persuade the bureaucracy to conform to his edicts.[62]

Of course, states have *tried* to organize the kind of single-minded and rational state bureaucracies that Weber described, and states in the core have generally been more successful than states in the periphery. But this has been more difficult to achieve than proponents of Weberian theories of the state concede. Rather than try to see whether states conform to some ideal type, I think it is more useful to examine how social and political relations within and between states have changed during the past two hundred years.

THE CONTAGION OF LIBERTY

By creating constitutional government based on popular sovereignty, the architects invited the citizens of the new republic to participate in self-government. Citizens enthusiastically responded to this invitation, organizing mass political parties, riotous mobs, and social movements to obtain state power, express their views, and demand social change.[63] The historian Bernard Bailyn argues that citizens who were invited to participate in self-government became infected by "the contagion of liberty," while his predecessor, J. Franklin Jameson, observes that "[t]he stream of revolution, once started, could not be confined within narrow banks, but spread broad upon the land."[64]

Citizens responded to this invitation by organizing political parties, mobs, and social movements to express their sovereignty.[65] As a result, citizens early on created what sociologist Sidney Tarrow calls "a social movement society."[66]

This was an important development because, for the first time, the state became something that citizens fought *for*, both in the sense that they fought to *obtain* political power in the state and in the sense that they fought on *behalf* of the state. Although citizens still organized people to participate in demonstrations and violent riots on the streets, they also organized political parties and social movements to make change through state institutions, an opportunity that dynastic states denied their subjects as a matter of principle.

Of course, the architects invited only *citizens* to exercise their popular sovereignty. Although they encouraged widespread participation in the revolution, they qualified and restricted the exercise of popular sovereignty to the citizen minority after it was won. As the antifederalist Herman Husband noted, "In Every Revolution, the People at large are called upon to assist true liberty," but when "the foreign oppressor is thrown off, learned and designing men" assume power to the detriment of the "laboring people."[67]

The architects defined popular sovereignty in narrow terms and extended their invitation only to the citizen *minority*, not to the denizen-subject *majority*. This development gave rise to considerable skepticism among historians about the character and extent of social change in the early republic. Barrington Moore asserts that the American Revolution "did not result in *any* fundamental changes in the structure of society," while J. Franklin Jameson argues that it transformed "the relations of social classes to each other, the institution of slavery, the system of landholding, [and] the course of business . . . all in the direction of levelling democracy."[68] Edmund Morgan agrees with Moore that there was "no radical rebuilding of social institutions at this time," though he thinks it brought "a host of incalculable, accidental, and incidental changes in society."[69] Alfred Young argues that historians in the 1990s worked "to restore *rebellion* to histories of the American revolution," stressing the ways various groups "shaped the revolution and were in turn shaped by it,"[70] while Gordon S. Wood observes, "If we measure the radicalism by the amount of social change that actually took place—by the transformations in the relations that bond people to each other—then the American Revolution was not conservative at all; on the contrary it was as radical and as revolutionary as any in history."[71]

Both sides have merit. The extension of liberty to the citizen minority contributed to meaningful social change, while the exclusion of the denizen and subject majority restricted the scope of social change. Moreover, social change cannot be understood only in terms of its meaning in the United States. It must be seen in a global context. From a global perspective, the social changes produced by the introduction of constitutional government in the United States, which was significantly limited, proved contagious and infected proponents of social change, first in France and then in Haiti. In the

1789 Declaration of the Rights of Man, delegates to the French National Assembly invited citizens to participate in social change and secure their rights. Like their American counterparts, the French delegates first extended the rights of man to male citizens. But they soon divided citizens into "active" and "passive" citizens and assigned "women, children, foreigners, and those others who contribute nothing to sustaining the public establishment" to the latter category.[72] The slaves who were excluded from the active or passive category made up a third category of "subjects."[73] The delegates subsequently extended "active" citizenship to both women and slaves, though not children. After Napoleon took power, these proclamations were rescinded. In France, as elsewhere, many residents—denizens and subjects— were excluded from participating as citizens either because they were seen as being "dependent on someone else in the exercise of their will, such as minors, women or servants," or because they could not be trusted to exercise their political rights responsibly and might be given to "mob rule."[74] Still, the clarion call for "liberty, equality, and fraternity" legitimized the efforts not only of citizens, but also of denizens and subjects, in republics and in dynastic states, to claim these rights for themselves and for others. Although denizens and subjects were not *invited* to do so, they nonetheless mobilized informal networks and organized social movements and political parties to make social change. From a global perspective, the relatively modest social changes made in the United States contributed to significant change in other countries. Liberty proved a contagion that infected people around the world.

The architects of constitutional government in the United States and France invited the few and then the many to exercise popular sovereignty, seek state power, and redeem the promise implicit in the call for "liberty, equality and fraternity." People responded to this call and fought to establish independent republics around the world, a development that we examine in the next chapter.

Chapter Three

The Rise of the Republics

Social movements fought to create republics, first in the United States and then around the world. It was a long, slow, and difficult process. World War II marked a turning point. Before 1945, dynastic imperial states controlled the interstate system. But the breakup of dynastic states and the creation of new republics in postcolonial states around the world during the postwar period led to the emergence of a new, republican interstate system.[1] Today, a vast majority of the 193-plus states in the world identify themselves as republics.

The rise of the republics had several important social consequences for people around the world.[2] First, the demise of dynastic empires brought an end to colonialism, which deprived billions of people of any real political voice and subjected them to economic exploitation. Second, it brought an end to the murderous rivalry between dynastic states for colonies and their resources, a ferocious competition that led to recurrent world wars and caused the deaths of tens of millions of soldiers and civilians from battle, disease, famine, and the Holocaust.

Third, it gave citizens in the new republics the opportunity to exercise popular sovereignty and promote economic development. Although it proved difficult to do, governments in some postcolonial states managed to practice democracy and/or promote economic development, as they did, for example, in Japan, South Korea, and Taiwan.[3]

The demise of dynastic states and the rise of the republics was the product of two major developments. First, independence movements fought to create republics around the world. In the late eighteenth and early nineteenth centuries, such movements established republics in the United States, Haiti, and across Latin America. During and after World War I, they founded republics in Ireland, Russia, Germany, Austria, Czechoslovakia, Hungary, and Poland. After World War II, they created republics in Europe, Africa, Asia, and the Middle East. The number of states grew from 79 in 1946 to 193 in 2011. Most of these states identified themselves as republics.

The social movements that fought to create republics often engaged in multisided struggles not only with imperial rulers but also with their peers. They drew support from diverse social groups—slaves, indigenous peoples, women, and ethnic minorities—but did not always include them as citizens in postcolonial states. And they adopted different political strategies (violent and nonviolent) and goals (state power for broadly defined social groups and state power for narrowly defined social groups).

Second, successive world wars undermined the ability of rival empires to meet the challenges posed by emerging independence movements, large republics in the United States and the Soviet Union, and new imperial rivals in Spain, Italy, Germany, and Japan. Although dynastic empires adopted different strategies to meet the challenges posed by republican insurgents and imperial rivals, they ultimately failed to do so. The successive failures of dynastic empires led to gains by republican states.

To appreciate how these two developments—the rise of the republics and the demise of dynastic empires—transformed the interstate system, it is important to recount how aspiring social movements fought to create new republics during the past two hundred years.

NEW REPUBLICS IN THE AMERICAS

Republics first emerged in the American colonies of dynastic European empires. During the late eighteenth and early nineteenth centuries, European settlers, African slaves, and American Indians fought against European states and, often, against one another to establish independent republics: "By the middle of the nineteenth century, virtually all of the [colonies in North and South America and Haiti] had been transformed into independent sovereign states."[4] These movements won their independence not only because they fought with determination and skill but because interimperial rivalries and world war compromised or crippled the ability of dynastic states to subdue republican insurgencies.

Of course, historians use the term "independence movement" as an umbrella to describe a wide variety of formal and informal social movements that participated in riots, rebellions, and wars for independence. Because many of these movements did not create the kind of formal, bureaucratic organizations that emerged after the mid-nineteenth century, many do not have formal names. The British historian Eric Hobsbawm describes the millenarian, peasant, bandit, mob, mafia, and anarchist groups of the early nineteenth century that engaged in riots and rebellions as "primitive rebels."[5] The American historian Paul Gilje describes the rowdy mobs of rioters in America as a "mobocracy,"[6] while Peter Linebaugh and Marcus Rediker describe the sailors, slaves, dockyard workers, and pub crawlers who raised riots, staged mutinies, and struggled for liberty and freedom as a "many-headed Hydra."[7] These diverse groups were often illiterate and disorganized, which means that while they elected their leaders and debated issues, strategies, and politics with the fervor of hard-working, hard-drinking workers, they did not appoint a secretary to keep minutes of their meetings. Social movement scholars might pay more attention to the important work done by historians of this period and keep in mind that beneath the large banners raised by "independence movements" marched diverse and contentious groups of people who fought the authorities and brawled with one another.

During the American War of Independence, widespread opposition to economic recession, rising taxes, and British restrictions on westward expansion made it possible for republicans to persuade diverse groups—merchants and planters, urban workers and rural farmers, and some Indians and slaves—to join the rebellion.[8] They organized effective political and military institutions (the Continental Congress and the army), waged successful military campaigns, and conducted a diplomatic campaign that enlisted foreign military support.[9] Military and naval assistance from France, which was supported by Spain and other dynastic states that were engaged in a long-running rivalry with Great Britain, made it difficult for British forces to defeat the republican insurgents. Timely French intervention during the American siege of British forces at Yorktown forced Britain to sue for peace. Although Great Britain lost the battle for the thirteen colonies, it nonetheless won the larger world war, which started in 1763 and ended in 1815.[10] The American War of Independence created the first republic in the colonies. It would not be the last.

In 1790, a multisided revolutionary war erupted between white settlers, mixed-race mulattoes, and black slaves in Haiti, a French colony that was "the leading sugar exporter in the Americas" and produced "one-third of all French trade."[11] The three-sided conflict triggered successive invasions by British, Spanish, and French forces, which represented the Republic of France and, after its demise in 1799, the dictatorship under Napoleon. Black slaves led by François-Dominique Toussaint L'ouverture raised armies and maneuvered them successfully against multiple and successive foes. Conflicts among their domestic opponents (whites and mulattoes savagely attacked one another as well as slaves) and imperial rivalries between European states that were then engaged in a bitter world war weakened the forces that wanted to reintroduce slavery. The island's tropical diseases—chiefly malaria—decimated European armies sent to crush the slaves. Yellow fever and malaria killed so many British troops that "British forces could only maintain defensive positions."[12] The British lost more soldiers—twenty thousand dead and one hundred thousand casualties—than they lost in all of their wars in North America (the French and Indian War, the American War of Independence, and the War of 1812) and suffered a defeat that ranked "among the greatest disasters in British military history."[13]

The multisided war for independence in Haiti was savage. Conventional armies and irregular militias slaughtered opponents in battle and civilians in their homes and on the streets. Captured black insurgents were executed after being forced to witness the murder of their wives. The French converted the hold of a prison ship, the *Stifler*, "into a gas chamber" where blacks and mulattoes were murdered by "noxious fumes" and "imported hundreds of killer dogs" from Cuba to attack and kill captured black and mulatto prisoners.[14] The island's population fell by half during the war.[15]

Although the British first invaded Haiti to assist the white planters and suppress the slave revolt, they later imposed a naval blockade on the island to prevent Napoleon from resupplying his troops and regaining control of the island. This time, British intervention helped black republicans defeat French troops and force their withdrawal. Again, black republicans took advantage of interimperial rivalries and shifting foreign policies to advance their cause.[16] On January 1, 1804, triumphant black insurgents "proclaimed the independence of Haiti, the second republic of the Western Hemisphere."[17]

The creation of a black republic in Haiti alarmed dynastic states that possessed slaveholding colonies (Great Britain, France, Spain, Portugal, and the Netherlands) and European settlers and free, mixed-race groups in colonies across Latin America, the Caribbean, and the United States.[18] "The creoles were frightened men: they feared a caste war, inflamed by French revolutionary doctrine and the contagious violence of [Haiti]."[19] They all feared that republican demands for independence might be heard and seized not only by black slaves but also by Indians, who labored in coercive conditions across Latin America. They had good reason to fear the Indians. In 1780, a fierce Indian insurrection led by Tupac Amaru "engulfed" Peru, which resulted in one hundred thousand deaths and inspired a revolt by Comuneros in New Grenada.[20] These aspiring social movements, which were sometimes aided by altruistic or sympathetic priests or intellectuals, threatened colonial overlords and white/creole settler populations, who were generally outnumbered by Indians, slaves, or both.

In Europe, revolution in France triggered a resumption of world war between the French republic, and then Napoleon, and dynastic empires across Europe. World war undermined Spanish and Portuguese rule across Latin America, contributed to the emergence of aspiring independence movements across the continent, and led to the creation of separate republics in Latin America.

In 1807, Napoleon invaded Spain and Portugal, forcing dynastic rulers in Spain to capitulate and rulers in Portugal to flee to Brazil.[21] The humiliation of Spanish and Portuguese rulers discredited metropolitan authority in Latin America. "Authority came traditionally from the king; laws were obeyed [in dynastic states] because they were the king's laws. Now there was no king to obey."[22] Royalist bureaucracies and elites in Spain's American colonies soldiered on, enjoying a kind of independent authority, though it was without higher sanction or legitimacy. "Confusion spread everywhere in Spanish America," Wallerstein argues. "Regional and local juntas took over in the name of [deposed Spanish king Ferdinand VII], in many cases ousting Spanish authorities. Creoles were now exercising de facto self-government in the name of loyalism."[23]

Aspiring independence movements took advantage of this opportunity to challenge dynastic authority. As one Mexican republican later explained, "Napoleon Bonaparte . . . to you Spanish America owes the liberty and independence it now enjoys. Your sword struck the first blow at the chain which bound the two worlds."[24]

In 1810, republican revolts triggered the outbreak of multisided conflicts in all four of the Spanish viceroyalties (Mexico, New Grenada, Peru, and Rio de la Plata). In these conflicts, royalists fought to preserve their power, which was derived, however loosely, from dynastic authority in Spain. Republican leaders such as Simón Bolivar and José de San Martin fought to establish great republics, which would consist of the viceroyalties at least, though perhaps *all* of the Spanish colonies together. They might be described as "federalist" republicans because they wanted to unite the different regions and create a large republic, like the United States, in Spanish America.[25] But federalist efforts were repeatedly stymied by republicans who fought for independence but wanted to obtain power in smaller, separate states.[26] These *regionalist* republicans might be described as "antifederalists" because they refused to surrender their power to a more centralized, federal state. They emphasized the differences among people living in different regions and urged them to think of themselves as "Venezuelans" or "Ecuadorans" or "Mexicans."[27]

Although the federalists and antifederalists disagreed about the final shape(s) of the republic(s), they agreed on two issues. They both wanted independence from Spain, and they both wanted to prevent the multitude—Indians and slaves—from achieving their independence from federalist and antifederalist creole elites.[28] In this regard, creole republican movements had both aspiring and restrictionist features.

The Indian and slave multitude also fought for their independence, both from Spanish authority and from federalist and antifederalist creole elites. In Mexico, for example, Miguel Hidalgo y Costilla, "a non-conformist and free-living parish priest," led a revolt by eighty thousand Indians, who killed two thousand Spanish and threatened the capital before they were defeated and dispersed.[29] Although Hidalgo was captured and executed, other altruistic priests organized an effective insurgency that returned "like the hydra in proportion to the number of times its head [was] cut off" and remained "the chief threat to royalist power until 1815."[30] The insurgents' "programme consisted of independence, a congressional form of [republican] government and social reforms—including the abolition of tribute, slavery, the caste system, and legal barriers to lower-class advancement [and] the introduction of an income tax."[31]

With the defeat of Napoleon and the end of the world war, the Spanish king returned to the throne. He moved quickly to reestablish dynastic authority in Spanish colonies.[32] But he proved unable to do so because many of his royalist supporters, who had enjoyed some autonomy in his absence, refused to submit to his authority and because "many Creoles who formerly were skeptical of independence felt obliged to jump on the bandwagon, not . . . to take power from the Spanish but, above all, to prevent the [indigenous and black multitude] from taking it."[33] Meanwhile, federalist and antifederalist

republicans deferred their disputes about the shape of the state after independence and fought together, offering concessions to Indians and slaves such as
the end of forced labor for Indians and eventual emancipation for slaves,
which reduced the threat of revolt from below.[34] The British and the United
States joined in, providing timely military, economic, and diplomatic assistance to the republicans, largely because they wanted to open trade relations
with postcolonial republics.[35]

After a protracted struggle, Bolivar and the federal republicans won the
war for independence but lost the battle to establish a grand republic: "Bolivar's dream of replicating the formula of unity achieved by the Thirteen [US]
Colonies failed."[36] Because the antifederalists won the battle for separate
states, the breakup of Spain's dynastic empire in America led to the creation
of eleven separate republics. They would be joined later by two others, in
Uruguay and in Brazil, which passed first through a constitutional monarchy
before becoming a republic in 1889.

1848: THE FAILURE OF REPUBLICAN REVOLUTIONS IN EUROPE

In 1848, republican insurgents staged spontaneous demonstrations and organized armed revolts in dynastic states across Europe: in Sicily and the kingdom of Naples; in France; in Spain; in Italian, Austrian, Hungarian, Bohemian, and Moravian territories of the Austro-Hungarian Empire; in German
kingdoms; and in papal Rome.[37] In Switzerland, which was already a republican confederacy, civil war between 1847 and 1848 resulted in the creation
of a federal republic.[38] In France, republicans organized a series of "reform
banquets" to celebrate republican values and protest the rising price of bread.
The regime's violent reaction to peaceful protest ignited widespread protests.[39]

During this "springtime of nations," as historians have called it, republicans demanded the creation of constitutional government in independent
states. As one German pamphleteer put it, "We want a republic and nothing
else."[40] When dynastic rulers fled in the face of rebellion, insurgents declared their independence and established sovereign republics. The Hungarian Declaration of Independence, which was modeled after the American
document, declared Hungary to be a free and sovereign state based on the
"inalienable rights" of its people.[41]

But republican insurgency did not long survive.[42] The Roman republic,
declared on July 4, 1848, lasted only one day.[43] Others lasted longer, but

only the Swiss republic survived.[44] The republican revolts led by aspiring social movements surprised dynastic rulers and caught them off guard. Some rulers fled into exile. But as soon as they recovered from the shock, they decided to defend their divine rights. As the king of Prussia said after the army crushed the revolt, "The assembly wished to take from me my Divine Right. . . . No power on earth is strong enough to do that."[45] He rejected an offer from the Frankfurt assembly to become king of a united Germany, saying he would not accept "a crown from the gutter . . . it would be a dog-collar fastened round my neck by a sovereign German people."[46]

Across Europe, dynastic regimes and their restrictionist allies deployed their armies to crush the revolts. In France, "approximately 500 insurgents lost their lives in the fighting . . . but after the last barricades were captured, the insurgents were hunted down . . . and almost 3,000 more were killed in cold blood. In addition, over 12,000 people were arrested, and about 4,500 of them were ultimately jailed and deported to labor camps in Algeria."[47]

Although the republicans were defeated, they were undeterred, and they learned several lessons from defeat. They decided that the clandestine secret societies—such as Giuseppe Mazzini's republican Carbonari, Young Italy, and Young Europe—and the spontaneous public riots and insurrections by urban mobs were not strong enough to wrest power from dynastic rulers and restrictionist economic, religious, and military elites.[48] "The adoption of [republican] forms and the development of mass-based organizations eventually distinguished independence movements from secret societies, clandestine fraternities, and spontaneously created mobs. Instead of plotting assassinations and organizing conspiracies, [republicans] began organizing public demonstrations, gathering petitions, electing delegates, and holding congresses to review their tactics and debate their goals."[49]

Second, they decided to develop durable, mass-based organizations and adopt long-term political strategies capable of seizing state power and creating republics in Europe and in the colonies. As Wallerstein argues, the republicans decided that "spontaneity was not enough. If one wanted to have a major political impact, systematic and long-term organization was a prerequisite. This would lead the 'movements'—an ephemeral concept—down the path of bureaucratic organization, with members and officers, with finance and newspapers, with programs and eventually with parliamentary participation."[50]

After 1848, republicans organized two kinds of aspiring bureaucratic social movements: "nationalist" and "socialist."[51] "Nationalist" republicans created broad-based, multiclass movements that organized adult males in Europe and in the colonies along ethnic, cultural, linguistic, and religious lines. In Ireland, Arthur Griffith in 1905 organized Sinn Fein (Gaelic for "Ourselves"), while nationalists in India organized the Indian National Congress in 1885.[52] Although most republicans advanced a secular politics and advocated the separation of church and state, some nationalists organized around religious identities: Zionists advocated the creation of a Jewish state in Israel, while Muslims in India created the All-Muslim League as a political vehicle for India's Muslim population.[53] Later, after states for Jews and for Muslims were created, the Bible (Old Testament) would become a constitutional document in Israel and the Koran a constitutional document in the Islamic Republic of Pakistan and later in the Islamic Republic of Iran.

Socialist republicans, by contrast, created class-based organizations that appealed to adult male wage workers, the "proletariat," in settings around the world, urging them to *shed* particular ethnic, linguistic, religious, and cultural identities and *adopt* a shared identity as "workers of the world." Moreover, they created international organizations to coordinate their efforts and facilitate change in Europe and their colonies and in the Americas.[54]

Nationalist and socialist republicans disagreed about whether to organize along ethnic or class lines. They disagreed too, both with each other and with themselves, about tactics, whether to engage in legal peaceful protest or violent armed struggle. But they *agreed* that dynastic empires should be abolished and that sovereign republics should take their place. In both cases, they had to make "national" or "class" identities salient or meaningful for people who did not *yet* regard themselves as "Italian" or "proletarian." *Moreover*, they all adopted republican institutions and practices: they sent delegates to congresses where they debated how best to achieve their goals. When the Indian National Congress convened its first meeting in Bombay on December 27, 1885, the seventy-two delegates, who were "well-acquainted with the English language," assembled "in their morning coats, well-pressed trousers, top hat and silk turbans to discuss the issues of the day."[55] Twelve years later, Theodor Herzl convened the first World Zionist Congress in Basel, Switzerland, where he "urged delegates attending the congress to wear formal black dress to observe the solemnity of the occasion."[56] The delegates to these and other republican congresses around the world consciously adopted the conventions of the Continental Congress in the United States and pursued similar goals: the creation of independent states in which the people, whom they imagined as adult males, could practice constitutional government.

WORLD WAR I: NEW REPUBLICS AND SELF-DETERMINATION

Economic competition and political rivalries among dynastic European states led to the outbreak of World War I. Like the world wars at the end of the eighteenth and beginning of the nineteenth centuries, World War I contributed to the emergence of new republics, this time in Europe and Asia. Republicans took advantage of the weakened condition of warring dynastic states to launch a nationalist rebellion in Ireland (1916) and a socialist revolution in Russia (1917). Both rebellions led to civil war and, eventually, to the creation of independent republics.[57]

The war destroyed dynastic states in the Russian, German, Austro-Hungarian, and Ottoman Empires. The breakup of these empires led to the creation of new republics, either at the hands of indigenous nationalist or socialist movements or at the behest of the victors, which included both dynastic states such as Great Britain, Belgium, and Italy and republics in France and the United States. As Billias observed, "The Allied victory resulted in a burst of democracy not seen in Europe since 1848. Many conservative monarchies were swept away. Before World War One, there had been 19 monarchies and three republics [in Europe], but after 1922, there were 14 republics, 13 monarchies, and two regencies."[58]

Aspiring social movements in Poland, Finland, Latvia, Lithuania, and Estonia created republics from parts of the German and Russian Empires and their successor states. Movements in Austria, Hungary, and Czechoslovakia created republics from the wreckage of the Austro-Hungarian Empire. Movements in Greece and Turkey created republics in parts of the Ottoman Empire, though the empire's colonial territories in the Middle East were seized by the French (Lebanon and Syria) and the British (Palestine and Iraq) and incorporated into their colonial empires.[59]

After the war, Woodrow Wilson and Vladimir Lenin, the leaders of the two largest republics, championed the spread of new republics. Although they had very different political backgrounds, they both advocated the idea of "self-determination." Wilson believed that "all nations have a right to self-determination," which he said was "an imperative principle of action, which statesmen will henceforth ignore at their peril."[60] Lenin agreed: "The right of nations to self-determination implies . . . the right of free political separation from the oppressor nation," and "the self-determination of nations means the separation of [national movements] from alien national bodies [empires] and the formation of an independent national state."[61] Lenin even included the right of self-determination in the Soviet constitution, giving constituent republics the right to secede from the union, a provision that antifederalist leaders in the republics eventually exercised, leading to the breakup of the Soviet Union in 1992.[62]

Wilson and Lenin advocated self-determination because they wanted republican movements to secede from empires and form independent states based on popular sovereignty and constitutional government. Their shared determination to encourage or assist republican movements grew out of their conviction that colonialism led to economic and political rivalry and world war. If oppressed peoples or "nations" exercised their right of self-determination and created new republics, it would then be possible to create a new republican interstate system that could provide collective security and reduce or eliminate the threat of world war.[63] In Wilson's view, the dynastic interstate system "had never produced anything but aggression, egotism, and war," and he argued that it should be replaced by "a league of powers, a universal organized peace instead of organized rivalries."[64] To this end, Wilson and Lenin created separate international institutions designed to realize these goals. Wilson established the League of Nations, and Lenin organized the Communist International, sometimes called the Third International (it was preceded by an anarchist-socialist First International and a socialist-only Second International).[65] However, neither organization lived up to its founder's aspirations, and both succumbed to global and domestic political forces. Dynastic empires and domestic US senators opposed Wilson's efforts to use the league to decolonize empires and provide collective security, and it soon lapsed into irrelevance.[66] Lenin's successor, Joseph Stalin, did not regard the Communist International as an effective instrument of Soviet policy, and it, too, became irrelevant.[67] Still, the idea of creating a new interstate system and international organization made up of republics that would provide collective security would be revived by US and Soviet leaders as a result of their collaboration as allies during World War II.

THE EMPIRES STRIKE BACK

Aspiring republican movements first challenged dynastic states in 1776. During the next two centuries, republican ideas spread, and the number of republican states grew. Faced with the growing republican threat, dynastic states adopted different military and political strategies to defend their empires and keep republican challengers at bay.

First, dynastic empires deployed their armies and navies to crush republican revolts in European homelands and in their colonies. Great Britain mounted campaigns against republics in the United States (in 1776 and again in 1812), France (1792), Haiti (1804), and Ireland (1916). It later waged antirepublican wars in Palestine, Kenya, South Africa, India, and Malaysia. Dynastic regimes in France fought republicans on the streets of Paris (1789, 1830, 1848, 1872) and in their colonies: Haiti (1790), Indochina (1945), and Algeria (1954). Spain waged antirepublican wars across Spanish America (1810) and in Cuba, Puerto Rico, and the Philippines (1896), which were assisted by the US republic. The Dutch fought republicans in Indonesia, the Portuguese in Guinea-Bissau, Angola, and Mozambique. Dynastic rulers fought tenaciously to prevent insurgent republicans from exiting their empire and establishing sovereign states of their own.[68]

Second, they made concessions and introduced political reforms to deter or deflect republican demands.[69] After republican revolts in 1848, dynastic rulers introduced constitutional monarchies that allowed adult males to elect representatives to parliaments, which were given limited "constitutional" authority to adopt legislation on some issues.[70] Dynastic regimes, particularly in Great Britain, took steps to upgrade the status of white settlers in some of their colonies, allowing them to participate in parliaments and legislate on local issues that did not infringe on the economic, political, and military jurisdiction of the parliamentary government in England.[71] They tried to defer republican aspirations in the colonies by promising eventual independence, though they refused to say just when that might occur. During World War I, Foreign Minister Arthur J. Balfour promised independence movements in India and in Palestine that the British government would work toward "the gradual development of self-governing institutions with a view to the progressive realization of responsible government," but gave no timetable.[72] When pressed to provide an estimate, British colonial minister Malcolm MacDonald said in 1938 that "the great purpose of the British Empire is the *gradual* spread of freedom. . . . It may take generations, or even *centuries* for the people in some parts of the Colonial Empire to achieve self-government" (italics added).[73]

In the meantime, regimes convened special committees to study the problem, issue white papers, and propose reforms. One British committee investigating possible reforms in India "met for 18 months, held 159 meetings, examined 120 witnesses, and interviewed one of them, Sir Quentin Hoare, for nineteen days, during which time he answered more than seven thousand questions."[74]

But military force, political concessions, and cosmetic reforms failed to prevent the gradual and abrupt breakup of dynastic empires. They failed for several reasons. First, dynastic states were unable to curb their own ambitions. Their ongoing rivalries led to recurrent world wars, which in turn led to military disaster and economic ruin. Second, they failed to develop a persuasive political response to republican demands for self-determination, for "liberty, equality, fraternity." Their alternative, which might be described as "service, inequality, and subordination," failed to inspire subject populations. Third, they were forced to seek help from the United States during World War I and from the United States and the Soviet Union during World War II to prevent defeat by their imperial and fascist rivals. These two republics then demanded the breakup of at least some empires as the price for their wartime assistance.

FASCIST FOES

During the 1920s and 1930s, restrictionist fascist social movements overthrew republican governments in Portugal, Spain, Italy, and Germany, and a like-minded militarist government seized power in imperial Japan. European fascist and Japanese militarist regimes rejected the idea of popular sovereignty, constitutional government, and democracy. "We are anti-parliamentarians, anti-democrats, anti-liberals," Dr. António de Oliveira Salazar, the Portuguese dictator, announced after he took power in 1932. He ridiculed the principles of "democracy, individual liberty and the rule of law as 'unfortunate' and 'doctrinaire.'"[75] Salazar's fascist contemporaries—Francisco Franco in Spain, Benito Mussolini in Italy, Adolf Hitler in Germany, and Hideki Tōjō in Japan—shared his views. "We did not win the regime we have today, hypocritically with some votes," Franco boasted. "We won it at the point of a bayonet."[76] Antirepublican fascist leaders viewed republican states as weak and incapable of addressing the economic problems associated with the Great Depression.

Fascist leaders also complained that dynastic empires (Great Britain and the Netherlands) and the large republics (the United States, France, and the Soviet Union) denied them the right to conquer lands and claim colonies of their own. Their determination to annex, conquer, or claim colonies made them "anti-imperialist imperialists." To secure their objectives, the regimes in Germany, Italy, and Japan decided to destroy both the old, dynastic European empires *and* the new republics. During the 1930s, Italy invaded Libya and Ethiopia and Japan invaded China, both to obtain new colonies. Germany then annexed Austria and Czechoslovakia. The subsequent German invasion of Poland and the Japanese attack on Pearl Harbor triggered the onset of World War II (Germany invaded Poland with the assistance of the Soviet Union and then turned on its ally and invaded the Soviet Union after completing the conquest of France and most of western and eastern Europe).

If the Axis powers had won the war, they would have destroyed the world-economy and the dynastic interstate system and created one or several world empires. Based on their wartime practices, it is clear they would have made slaves of subject peoples and exterminated many of the peoples whom they regarded as racially inferior. Their capacity for cruelty was unfathomably deep. Franco ordered the execution of 250,000 republicans after the Spanish Civil War, most of them slowly strangled by garrote.[77] Japanese military forces slaughtered civilians and beheaded captured soldiers.[78] German forces slaughtered civilians and captured soldiers. They murdered six million Jews, another six million civilians, and 3.3 million Soviet prisoners of war during the Holocaust.[79]

THE TURNING POINT: WORLD WAR II AND THE NEW REPUBLICAN INTERSTATE SYSTEM

In 1941, Germany attacked the Soviet Union and Japan attacked the United States. These two surprise attacks joined the great republics as allies and persuaded their leaders to dismantle the "colonial system," which they thought was responsible for world war, and create a new republican interstate system, made up of independent republics, that would provide collective security and promote economic development for constituent states. US officials adamantly opposed a return to the dynastic interstate system, which President Roosevelt described as "the system of unilateral action, exclusive alliances, and spheres of influence and balances of power, and all the other expedients which have been tried for centuries and have always failed."[80] Roosevelt argued that "the colonial system means war," and warned British prime minister Winston Churchill, "I can't believe we can fight a war against fascist slavery, and at the same time not work to free people all over the world from a backward foreign policy."[81] As Roosevelt observed, "There are 1,100,000,000 brown people [in the colonies]. They are ruled by a handful of whites and they resent it. Our goal must be to help them achieve independence."[82] US policy makers argued that "victory must bring in its train the liberation of all peoples. . . . The age of imperialism has ended."[83]

US and Soviet leaders took a series of steps to achieve their goals. First, they assumed "plenipotentiary" or supersovereign powers, which gave themselves and their partners (Great Britain and sometimes China) the constitutional authority to construct a new republican interstate system. Second, they convened a series of summit meetings during and after the war—in Newfoundland, Cairo, Tehran, Potsdam, Bretton Woods, Dumbarton Oaks, and San Francisco—to create the operating systems and organizations needed to make the new system work.[84] The 1942 Atlantic Charter provided a first draft of the system, which might be regarded as 1.0.[85] The 1945 United Nations Charter, 2.0, represented the finished product.[86] It created political and economic institutions designed to provide collective security for its members (the Security Council and the General Assembly), promote economic development (the International Monetary Fund, World Bank) and public health (the World Health Organization and the Food and Agricultural Organization), and promote decolonization by requiring European empires to promise they would eventually introduce self-government and later agree, albeit with reluctance, to grant independence to their colonies.[87] US and Soviet leaders insisted that participation in UN organizations be "based on respect for the principle of equal rights and self-determination of peoples," which meant they must agree to permit people in the colonies to depart from empires and establish republics of their own.[88]

US and Soviet diplomats then used the United Nations to promote decolonization, authorizing special commissions to investigate colonial conditions and encouraging colonial people to petition the General Assembly for relief, which forced empires to fix timetables for eventual independence.[89] By limiting membership, more or less, to independent states, US and Soviet officials created an organization in which republics outnumbered dynastic states by a two-to-one margin.[90]

Although relations between the United States and Soviet Union deteriorated after the war ended, primarily because they quarreled over the exact boundaries of each other's "spheres of influence" in the new interstate system, which led to the Cold War between 1948 and 1960, they nonetheless *agreed* on the central features of the system and *together* promoted decolonization despite the onset of the Cold War.[91] Indeed, twenty-six countries in Africa and Asia gained their independence with US and Soviet assistance between 1956 and 1960, during the *height* of the Cold War.[92]

After World War II, US and Soviet leaders moved quickly to decolonize the empires of their wartime enemies, depriving Axis states of the colonies they had acquired before and during the war. They detached Austria, Czechoslovakia, and Poland from Germany; Tunisia, Libya, Somalia, Eritrea, and Ethiopia from Italy; and Formosa (Taiwan), Manchuria (China), and Korea from Japan. European states also forcibly deported eight million German-speaking residents to Germany, and Asian states deported 2.6 million ethnic Japanese to Japan after the war, largely because they regarded them as representatives of the German and Japanese empires.[93] US and Soviet governments then pressured their erstwhile allies to decolonize while encouraging aspiring nationalist and socialist movements in the colonies to press their demands for decolonization and self-determination.

While the United States and Soviet Union demanded decolonization from above and myriad republican movements demanded independence from below, dynastic European states found themselves in difficult straits.[94] Although European empires survived the fascist onslaught, the war exhausted their economic resources, military defeat shredded their aura of invincibility, and their reprehensible behavior during the war—British and French concessions to Hitler at Munich, French collaboration with German occupation in France and with Japanese occupation in Indochina—ruined their political reputations and legitimacy as great powers. As de Gaulle lamented, "All the nations of Europe lost [the war]. Two were defeated."[95]

Although the world war had wrecked dynastic empires, it emboldened nationalist and socialist republicans in the colonial world. Older nationalist movements—the Indian National Congress (1885), Muslim League (1906), Zionist movement (1896), Arab National Congress (1913), and Chinese Nationalist Party (1922)—and socialist movements—the Chinese Communist Party (1921) and Vietnamese Communist Party (1925)—were joined by new republican movements in French, British, Dutch, Spanish, Portuguese, and Belgian colonies around the world. Many of these movements fought against the Japanese during the war and were prepared to wage war to secure their independence. As Muslim League leader Ali Jinnah said of his commitment to use "direct action" in India to secure independence, "We have forged a pistol and we are in a position to use it."[96] Although some movements adopted nonviolent strategies to win independence, colonial authorities regarded independence movements everywhere as potentially armed and dangerous.

In some places, European empires fought hard to retain their colonies. The United Kingdom waged brutal counterinsurgency campaigns against aspiring Jewish and Arab insurgents in Palestine, communists in Malaysia, and Mau Mau in Kenya. France fought the Viet Minh in Indochina and nationalist insurgents in Algeria. The Netherlands struggled against nationalist insurgents in Indonesia. Portugal fought communist movements in Guinea-Bissau, Angola, and Mozambique. Belgium fought with nationalist insurgents in the Congo. Although European empires sometimes managed to defeat their multiple republican adversaries in the field, they were eventually forced to retreat and surrender their colonies. Decolonization proceeded rapidly during the late 1950s and then continued at a slower pace. As a result, the number of states in the interstate system grew from 50 in 1945 to 100 in 1960, to 150 in 1990, and to 193 in 2012.[97] The great majority of these new states identified themselves as republics.

The creation of a new republican interstate system after World War II, which contributed to widespread decolonization and the rise of the republics, had important global consequences. First, it brought an end to colonialism, which for centuries had facilitated the political degradation and economic exploitation of billions of people around the world. Second, it brought an end to the murderous interimperial rivalries that were responsible for the outbreak of recurrent world wars that had resulted in immeasurable violence and suffering for the billions of people who were exposed to war, genocide, and famine. Third, it created global institutions that provided collective security for constituent states, facilitated the emergence of states based on popular sovereignty and constitutional government, and promoted, for the first time, economic development in some postcolonial states. Of course, the new republics did not always provide political democracy or achieve economic development.

Unfortunately, the rise of the republics was accompanied from the outset by two related problems: dictatorship and division. In some settings, these developments deprived people of political choices and economic opportunities and contributed to conflicts within and between the new republics. To appreciate these developments, it is necessary to examine these two problems in greater detail.

Chapter Four

Dictatorship and Division

The rise of the republics was accompanied by two onerous problems. First, minority political factions in many postcolonial states seized power, established dictatorships to enhance their own wealth and power, and inflicted terrible cruelties on majority populations. Second, minority political factions that competed for political power with domestic rivals in colonial and postcolonial states sometimes precipitated the division of postcolonial republics. This often led to conflicts and wars within and between divided states. Dictatorship and division both compromised the meaning of citizenship and sovereignty in the new republics and contributed to domestic violence and interstate war.

The architects of constitutional government in the United States worried that a minority faction might capture the state. To prevent this, they divided government and created institutional firewalls designed to prevent one faction from breaching these barriers and capturing the state as a whole. They also feared that the multitude might capture the state and establish a "tyranny of the majority" over the "minority," the economic and political elite who made up only 10 percent of the population. To prevent this, they divided civil society, reserved citizenship and the franchise for themselves, and barred the multitude—denizens and subjects—from exercising popular sovereignty. In retrospect, given the ease with which minority factions established dictatorships in many republics, the architects probably worried too *much* about the danger posed to constitutional government by the multitude and too *little* to the threat presented by faction. The republics, it turned out, were more vulnerable to capture by faction than by the multitude.[1]

DICTATORSHIP IN THE REPUBLICS

In Latin America, where republican government first emerged in the early
nineteenth century, individual strongmen, or caudillos, used personal social
networks to create social movements that seized power in postcolonial states.
Caudillos such as Antonio López de Santa Anna in Mexico and Juan Manuel
de Rosas in Argentina were landlords who organized dependent tenant farmers into militias that enabled them to become regional warlords and then
national dictators.[2] As the historian John Lynch observes, "An exaggerated
form of presidentialism, known as *caudillismo*, emerged. . . . Caudillismo
was marked by certain characteristics: personal rule by a man with a charismatic personality, a repressive dictatorship, a resort to military force to gain
political power, and the centralization of authority. . . . This phenomenon
lasted well into the twentieth century."[3]

Dictators relied on social networks and on relatives to take power and
maintain their faction's hold on power after their deaths. In Argentina, Rosas
asked that power be passed to his daughter in the event of his death, and in
Paraguay, the Congress allowed the dictator Carlos Antonio López the right
to name his own successor.[4] Although Lynch argues that "hereditary caudillismo . . . was a rare phenomenon," it became a common feature in many
republics, where factions rooted in familial social networks subsequently
emerged: the Somozas in Nicaragua, Peróns in Argentina, Chiangs in Taiwan, Castros in Cuba, Bhuttos in Pakistan, Assads in Syria, and Kims in
North Korea.[5]

In Latin America, it was relatively easy in the early nineteenth century for
factions rooted in small social networks to seize and maintain power. They
simply "waited for, and took advantage of moments of government weakness
in order to overthrow the ruling group," Frank Safford observes.[6] But as time
passed, it became more difficult for factions with narrow social support to
obtain power, both to prevent other elite factions from seizing power and to
keep the multitude at bay.[7] Caudillismo gave way to factions that organized
larger, more impersonal social networks and recruited different social
groups—the church, military, bureaucracy, and domestic and foreign elites—
that created elite coalitions, a development that Lynch says occurred in Latin
America after 1870.[8]

In other regions, minority political factions relied not only on charismatic
leaders and social networks but on mass-based political parties and organized
social movements to demand power from colonial empires and to compete

for power with domestic rivals. In many colonies and postcolonial republics, competing republican independence movements emerged. In Russia, Menshevik and Bolshevik factions of the same party simultaneously battled each other, the regime, anarchists, liberals, social democrats, conservatives, royalists, and foreign invaders. In India, the Indian National Congress and the Muslim League engaged in a contentious, collaborative, and combative relation in the decades before independence.[9] In China, the nationalist movement led by Chiang Kai-shek and the Communist Party led by Mao Zedong engaged in a competition both as allies and as enemies on the mainland between 1920 and 1949 and then as opponents in separate states in the years since then.[10]

To compete successfully against foreign and domestic opponents, political factions recruited the members of ethnic-religious groups and/or social classes to create movements that could seize power in postcolonial states. For instance, in Iraq, Saddam Hussein recruited members of the Sunni minority into the Baath Party while in Syria, Bashar al-Assad enrolled members of the Alawite minority in the Baath Party to create a dependable constituency for the regime. The apartheid regime in South Africa, which was established by the National Party in 1948, relied on members of the white settler community, which made up about 20 percent of the population, for political support, a group that had both ethnic and class dimensions.[11]

By contrast, the Chinese dictatorship in 2002 recruited seventy-three million people from different social classes as members of the Communist Party—this is more people than live in California, Texas, and Illinois—and then, in the 2000s, enlisted a roughly equal number of people from bourgeois and entrepreneurial classes and partnered them with state bureaucrats and party members in a new, wider collaborative alliance, though still representing only about 10 percent of the population in China.[12]

These numbers are telling. Most dictatorships have difficulty creating a faction that represents as *much* as 20 percent of the populace. Some regimes—the apartheid government in South Africa, the regimes led by Marshal Broz Tito in Yugoslavia or Gamal Nasser in Egypt—could count on relatively large class or ethnic constituencies.[13] But this is rare. Most of the factions that seize power count on much smaller constituencies, perhaps 10 percent, like those in China, and perhaps only 1 percent in regimes run by caudillos.

Given the fact that the dictators who took power in the republics represented social and political *minorities*, how did they manage to seize power and dissuade or prevent the majority from challenging their authority? They adopted republican practices to enhance their *legitimacy*, and they used *violence* to seize and defend their authority and cow the majority.

Legitimacy

The minority factions that established dictatorships in the republics insisted that they believed in constitutional government. When they took power, dictators did not abolish constitutional government—they *changed* it. In Latin America, this was easy to do. As Keith Rosenn argues, "Built into almost all Latin American constitutions are provisions that permit democracy *and* dictatorships."[14] This was a problem because the men who drafted constitutions in postcolonial Latin American republics borrowed heavily from the US Constitution and adopted a *presidential* model that placed extraordinary powers into the hands of the executive. Billias wryly observes that the US Constitution was "like a lock ordered by catalog from the United States that came with the wrong instructions and no keys."[15] As a result, when one faction won the presidency, it used executive power to rewrite the constitution, emasculate the judiciary, subdue the legislature, and strip the citizenry of any real voice in government. This practice is also a problem in contemporary Egypt, where the Muslim Brotherhood candidate Mohamed Morsi won the presidential election following the overthrow of Hosni Mubarak and then used presidential powers to draft a new constitution, sideline the opposition, and muzzle the judiciary.

In Latin America, factions regularly discarded, rewrote, and adopted new constitutions to cripple their rivals.[16] Between 1811 and 1989, "Latin American countries produced a total of 253 constitutions . . . or 12.6 per country on average, compared with two in the United States during the same period. . . . Latin American constitutions were notoriously easy to change."[17]

Where independence movements created "dictatorships of the proletariat," as the Bolsheviks did in the Soviet Union and the Communist Party did in China and Vietnam, they drafted elaborate constitutions that provided for one-party democracy and, in the Soviet Union, allowed constituent republics to exercise their self-determination and secede from the union if they wanted, a provision that the republics exercised in 1992.[18]

Dictators in postcolonial republics did not typically abolish elections, though they often suspended elections and, when they were held, rigged the results. They restricted the formation of rival political parties, obstructed rivals' campaigns, assassinated rival candidates, and stuffed ballot boxes to ensure their own victories. In Argentina, Rosas won the 1833 election, giving him dictatorial powers with 99.9 percent of the vote, a ridiculous number.[19] They did not dissolve parliaments or close legislatures; they filled them with their cronies, who debated the issues, voiced their support for government policy, and solemnly voted for measures to enhance presidential powers, extend states of emergency, and abolish term limits so that their leaders could become "presidents for life."

By contrast, fascist leaders described themselves as "antiparliamentarians" and vowed to end constitutional government, which they viewed as weak and corrupt. But dictators in most of the republics adopted a different approach. They embraced constitutional government and then smothered it. They preserved the institutions (constitutions and congresses) and observed the practices (elections) of republican government because it enhanced their legitimacy, both at home and abroad. In a world where the republics were growing in number, it was politically advantageous for dictators to adopt republican values and norms. Powerful republics such as the United States and the Soviet Union often insisted that dictators profess republican principles as a condition for admission to the United Nations and for receiving economic or military aid. Between 1945 and 1988, the United States provided $94.8 billion in economic aid to the new republics, most of them dictatorships in the US sphere of influence, while the Soviet Union provided $17.1 billion in aid to regimes in eastern Europe, Southeast Asia, and Africa.[20]

By paying lip service to republican values by holding the occasional election, dictators could obtain foreign investment and secure Olympic Games, which allowed regimes in the Soviet Union (1980), Yugoslavia (1984), South Korea (1988), and China (2008) to showcase their regimes and persuade observers that they were not as bad as their detractors claimed, much as Nazi Germany had done during the 1936 Olympic Games in Berlin. During the 2008 Olympics in Beijing, McDonald's ran "Cheer for China" television ads and Pepsi "painted its familiar blue cans red [as part of] a limited edition, 'Go Red for China' promotion."[21]

Dictatorships also took economic steps to enhance their political legitimacy. Although factions typically used state power to enhance their own wealth and engaged in widespread corruption—President Mobutu Sese Seko of Zaire stole five billion dollars, virtually all of the money given to Zaire by foreign donors—they also promised to promote economic development, provide jobs, and deliver "welfare" benefits to majority populations.[22] Most dictators, even poor ones, subsidized staple foods, cooking and heating oils, primary education, and public transportation.[23] Because dictators made these goods available to everyone without restriction and made cheap goods available to "free riders" (people who could otherwise afford them), they did not have to pay for costly bureaucracies to administer them.

Violence

The factions that installed dictatorships in the republics shared a common feature: a willingness to use violence to dissuade the majority from challenging their authority. In contrast to other republicans, who expressed a yearning for "liberty, equality, fraternity," the bullies and braggarts who became dictators expressed contempt for their opponents, took pride in their ruthlessness, and bragged about their willingness to murder without remorse.

In 1835, when Vicente Rocafuerte took power in Ecuador, he "declared that 'only terror' could reduce the rebels to order and 'conserve the first of all laws [*sic*] which is that of public tranquility. The only course that I have is that they tremble before me. . . . I will convert myself into a Sylla [a Roman dictator] to save my country from the anarchy that is trying to devour it. A true lover of enlightenment and civilization, I consent to pass for a tyrant."[24]

Georgios Papadopoulos, the leader of the Greek military junta in 1973, ordered his soldiers to "slug the flesh" of unarmed student demonstrators.[25] His successor, Dimitrios Ioannidis, demanded that Nicos Sampson, a collaborator who mounted a coup against the democratic government of Cyprus, kill its president, Archbishop Makarios III, and cut off his head: "Nicky," Ionnidis told Sampson, "I want his head. You shall bring it to me yourself, okay Nicky?"[26]

When Argentina's military dictatorship began its "dirty war" against dissident civilians—kidnapping, jailing, torturing, and murdering its opponents, sometimes pushing drugged prisoners out of airplanes over the Atlantic—General Ibérico Saint-Jean bragged about the regime's ruthless commitment to violence: "First we'll kill the subversives, then their collaborators, then . . . their sympathizers, then . . . those who remain indifferent, and finally we'll kill the timid."[27]

Dictators used the army, government bureaucracies, and the courts to arrest, imprison, torture, murder, and massacre. It would be taxing to recount all the horrors inflicted on civilian populations by dictators in the republics: ethnic cleansing in Yugoslavia; genocide of Tutsis by the Hutu regime in Rwanda; dirty wars across Latin America. It may suffice to inventory the violence inflicted by only one regime, in China, during the period after it took power in 1949. According to scholars and US State Department reports, the dictatorship killed two million landlords during the land reforms of the early 1950s, killed one million people during the purges triggered by the Great Proletarian Cultural Revolution, massacred two thousand unarmed demonstrators in Tiananmen Square in 1989, and in recent years annually executed between seven thousand and fifteen thousand people, though most of these people committed "crimes" that are not punishable by death in any other country, and in many cases, neither the defendants nor their lawyers were allowed to *speak* in court.[28] This summary of the regime's purposeful violence does not include the fifteen to forty-five million who died of famine as a result of its failed economic policies during the Great Leap Forward (1958–1960) or the uncounted deaths of women and girls who died as a result of the regime's forcible sterilization and abortion practices, which were part of its ongoing one-child policy, or the practice of abandoning infant girls in orphanages, where high mortality rates have resulted in the deaths of hundreds of thousands of girls.[29]

Dictators did not rely only on state officials and government bureaucracies to dispense violence on civilians. They also enlisted nonstate actors to participate. Regimes in Latin America allowed vigilante death squads to torture and murder opponents of the regime. The Hutu regime in Rwanda persuaded young men in soccer clubs to join the Interahamwe ("Let us strike together"), which was tasked with the murder of Tutsis during the genocide in 1994. The regime in East Germany recruited civilians to inform on family members, friends, and coworkers. The regime in China recruited women in villages to record the menstrual cycles of neighboring women and report unauthorized pregnancies to the authorities; it paid civilian bounty hunters to kidnap and imprison, in unofficial "black jails," people who tried to deliver petitions seeking redress to government officials. Of course, when regimes invited nonstate actors to engage in violence without supervision, those nonstate actors invited their subcontractors to abuse their petty authority.

THE SILENCED MAJORITY?

The willingness of dictators to inflict violence on civilians helps explain why the multitude might be willing to concede political power to small factions. Although violence was an important reason that the multitude might refrain from challenging authority, it was not the only one. There were other reasons that the multitude was not only unable but also unwilling to wrest popular sovereignty from venal, predatory factions.

Thomas Jefferson in 1821 offered a possible explanation why they might not. "I feared from the beginning that these people [in Latin America] were not sufficiently enlightened for self-government; and that after wading through blood and slaughter, they would end in military tyrannies, more or less numerous."[30]

Jefferson gives the people of Latin America too little credit for rational behavior. Recall that the *majority* of people in the republics across the Americas were *dis*enfranchised and treated as denizens or subjects by the citizen *minority*. The majority had little reason to defend a democratic faction of citizens from their predatory, undemocratic brethren. The disenfranchised multitude had little to gain from such a fight (though they frequently fought for the independence movements that disenfranchised them—see chapter 3), particularly where neither citizen democrats nor citizen dictators were willing to enfranchise them. The multitude had much to lose by joining a fight between dueling citizenries.

This may also have been true for disenfranchised groups in more recent years. In many countries today, immigrants and ethnic minorities do not challenge the authority of dictators or join with the opponents of the regime because it is not clear that the challengers would include them in a more "democratic" polity. The noncommittal behavior of Kurdish minorities during the recent civil wars in Iraq and Syria and of Christian minorities during the recent democratic "opening" in Myanmar/Burma are instructive in this regard.

The multitude may also be unwilling to challenge regimes because they depend on the benefits that the regime grudgingly provides. Dictators around the world put food on the table, literally, by providing subsidies to keep the price of bread and other necessities affordable for the impoverished multitude. Economic dependence may weaken or inhibit the multitude's willingness to challenge authority, though as we shall see in the next chapter, if regimes allow these prices to rise (for whatever reason), the multitude's sense of entitlement to (or dependence on) these benefits may encourage them to challenge the regime.

As the representatives of minority factions, dictators work hard to maintain their political legitimacy, both at home and abroad, by portraying themselves as republican and by demonstrating their capacity to use violence against any challenge to their authority, however "timid" it might be. This is a difficult task. As Egyptian dictator Gamal Nasser admitted in a moment of candor, "You imagine that we are simply giving orders and the country is run accordingly. You are greatly mistaken."[31]

If their legitimacy or capacity for violence is diminished, dictators become vulnerable, and the multitude, or small groups among it, might demand change. When it does, dictators fall. Although dictators kept republican institutions and practices intact—rewriting constitutions, holding rigged elections—for cynical reasons, to burnish their credentials and secure foreign and domestic support, their decision to do so had important consequences. When dictators fell, civilian democrats revived moribund republican institutions and used them to facilitate a relatively peaceful transition to democracy in southern Europe, Latin America, eastern Europe, the Soviet Union, and South Africa. More recently, the republican institutions that Nasser, Sadat, and Mubarak used as instruments for dictatorship in Egypt actually played a key role in the *initial* transition from dictatorship to democracy during the Arab Spring.

FACTION AND DIVISION

Although political factions seized power and established dictatorships in postcolonial states, factions in other countries sought to *divide* political power in postcolonial states so that they could rule, as a majority, on their own terms. The division of the republics was a problem that the architects of constitutional government did not fully appreciate.

For example, after the Revolutionary War, the architects of constitutional government in the United States labored to create a unitary federal republic that assigned some power to the thirteen constituent states. During the debates about the Articles of Confederation and the Constitution, the federalists advocated the creation of a strong central government. The antifederalists argued that considerable power should be devolved to the states so that the citizens of each state could rule on their own terms, as a majority, rather than as a minority in a larger union. In addition, the antifederalists "opposed the new national government because its structure and distance from the people would . . . 'prevent those who were not rich, well-born or prominent from exercising political power.'"[32] There was also a "strong drive to separatism on the part of frontiersmen" in the territories west of the Appalachians.[33] The frontiersmen wanted to create republics of their own in western territories so that they could escape the authority both of the federal government and of the original thirteen states, which made them both antifederalist and anti-antifederalists.

The antifederalists and the frontier separatists lost this battle when the states ratified the Constitution, though they obtained a strong Bill of Rights that prevented the rights of minority factions and individuals in the states from being trampled by a political majority in the new Union.[34]

In Latin America, the debate between federalist and antifederalist republics took a different turn. Federalist republicans such as Bolivar and San Martin fought for independence from Spain and for union, the creation of a great republic consisting of different viceroyalties in Spanish America.[35] The antifederalists in the colonies fought for independence and also division, the creation of separate republics in Spanish America, and some fought, like the frontiersmen in North America, for division *and* subdivision. In Argentina, Estanislao López announced in 1819, "We wish to form a small republic in the heart of our territory," and "a number of small, micro-republics emerged, their governments sustained by dominant interest groups and led by a local chief."[36]

In the end, the *anti*federalists prevailed, and the devolution of dynastic power was accompanied by the *division* of Spanish America into separate republics, where minority factions frequently seized power and established dictatorships, as we have seen.

After World War I, the defeated dynastic empires were divided into multiple republics. The division of the Austro-Hungarian Empire led to the creation of separate republics in Austria, Hungary, and Czechoslovakia, though Croatia was attached to the Kingdom of Yugoslavia. The division of the German Empire led to the creation of republics in Germany and Poland. The collapse of the Russian Empire led to the creation of states in the Soviet Union, Latvia, Lithuania, Estonia, Finland, and Poland. The division of the Ottoman Empire led to the creation of a republic in Turkey, though its possessions in the Middle East were assigned to the empires of Great Britain, France, and the new Kingdom of Saudi Arabia.

In general, the devolution and division of power in dynastic states in Europe resembled earlier events in Spanish America, where division of dynastic authority led to the creation of multiple successor republics. But this needs to be qualified. In Russia, the Bolsheviks fought hard, like federalists in North and South America, to create a strong unitary republic that consisted of multiple states (the Bolsheviks called them "republics"), and provided each of them with the constitutional authority to secede from the Soviet "Union."

At the same time, rebellion and civil war in Ireland forced Great Britain to devolve and divide its authority between competing political movements on the island. Catholic republicans fought for a unitary republic in Ireland, while Protestant royalists fought for "union" with Great Britain. The protestant minority argued that their political interests would not be protected or served by a Catholic majority in a unitary republic. They wanted a state in Northern Ireland where they could exercise power on their own terms as a majority, the Catholic minority in Northern Ireland notwithstanding. The British agreed with the Protestants and divided the island, creating an Irish "Free State," which eventually became a republic, and a semiautonomous state in Northern Ireland that had its own parliament but remained a part of the British Empire. British officials created similar accommodations for white settler minorities in South Africa, New Zealand, Australia, and Canada. Of course, the Catholic minority in Northern Ireland objected to political domination by the new Protestant "majority."[37]

After World War II, the great powers dissolved the German, Italian, and Japanese Empires and transferred power to republics in their homelands and new republics in their colonies.[38] The United States and the Soviet Union, along with the republican independence movements in the colonies, then forced the British, French, Dutch, Belgian, Spanish, and Portuguese empires to decolonize. In most cases, decolonization led to the devolution of power from dynastic empires to single, unitary republics, a *federalist* model of change. So, for example, the Belgian Congo became the Republic of the Congo, Dutch Indonesia became the Republic of Indonesia, and French Algeria became the Republic of Algeria.

But the great powers *sometimes* adopted the *antifederalist*, Latin American model and *divided* power between competing republican independence movements.[39] They divided Korea, China, Vietnam, and Germany between nationalist and communist independence movements and gave them each a state of their own. Great Britain divided India and Palestine between competing ethnic-religious movements (Hindus and Moslems in India, Arabs and Jews in Palestine), much as it had done in Ireland, and created separate states for each, though the one assigned to the Arabs in Palestine did not come into being.[40]

The great powers divided these states because they thought it would end conflict between competing independence movements, protect minority movements from being dominated by majority movements in unified states, and protect great-power interests, which were tied to different movements. They were mistaken. Instead of reducing conflict, division created new problems that led to conflict and war between divided states. This should not have surprised them. Philosophical and practical problems associated with partition emerged early on, first in the United States.

Philosophical Problems

The problems with partition first became evident in the United States in the 1850s, when a slave-owning minority faction in the South argued that division would *solve* the deepening political differences between southern states that allowed slavery and states in the North and West that did not. Recall that the slaveholding citizenry represented both a minority of adult white males in the United States as a whole and a minority of the inhabitants (which included women, children, immigrants, and slaves) in every southern state. The Constitution allowed this double minority to count their slaves as three-fifths of a man to boost their representation in Congress, and this, together with two senators for each state, helped them use republican institutions—the executive (most of the presidents elected before the Civil War were slave owners), Congress, and the Supreme Court—to wield greater political power than their numbers would otherwise afford, to protect slavery, and even to extend slavery to new territories in some western states. But with the emergence of the Republican Party, which opposed the *extension* of slavery but did not advocate the *abolition* of slavery where it already existed, and the election of Abraham Lincoln in 1860, the southern minority feared that they would lose their ability to act like a majority and that the new majority would restrict the expansion of slavery in new territories, obstruct the return of fugitive slaves, and eventually abolish slavery. The only way to defend *their* liberty (not the liberty of the multitude, either in southern states or the nation as a whole) was to divide the Republic and create a "Confederacy" that would resemble the kind of republic the antifederalists earlier imagined.

Lincoln disagreed with the Confederates' view of democracy in a republic and advanced three philosophical arguments. First, he argued that the Confederate minority was acting without legal authority. When they signed the Constitution, the delegates of southern states agreed to bind themselves in perpetuity to the Union. This contractual obligation, voluntarily made, could be undone only by *amending* the Constitution. To secede lawfully, the Confederate minority would have to obtain the *consent* of the majority, which, of course, they were unwilling and, probably, unable to do. If they abandoned their contractual, constitutional obligations, the Confederate minority would be acting without lawful authority.

Although Lincoln argued that the Confederate minority could not unilaterally abandon the *Union*, the new Republican majority could not unilaterally abandon *slavery*, which was given constitutional protection, unless it amended the Constitution. This was unlikely, given the number of slave states and the requirement that two-thirds of all states ratify such a change.

Second, Lincoln argued that the southern minority's determination to create a confederate republic where they could rule on their own actually undermined democracy, which was based on the principle of "majority rule." As Lincoln explained in his inaugural address, a minority possessed the right to revolt if "a majority should deprive a minority of any constitutional right."[41] But he said that no such right had been denied to the southern minority. "All the vital rights of minorities and of individuals are so plainly assured to them . . . in the Constitution, that controversies never arise concerning them."[42] He said that since the extension of slavery to new territories was not expressly protected by the Constitution, southern slaveholders could not claim this as their "right" or as a justification for revolt. "If the minority will not acquiesce [on nonconstitutional issues], the majority must, or the government must cease."[43]

In effect, Lincoln argued that the Confederates rejected the *principle* of majority rule, a cornerstone of democracy:

> If a minority . . . will secede rather than acquiesce [to majority rule], they make a precedent which in turn will divide and ruin them, for a minority [faction] of their own will secede from them whenever a majority refuses to be controlled by such a minority. . . . Why may not any portion of a new confederacy, a year or two hence, arbitrarily secede again, precisely as portions of the present Union now claim to secede from it? All who cherish disunion sentiments are now being educated to the exact temper of doing this.[44]

(This is what happened in Virginia, where the mountaineers in 1863 seceded from Virginia, created their own state, West Virginia, and fought for the Union.)

Although Lincoln argued that the practice of democracy required both advancing majority rule and protecting minority rights, he did not imagine that the "majority" or the "minority" were fixed or permanent social identities, etched in stone. Instead, he argued that people possessed multiple and overlapping social and political identities (much as contemporary "intersectional" feminists argue) that changed over time. He had witnessed these changes himself. During Lincoln's lifetime, political factions had undergone a dramatic transformation from Federalists and Whigs to Democrats and then Republicans. Moreover, these political identities have continued to change so that today, constituencies in southern states identify themselves as "Republicans" and constituencies in the North and West as "Democrats," a complete and, for Lincoln's contemporaries, unimaginable turn of events. As Lincoln observed, "A majority held in restraint by constitutional checks and limitations, and *always changing easily* with deliberate changes of popular opinions and sentiments, is the only true sovereign of a free people. . . . The rule of a minority, as a permanent arrangement, is wholly inadmissible."[45]

Confederates responded to these arguments with gunfire. The result was a long, bloody civil war that preserved the Union, abolished slavery, and enfranchised adult black men (see chapter 6). Although the Civil War averted the division of the United States, it has not done so elsewhere. Indeed, the division of states has waxed, even while dictatorship in the republics has waned. Lincoln called attention to the philosophical problems associated with division. But there were also practical problems that he did not anticipate.

Practical Problems

The great powers adopted "partition," or the devolution *and* division of power, in many countries after World War I and World War II because they thought that assigning separate states to each would protect "minority" movements from being dominated by their "majority" peers and reduce conflict between them.[46] But instead of reducing conflict, partition created three problems that led to conflict and war.

First, partition triggered disruptive migrations across newly created borders. After Korea was divided, nearly three million people, or about 25 percent of the population, fled North Korea and moved to the south.[47] The 1.5 million Chinese who fled the mainland for Taiwan in the late 1940s increased the island's population of 8 million by 20 percent.[48] In Palestine, UN observers estimated that 726,000 Arabs moved across newly drawn borders after partition, some voluntarily, many by force, and the Arab population inside Israel dropped by 11 percent.[49] After Britain divided India, seventeen million people fled across newly drawn borders between India and Pakistan, the largest and fastest migration in human history.[50]

People fled because they feared they would be subjected to discrimination by the leaders of the new state or by tyrannical majorities; majorities encouraged or forced minorities to leave so that they could rule without restraint. But violent and socially disruptive migrations and ethnic cleansing, which killed one to two million people during postpartition migrations in India and Pakistan, did not create homogeneous populations.[51] Millions of Moslems remained in India, and today, more Moslems live in India than in Pakistan, an Islamic country.[52] After the partition of Palestine, tens of thousands of Arabs remained in Israel, and when Israel captured the West Bank and Gaza during the 1967 war, hundreds of thousands of Arabs were reincorporated.[53]

Second, many of the postpartition republics were seized by factions that installed dictatorships, and both authoritarian and democratic republics discriminated against residual minority populations. State officials denied minorities the right to vote or bear arms or serve in the military. They imposed martial law on minority populations and authorized majority populations to use violence against minorities. So, for example, the British gave the Protestant Ulster Defense Force unofficial sanction for its campaign against the Irish Republican Army and its Catholic sympathizers in Northern Ireland, and the Israeli government gives armed Jewish settlers in the occupied territories the authority to defend themselves, a right it does not extend to the Arab inhabitants. These kinds of developments undermined the meaning of citizenship in these states.

In response, minorities organized social movements—the Palestine Liberation Organization and later Hamas in the Israeli-occupied territories, the Awami League in eastern Pakistan, Islamic movements in the Indian-controlled sector of Kashmir—to protest the treatment of disenfranchised groups, and some engaged in violent campaigns that resulted in hijackings, hostage taking, bombing campaigns, and assassinations.

The discriminatory practices of officials and nonstate actors in divided states antagonized not only resident minority populations, they also antagonized their compatriots in neighboring states.[54] Moslems in Pakistan traveled to Kashmir to fight on behalf of their compatriots, and Arab Palestinians in Lebanon, Jordan, and Egypt joined the PLO, Hamas, and Hezbollah.

Third, postpartition republics contested the partition process, both because they were excluded from decision making and because many wanted to secure power in a *unitary* state. So they challenged the sovereignty and legitimacy of their rivals and claimed the authority to reunify their country, by force if necessary. For example, the leaders of postpartition states in

Vietnam both adopted constitutions that claimed each other's territories; the communists on the Chinese mainland laid claim to Taiwan, and the nationalists in Taiwan laid claim to the mainland.[55] Competing territorial claims undermined the meaning of sovereignty in divided states.

Disruptive migrations, the rise of dictatorships and discriminatory policies against minority populations, and bitter fights over postpartition boundaries led to conflicts within and between divided states. Large-scale wars erupted between states in North and South Korea and between North and South Vietnam. Conflicts between the two Chinas and between East and West Germany triggered political crises that very nearly led to war. India and Pakistan have waged three wars since partition. Israel and its Arab neighbors have fought five wars since partition, while Palestinian Arabs have staged two uprisings, or *intifadas*.

Moreover, these conflicts triggered superpower military intervention. The United States intervened in conflicts in Korea, China, Vietnam, Germany, India, Pakistan, and the Middle East. The Soviet Union intervened in conflicts in Germany and in the Middle East.[56]

During these conflicts, the superpowers sometimes threatened to use nuclear weapons, as the United States did on a number of occasions.[57] After the United States threatened China, Mao Zedong vowed to develop nuclear weapons, which China did not then possess, to "boost our courage and scare others."[58] But the development of nuclear weapons by China "scared" India, which then developed nuclear weapons, a development that in turn threatened Pakistan, which then developed nuclear weapons of its own.[59] This chain reaction led to the proliferation of nuclear weapons in divided states, which have a long history of waging war with their neighbors, an extremely troublesome development.[60]

During the early twentieth century, republics urged colonized people to exercise their right to self-determination, which meant breaking away from dynastic empires and creating independent republics of their own. Minority factions in some republics demanded the right to exit those republics and establish states of their own. Note, however, that self-determination in the first instance meant separation from dynastic *empires*, while self-determination in the second instance meant secession from *republics*.

In 1971, Bangladesh seceded from Pakistan after a bloody civil war. Then, in 1974, the Turkish minority in Cyprus broke away from the republic, with Turkish assistance, and established a separate state on the island called North Kibris.[61] Then, in the late 1980s and early 1990s, the fall of communist dictatorships in eastern Europe, the Soviet Union, and the Horn of Africa led to the division of some republics into multiple states. Czechoslovakia divided into two republics, Yugoslavia into five republics, more or less, the Soviet Union into fifteen republics, and Ethiopia into two successor states.[62]

The division of these republics differed from previous partitions in two important respects. First, division was generally a product of internal developments, not engineered by the superpowers. Although NATO forces intervened in Bosnia and Kosovo and forced a settlement between warring parties, the superpowers did not participate in the division of the other states.[63]

Second, the division of these republics did not always or everywhere create the kind of problems associated with earlier partitions. Czechoslovakia divided peacefully, and relations between successor states have been relatively amicable.[64] Many of the republics from the former Soviet Union have avoided postpartition problems. But these problems still emerged in some places. The division of Yugoslavia led to conflict and ethnic cleansing, the division of the Soviet Union led to conflicts in Georgia, Chechnya, Armenia, and Azerbaijan, and the division of Ethiopia led to war between Ethiopia and Eritrea. Although partition and secession have long been closely associated with conflict within and between states, it is still being advanced as a *solution* to conflict in many settings. In 2011, Sudan was divided, and South Sudan emerged as a new republic. However, fighting soon erupted, and all of the problems associated with partition have reemerged.[65]

In general, the rise of the republics was associated with decolonization around the world, the creation of democratic republics, and the expansion of citizenries within them. The demise of the dynastic interstate system and the creation of a republican interstate system substantially reduced the threat of world war and the horrific violence associated with it. Still, the rise of the republics was accompanied by two problems: the rise of dictatorships in many republics, and the division of some postcolonial states. As we have seen, both developments compromised the meaning of democracy, citizenship, and sovereignty and contributed to violence within and between states. During the past forty years, social movements ousted dictatorships around the world. Although dictators retain power in China, the world's largest state, dictatorship in the republics has waned, an important and positive development. The same cannot be said of division. Social movements have emerged to demand power in states of their own. Scots in the United Kingdom, Basques and Catalans in Spain, Lombardians in Italy, Karen in Burma, and

Quebecois in Canada now demand the right of "self-determination," which in this context means the division of existing republican states, a troubling prospect.

Let us next examine the democratization of the republics during the past forty years.

Chapter Five

The Democratization of the Republics

In the last quarter of the twentieth century, social movements toppled dictators in dozens of republics around the world. Harvard political scientist Samuel Huntington argued that the "transition of some 30 countries from nondemocratic to democratic political systems between 1974 and 1990 . . . was perhaps the most important global political development in the late twentieth century."[1] The fall of dictators in eastern Europe was soon followed by democratization in the Soviet Union (1992), South Africa (1994), Indonesia (1997), Turkey (2000), Burma (2011), and, during the Arab Spring (2011), in Tunisia, Libya, and Egypt.[2]

The democratization of the republics extended citizenship to people who had long been treated as the subjects of authoritarian rule and brought an end to the violence that dictators used to protect minority political power. Today, a majority of the republics in the interstate system are democratic.

SUPERPOWER SPHERES

After World War II, the United States and Soviet Union created a new republican interstate system and used it to promote decolonization. But they also divided the world into competing spheres of influence and frequently supported dictators in the new republics to secure superpower interests and defend the boundaries of their spheres. Although Roosevelt told Churchill, "We must be careful to make it clear that we are not establishing any postwar spheres of influence," he nevertheless agreed with Stalin to divide the world into US and Soviet spheres.[3] At the inaugural UN conference in San Francisco, US officials persuaded delegates to adopt articles that preserved the Monroe Doctrine and permitted the creation of political and military blocs outside the United Nations, which effectively authorized US and Soviet officials to organize a series of military alliances designed to defend these spheres. "We have preserved the Monroe Doctrine and the Inter-American System," Senator Arthur Vandenburg, author of the UN articles, boasted.[4]

US and Soviet officials then moved to establish separate spheres of influence around the world. But disputes over the boundaries of their respective spheres led to a series of conflicts between the United States and the Soviet Union, which became known collectively as the Cold War.[5]

During the Cold War, US and Soviet leaders recruited, supported, and installed dictatorships within their spheres. They did so to protect their interests in the region and prevent indigenous social movements from seizing power and then defecting from their assigned place in the sphere. For example, US officials worried that communist insurgents in Greece might win the civil war, exit the US sphere, and join the Soviet bloc; Soviet leaders feared that independent-minded communists in Yugoslavia and nationalist movements in Hungary might exit the Soviet bloc and join the US sphere. US and Soviet leaders worried that the departure of independent-minded republics would weaken the "collective security" that spheres of influence were supposed to provide for their members. So they frequently supported dictators to prevent this from happening. George Kennan, an architect of US foreign policy during the Cold War, explained why the United States supported client regimes: "Where the concepts and traditions of popular government [constitutional government based on popular sovereignty] are too weak to absorb successfully the intensity of communist attack, then we must concede that harsh government methods of repression may be the only answer."[6] As a result, "the sweeping terms of [Cold War policy] obliged [the United States] . . . to recruit, subsidize, and support a heterogeneous army of satellites, clients, dependents, and puppets."[7]

Although US officials promoted and assisted the creation of strong, stable, democratic republics in western Europe and Japan during this period, they also supported dictators in southern Europe, across Latin America, and in many of the new republics that emerged from colonial rule across Asia, Africa, and the Middle East.

The Soviet Union followed suit, creating puppet dictatorships across eastern Europe and making alliances with communist regimes that came to power on their own in China, North Korea, North Vietnam, and Cuba. Both superpowers then provided economic and military aid to client regimes, which enabled those regimes to develop their economies and provide some economic benefits to subject populations.

Significantly, leaders in some of the new republics objected to the emergence of superpower spheres of influence and refused to assume the roles assigned to them. During the 1950s, the communist regime led by Marshal Broz Tito broke with Stalin and took Yugoslavia out of the Soviet sphere in eastern Europe. Mao Zedong subsequently broke with Stalin and decamped as well. In Egypt, Gamal Nasser objected to Egypt's treatment by the United States and its allies during the 1956 Suez War. So he took Egypt out of the US sphere and joined the Soviet bloc, though as a *non*communist member. In India, Jawaharlal Nehru's socialist government refused to participate in *either* sphere and adopted a nonaligned foreign policy.[8] "We will not attach ourselves to any particular [superpower] group," Nehru announced, "or align ourselves with this great power or that and [become] its camp followers in the hope that some crumbs might fall from their table."[9]

After abandoning their assigned places in superpower spheres, Tito, Nasser, and Nehru then joined together and created a nonaligned movement, a political space *outside* superpower spheres, and invited the leaders of other postcolonial republics to join them.[10]

US and Soviet leaders denounced the nonaligned movements and their efforts to persuade other republics to exit their assigned places in the US and Soviet spheres. US officials defended "collective security" and attacked nonalignment as a form of "neutralism," which "pretends that a nation can best gain safety for itself by being indifferent to the fate of others. This has increasingly become an obsolete conception and, except under very exceptional circumstances, it is an immoral and short-sighted conception."[11] Soviet leaders agreed: "Neutralism, or the idea that these new states [republics] could be a 'third force' between the two sides, was a 'rotten idea' that served only the interests of imperialism."[12]

Moreover, US and Soviet leaders took steps to shore up their respective spheres and prevent social movements within them from seizing power and then defecting. US officials deployed military forces, mercenaries, and clandestine agents in Greece, Congo, Iran, the Philippines, Cuba, Guatemala, South Korea, South Vietnam, Cambodia, Nicaragua, El Salvador, Chile, Grenada, and Panama to prevent indigenous social movements or independent-minded governments from taking power. During the same period, the Soviet Union deployed its military forces in East Germany, Hungary, and Czechoslovakia to prevent social movements or governments from exiting the Soviet sphere, in Egypt to support Nasser, and in Cuba to support Castro. The Soviet Union also supported Castro's deployment of Cuban troops in Ethiopia and Angola and invaded Afghanistan to expand its sphere.

But in the early 1970s, global political and economic conditions changed abruptly. Political and economic crises undermined dictatorships in both the US and Soviet spheres. Social movements and political parties then took advantage of the crises to press for change, and they forced dictators from power in countries around the world.

DICTATORS, CRISES, AND SOCIAL MOVEMENTS

Three important political and economic developments undermined dictators in the US and Soviet spheres during the 1970s and 1980s. First, President Richard Nixon decided to abandon Chiang Kai-shek's nationalist dictatorship in Taiwan, a longtime ally, and recognize Mao Zedong's communist regime in China. Nixon did so to enlist China in his effort to force a peace treaty on North Vietnam and bring an end to the war in Vietnam.[13] The US recognition of China had two important consequences for dictators around the world. It called into question US support for spheres of influence, which were based on the idea that the world was divided into a US-supported capitalist sphere and a Soviet-dominated communist sphere. By recruiting *communist* China as its ally, Nixon abandoned the idea that the two spheres were based on important political, economic, and ideological differences. Would the United States support dictators in their fight against communism if the United States no longer objected to communism in China?

By recognizing China, US officials also demonstrated that they were prepared to abandon the dictatorship in Taiwan, which had long been a stalwart ally, because this alliance no longer served the long-term interests of the United States. Might there also come a day when US officials abandoned dictatorships in Spain, Brazil, South Korea, or South Africa, and for the same reasons? As we will see, during moments of crisis, US officials subsequently abandoned regimes in South Vietnam, Greece, Argentina, and the Philippines. The withdrawal of US support contributed to the fall of these regimes *and* undermined *other* dictatorships in the US sphere.

Soviet officials subsequently adopted a similar approach to dictatorships in their sphere. In 1989, Mikhail Gorbachev announced that he was going to withdraw unconditional Soviet support for client regimes in eastern Europe and Afghanistan. This proved to be a crippling blow for dictatorships in eastern Europe, as we will see, though not immediately in Afghanistan, where the communist regime actually survived the withdrawal of Soviet troops and fought on, alone, for several years before it collapsed in 1992.[14]

By withdrawing their support for dictatorships in their spheres, US and Soviet leaders intentionally and unintentionally undermined the regimes they created and for many years supported. This tectonic shift destroyed the whole idea of spheres of influence as an organizing principle of global politics.[15] As sphere-of-influence politics collapsed, the United States and Soviet Union no longer had any real reason to support client dictators, though they would continue to do so in some cases on an ad hoc basis.

Second, global economic crises in the 1970s and 1980s sabotaged the efforts of dictators in both spheres to promote economic development and provide benefits to the multitude. During the early 1970s, rising gas and food prices triggered both an inflationary spiral that increased prices for goods and services around the world and a recession that increased unemployment. Economists described this dual economic crisis (stagnant economic growth and rising prices) as "stagflation."[16] Regimes in Latin America and eastern Europe borrowed money to spur economic growth, keep employment levels high, and continue to provide benefits (cheap staple foods, energy, transportation, and education) for the multitude. But growing indebtedness simply deferred the crisis. When US officials raised interest rates in the 1980s to battle inflation, the regimes that had borrowed money could not repay their debts, and a debt crisis ensued. Lenders in the United States and elsewhere assigned the International Monetary Fund the task of collecting the debts, and the IMF imposed "structural adjustment programs" or "austerity measures" to ensure that dictators repaid the money they borrowed. In general, the IMF required regimes to cut state benefits and raise the price of food, fuel, transport, and education. As their economies slowed, unemployment and food prices rose, which *lowered* the living standards for poor and working people in the US and Soviet spheres. This development undermined the economic and political legitimacy of dictators who had borrowed money and allowed living standards to fall. In response to *economic* crisis, people gathered in the streets and demanded *political* change.

Third, dictators in the US and Soviet spheres often took steps that created political problems for their own regimes. Dictators in Greece, Portugal, Argentina, the Soviet Union, and South Africa engaged in wars that led to humiliating military defeats, which discredited these regimes. Dictators in the Philippines, Paraguay, and Chile called "snap" elections to demonstrate their popularity but then lost those elections to hastily organized opposition movements, despite the regimes' efforts to rig the elections and steal the vote. In the Philippines, Nicaragua, and Panama, dictators assassinated political rivals, which turned wealthy elites against them. In Spain, Brazil, and the Soviet Union, the deaths of dictators led to crises of succession, which compromised the regimes' ability to manage economic and political crises and gave the opposition an opportunity to mobilize. These self-inflicted wounds undermined dictatorships and made it difficult for them to address multiple and ongoing problems.

Political and economic crises undermined the legitimacy of regimes in the US and Soviet spheres. When crises struck, social movements took advantage of economic and political opportunities to act, some for the first time, others as part of ongoing campaigns against a given regime. When regimes cut back programs to assist the poor, people took to the streets and engaged in what sociologists John Walton and David Seddon called "austerity protests."[17] When regimes suffered military defeat in foreign wars, soldiers in Portugal and Greece mutinied, and demonstrators gathered in public squares in Argentina to demand the ouster of the military junta responsible for the invasion of the Malvinas/Falklands and subsequent defeat by British forces. In East Germany, millions of people simply fled the country and made their way to West Germany, a migration that brought the economy to a standstill and the regime to its knees.

Although the social movements that first braved government violence to confront brutal regimes were often quite small—in Argentina, the handful of women who joined the Mothers of the Plaza de Mayo and marched in silence on behalf of their children who were kidnapped during the regime's dirty war; the small group of playwrights and dissidents who joined Charter 77 in communist Czechoslovakia; the college students who faced police tear gas and bullets in Greece—they could be quite powerful because they acted as proxies for the silenced multitude, who might join them at a moment's notice.

Social movements also organized large and determined coalitions of students and workers—the *minjung* movement in South Korea, Solidarity in Poland, the African National Congress in South Africa—to demand change. Although dictatorships effectively suppressed, contained, or drove these movements into exile for many years, economic and political crises weakened their ability to do so. These movements eventually forced regimes to recognize and then invite them to negotiate a transfer of power, which resulted in democratization. Although *anti*communist dissident movements emerged in the Baltics and in many Eastern European states, in the Soviet Union, Czechoslovakia, and Yugoslavia, *former* communist leaders also organized social movements that contested for power in the Soviet Union and eastern Europe, a development that complicates our understanding of social movements in this period.

In the early 1970s, the political and economic conditions that allowed dictators to survive and thrive during the postwar period changed dramatically. The end of superpower spheres and the onset of persistent economic problems undermined the political and economic foundations of regimes in the US and Soviet spheres, making them vulnerable to political change by social movements small and large. Let us now examine some of the developments that contributed to democratization around the world, starting in 1974 with the fall of regimes in southern Europe.

Southern Europe

After 1945, fascist dictators in Portugal and Spain became US allies. They were later joined by a fascist-style military regime in Greece. Economically, they relied on US military aid as members of NATO during the 1950s and then on income from millions of workers who migrated to northern Europe and sent money home and on income from tourists who spent their vacations on beaches in southern Europe: "The economy [of Greece, Spain, and Portugal] was refueled from abroad: by tourist earnings, by the remittances of émigrés working abroad, and by foreign loans."[18] But with the onset of inflation and recession in western Europe in the early 1970s, émigré workers were sent home, tourists canceled vacations, and all three regimes ran out of money.[19]

Economic crisis in all three countries was compounded by different military and political problems. In Portugal, military defeat by insurgent republicans in Portugal's African colonies persuaded dissident Portuguese military officers to launch a successful coup. According to Samuel Huntington, "The Third Wave of democratization in the modern world began, implausibly and unwittingly, at twenty-five minutes after midnight, Thursday April 25, 1947, in Lisbon, Portugal, when a radio station played the song, 'Grando la Vila Morena,' which signaled the go-ahead for leaders of the coup."[20] The coup toppled a fascist regime that first took power in 1930. But instead of forming a new military regime, the leaders of the coup organized elections that brought the newly created Socialist Party to power and then retired, leaving government in the hands of civilian authorities.[21]

A few months later, the military junta in Greece supported a coup against the democratically elected government in Cyprus, an independent island republic with a large Greek-speaking population.[22] The leaders of the coup planned to assassinate the Cypriot president, Archbishop Makarios III, and merge Cyprus into Greece. But Makarios escaped, fighting broke out between the Greek-speaking majority and the Turkish-speaking minority, and Turkish forces invaded the island to protect the Turkish minority, developments that brought Greece and Turkey (both of them members of NATO) to the brink of war. The regime's misadventure in Cyprus brought antigovernment demonstrators into the streets and persuaded Greek military leaders to depose the "colonels" and return power to a civilian government. Leaders of the political opposition returned from exile, and social movements organized and reorganized domestic political parties. Elections brought a socialist party to power, and constitutional government was restored in the birthplace of democracy.

In Spain, the death of Francisco Franco in 1975 resulted in the transfer of power to King Juan Carlos, who defied expectations by dismantling the regime's fascist institutions and moving to reestablish constitutional, republican government. King Carlos allowed antifascist social movements in Spain and in exile to reemerge and then presided over a process that led eventually to the election of a socialist government and the entry of Spain into the European Community, which also admitted new republican governments from Greece and Portugal.[23] Membership in the European Community promoted rapid economic growth in all three countries, at least until the financial crisis of 2008.

Latin America

During the 1970s, dictators in Latin America and the Philippines collectively borrowed $400 billion to avert the economic problems associated with rising food and energy prices.[24] But when US officials raised interest rates in 1979, they triggered a debt crisis that created serious economic and political problems for indebted regimes. By insisting that regimes adopt painful austerity measures so that they could repay their debts to US banks and international lending agencies, US officials undercut client regimes and exposed them to public wrath.[25] Across Latin America, poor and working people poured into the streets and organized violent and nonviolent protests against the austerity programs imposed by dictators and the International Monetary Fund. For example, protesters organized by the Committee Fighting against Unemployment in Brazil united around the slogan "We won't die of hunger and be quiet about it."[26]

Under these conditions, dictators took desperate measures to retain power. In Argentina, the generals invaded the Falkland Islands to boost popular support for the heavily indebted regime. But the 1982 invasion, much like the Greek colonels' misadventure in Cyprus, turned into disaster after British forces destroyed Argentina's navy, recaptured the islands, and forced the Argentine garrison to surrender.[27] Protesters demanding an end to dictatorship filled the streets of Buenos Aires and forced the generals to surrender political power and hold elections, which paved the way for the return of civilian, constitutional government in 1983.[28]

The collapse of the dictatorship in Argentina reverberated across the continent. Dictators in other countries realized that they, too, faced a serious economic crisis, that their efforts to repay their debts would antagonize the multitude, and that they had conducted dirty wars against political dissidents, which made government officials vulnerable to arrest or retribution if they were forced from office. They realized, too, that they could no longer count on US support if push came to shove. These problems persuaded regimes to initiate and, where they could, manage a transfer of power to opposition social movements, resurgent political parties, and civilian authorities in return for protection or immunity from legal prosecution. They did not always succeed. In Nicaragua and El Salvador, dictators were forced from power by armed insurgents and in the Philippines by nonviolent protests in the streets, after which the dictators fled into exile.[29] Still, by 1990, "17 of the 20 countries and over 90 percent of the population [could be said] to live under democratic governments," Robert Pastor observed. "More of Latin America is now democratic . . . than at any time in the previous 160-year period of the continent [since] the struggle for separation from Spain and . . . Portugal."[30]

East Asia

Between 1945 and 1978, US officials gave more economic and military aid to front-line, anticommunist dictatorships in South Korea and Taiwan than to all US allies in Latin America.[31] US aid and easy access to American markets spurred rapid economic growth in both countries.[32] But when Nixon recognized China, the political and economic conditions that contributed to economic growth in Taiwan and South Korea changed dramatically. In *polit-ical* terms, the United States refused to provide unconditional military support for the regime in Taiwan, and the regime was kicked off the UN Security Council and out of the United Nations, a development that made it politically vulnerable. US officials continued to support South Korea against the threat of invasion by North Korea, but the new US friendship with China diminished the threat of attack by North Korea (which was close to China) and diminished the importance of the South Korean regime as a bulwark against communism.

Changed relations between the United States and China also had important *economic* consequences for South Korea and Taiwan, which had built their economies by exporting cheap manufactured goods to the United States. After 1978, US firms invested heavily in China, low-cost Chinese exports soon replaced goods from South Korea and Taiwan in US markets, and these developments threatened continued economic growth in both countries. Moreover, workers and students in both countries joined together and created a large antigovernment coalition, what the Koreans called *minjung*, "the people" or "the masses," that organized determined and ongoing protests, riots, and strikes against the dictatorships and martial law. They argued that the regimes denied them the benefits associated with rapid economic growth and barred them from a meaningful say in government.[33] As their economies slowed, Cho Soon, South Korea's minister of economic planning, warned that without economic or political reform, "our country will collapse like some of the Latin American countries."[34]

In South Korea, the military leader of the regime, Roh Tae Woo, in 1987 announced that "this country could develop a more mature democracy," and took steps to hold elections and return the country to constitutional government.[35] In Taiwan, the dictatorship lifted martial law in 1987 and embarked on a slow, controlled process of democratization, which led to open elections in 1992.[36]

During this period, demonstrators gathered in Tiananmen Square and demanded that communist China democratize. But the regime slaughtered protesters and crushed efforts to reform the political system.[37] Since then, the regime has grown stronger, in part because it received massive amounts of foreign investment, much of it from countries that recently democratized.[38]

Eastern Europe and the Soviet Union

After 1945, the Soviet Union installed communist regimes in eastern Europe and worked to rebuild war-torn industries and infrastructures, which contributed to modest economic growth during the 1950s and 1960s. But Soviet leaders, determined to defend their sphere of influence during the Cold War, devoted much of the country's available economic resources, as much as 20 to 28 percent of the gross national product, to the military.[39] They created impressively large but relatively ineffective conventional military forces.[40] Heavy military spending reduced Soviet investment in agriculture and industry. Crop yields fell, and in the mid-1970s grain harvests failed, which created domestic food shortages and forced the regime to purchase costly imported food.[41] Meanwhile, the resources diverted from industry prevented the introduction of more productive technology and resulted in the production of shoddy goods that were not competitive on world markets.[42] When Mikhail Gorbachev took office in 1985, he found the Soviet Union "in a state of severe crisis which has embraced all spheres of life."[43] He blamed heavy military spending and the war in Afghanistan for the crisis, saying they had "exhausted our economy."[44]

Gorbachev adopted a series of economic and political reforms to address these problems, arguing that he had no choice: it was "either democracy or social inertia and conservatism."[45] To cut military spending, he abandoned support for the Soviet Union's client dictatorship in Afghanistan and withdrew Soviet troops, cut aid to client regimes in other countries, negotiated arms-control and troop-reduction agreements with the United States and its NATO allies in Europe, and pursued détente with the United States and China.[46] Perhaps most important, he renounced the Soviet Union's right to use military force to support client regimes in eastern Europe. On October 25, 1989, Soviet foreign minister Gennady Gerasimov was asked whether he still adhered to the Brezhnev Doctrine, which the Soviets invoked to justify their invasion of Czechoslovakia in 1968. He said he did not. Instead, he said that the new Soviet policy might be described as the "Sinatra Doctrine," because the American singer Frank Sinatra "had a song, 'I Did It My Way.' So every country decides in its own way which [economic and political policy] road to take."[47]

By adopting the Sinatra Doctrine, the Soviets abandoned their client regimes in eastern Europe. These unpopular regimes had long relied on Soviet support to stay in power. Moreover, during the 1970s, they had borrowed heavily, like their counterparts in Latin America, to cope with economic problems and now found that they could not easily repay their debts without imposing severe austerity programs on restive populations. When it became apparent that Soviet leaders had withdrawn their support for communist regimes, old dissident movements joined with new opposition movements to demand an end to Communist Party rule. Searching for a way out, communist regimes quickly opened negotiations with dissident movements to hold elections and surrender power. Except for Romania, where the dictator fought to retain his grip on power, democratization was conducted peacefully. By the end of 1989, civilian political parties and constitutional government had returned to the republics in eastern Europe.

In the Soviet Union, meanwhile, Gorbachev tried to introduce economic and political reforms. But social movements and political parties organized along ethnic-national lines in the Soviet Union's constituent republics—Russia, Ukraine, the Baltic republics—and demanded that the Soviet Union both democratize and divide.[48] An August 1992 coup by a hard-line faction determined to reverse Gorbachev's reforms and crush emerging social movements in the republics failed to restore one-party dictatorship, as factions in the army rallied behind Russia's president, Boris Yeltsin. These developments led, by the end of 1992, to the democratization and division of the Soviet Union into fifteen independent republics.[49]

Democratization also led to division in Czechoslovakia, where it was peacefully achieved, and in Yugoslavia, where it led to a series of multisided conflicts, ethnic cleansing, superpower intervention, and subdivision.[50]

DEMOCRATIZATION IN THE 1990s AND 2000s

After the fall of dictatorships in eastern Europe and the Soviet Union, democratization continued, though at a slower pace, in republics around the world.

South Africa

In South Africa, the white-minority government excluded the black and mixed-race "colored" majority from citizenship under a strict system of apartheid, which segregated the races and banned interracial marriage and opposition political parties, and made it a crime for blacks to touch and thereby "desecrate" the South African flag or to "campaign for the repeal or the modification of *any* law" or to promote "the communist doctrine of racial equality."[51] The regime subjected the majority population to severe economic exploitation and treated them as illegal aliens in their own country.[52] During the 1980s, opponents of the regime persuaded Western governments to embargo South Africa and foreign investors to divest their holdings and exit the country, which resulted in "an outflow of $3.7 billion between 1981 and 1985."[53] Falling gold prices and mounting debt contributed to a growing economic crisis. At the same time, students and black workers together conducted a series of illegal school boycotts and strikes that hastened the exit of foreign investors and contributed to a deepening political crisis.[54]

The regime reacted violently to domestic protest, declaring a state of emergency, arresting tens of thousands of dissidents, and deploying military forces and ethnic vigilantes to suppress the nonviolent insurgency.[55] Six thousand people were killed in the violence between 1985 and 1990.[56] After bitter political infighting for control of the National Party, which controlled the regime, Frederik de Klerk forced out the old leadership and in 1990 announced that he would legalize the banned African National Congress, free its leader, Nelson Mandela, and open negotiations to dismantle apartheid, expand the citizenry, and create constitutional government based on majority rule. "The well-being of all in this country is linked inextricably to the ability of leaders to come to terms with one another on a new dispensation," de Klerk announced. "The aim is a totally new and just constitutional dispensation in which every inhabitant will enjoy equal rights, treatment, and opportunity in every sphere of endeavor—constitutional, social, and economic."[57]

Although the process of negotiating terms and rewriting the constitution took four years and was marred by ongoing violence, primarily between rival black African social movements and political parties, it resulted in 1993 in the adoption of a new constitution and the country's first nonracial general election, which in 1994 brought the ANC to power and made Nelson Mandela the country's first black president. When he was inaugurated in 1994, joyous black crowds chanted, "Amandla! Nguwethu! (Power! It Is Ours!)."[58]

Indonesia

In 1968, General Suharto (Soeharto) seized power in Indonesia, the world's largest Muslim country. During the 1970s and 1980s, the regime used rising oil revenues to promote economic growth and enrich family members and business and military elites associated with the regime.[59] Oil prices declined after 1985, but foreign businesses invested heavily in Indonesia, which kept the economy growing and strengthened the currency (the rupiah).[60] The appreciation of the rupiah encouraged consumers to buy imported goods but also made Indonesian goods more expensive on foreign markets, leading to growing trade deficits, a common problem for countries across South Asia during the late 1990s.[61] In 1997, a currency crisis, which began in Thailand, engulfed Indonesia. The value of the rupiah fell by 70 percent, foreign investors fled, the Indonesian economy collapsed, unemployment rose, standards of living fell (though as a result of the currency crisis, not debt), and the number of people in poverty tripled.[62] As in other countries, economic disaster triggered riots, protests, and the emergence of social movements and opposition political parties across the country. Sustained and determined protests soon forced Suharto from office.[63] Military and political elites then obtained economic assistance from the International Monetary Fund, which demanded that the government adopt strict austerity measures, and moved to democratize the political process, both in response to public demands for an end to dictatorship and corruption and to create a government with the political legitimacy necessary to pursue the painful economic restructuring required by the IMF. Democratization led to elections, the departure of military representatives from the country's parliament, declining levels of public corruption, and, after some years, renewed economic growth.[64] It also led to the withdrawal of Indonesian forces from East Timor, a former Portuguese colony that was annexed by the Suharto regime in 1975, a development that triggered an armed insurgency by people in the occupied region.[65] The departure of Indonesian forces led to the creation of a new republic in East Timor.

Turkey

When the Ottoman Empire dissolved after World War I, military elites led by Kemal Atatürk created a secular republic in Turkey. Like many Latin American countries in the nineteenth and twentieth centuries, the military dominated political life in Turkey, though civilian political parties often formed governments under the watchful eyes of the military elites. The military permitted conservative political parties to participate in elections and Parliament so long as they did not challenge secular military authority, a political system that effectively disenfranchised secular leftists, Islamic political parties, and Kurds, an ethnic minority, some of them separatists.

After the collapse of communist dictatorships in eastern Europe, the European Union invited civilian governments in some countries to apply for membership, which would give them access to important economic, political, and social benefits.[66] In 1999, the EU invited Turkey to apply for membership on the condition that the government democratize and extend real political power and civil rights to groups that had long been excluded from meaningful political participation.[67] Military and political elites decided to democratize, both because they wanted to take advantage of the economic benefits associated with EU membership and because they wanted to develop broad political support for adopting the painful austerity measures imposed by the IMF in the wake of a 2001 currency crisis (a crisis very similar to the one that earlier struck Thailand and Indonesia). Military authorities and civilian political parties then rewrote the constitution and adopted legal measures designed to expand the electorate and extend political and civil rights to excluded groups. This led to the election and subsequent reelection of an Islamic party, which the military had long viewed as a threat to the secular character of the republic.

Iraq and Afghanistan

After the attacks of September 11, 2001, the United States and some of its allies invaded Iraq and Afghanistan and toppled Saddam Hussein's Baathist regime in Iraq and the Taliban dictatorship in Afghanistan. US forces then established provisional, US-run occupation authorities in both countries, which created a set of republican institutions and then transferred power, more or less, to indigenous civilian authorities, pending the withdrawal of US military forces (the United States withdrew the bulk of its forces from Iraq in 2011; US troops remain in Afghanistan).[68] The top-down US approach to the creation of constitutional government in Iraq and Afghanistan was modeled on the US military occupations of Germany and Japan after World War II. But in Iraq and Afghanistan, the creation of new republics and the transfer of power to indigenous political parties occurred during violent, multisided civil wars, which were conducted by domestic and foreign insurgents. Although civilian, constitutional governments have been established in both countries, it is unclear whether they can end the violence, expand citizenship to include groups that had been excluded from the government—women and members of different ethnic groups—and resist capture by factions determined to seize power and establish a dictatorship and/or divide power and create dictatorships in separate states.

Burma

The military dictatorship that took power in 1962 turned Burma, one of the biggest rice-exporting countries in the world, into one of the planet's poorest countries.[69] Military elites plundered the country's natural resources, adopted insular political and economic policies, impoverished the population, crushed secular and religious antigovernment protests, and tried to suppress, without much success, armed insurgencies by minority groups in the country's interior.[70] In 2001, Than Shwe, the leader of the junta, chose General Thein Sein as his successor. In a surprise move, Thein Sein in 2011 called for an end to corruption and ongoing civil wars, released political prisoners, rewrote the constitution, and organized elections in which dissident students and Buddhist monks, social movements, and opposition parties participated, including a party led by Aung San Suu Kyi, a long-incarcerated activist who won the Nobel Peace Price in 1991.[71] Thein Sein may have democratized because he wanted to persuade foreign governments to lift trade embargoes and political sanctions and encourage investment in Burma, which might then create the conditions for economic growth.

The Arab Spring

The sudden fall, in rapid succession, of dictators in Tunisia, Egypt, and Libya led to democratization in all three Arab republics during 2011. The individual protesters, social movements, and political parties who gathered in the streets of Tunis and Cairo and the rebels who took up arms against Muammar Qaddafi in Libya all objected to their governments' economic policies and political constraints. During the 1980s and 1990s, dictators in Tunisia and Libya used oil revenues to generate modest economic growth, while the Mubarak regime in Egypt relied on income from tourists and from workers who found employment overseas (mostly in the Gulf states) and sent money (remittances) home.[72] But corrupt family members and elites captured most of the wealth, and governments did little to provide employment for young, educated domestic workers, the "hittiste" (young men who lean against walls waiting for work) who could not find meaningful employment or earn enough to move away from their parents, establish independent households, marry, and raise families of their own.[73]

The global recession that began in 2008 reduced oil prices and revenues for oil-producing states such as Tunisia and Libya, tourists stayed home, and workers in the Persian Gulf were sent home, which reduced Egypt's revenues from tourists and workers living abroad, its most important sources of revenue.[74] At the same time, the price of wheat and bread rose sharply, which reduced living standards for a majority of people living in the region.[75]

Meanwhile, the behavior of political elites—their determination to enrich family, friends, and tribes from the public coffers, to pass power to family members and establish "republarchies" (republican monarchies)—alienated secular opponents of the regime, who believed that economic and political advancement should be based on merit, not privilege. Meanwhile, their campaigns against Islamic dissidents antagonized poor people who clung to conservative traditions.[76] In Egypt, the Mubarak regime arrested, jailed, and tortured members of the Muslim Brotherhood, who had assassinated Mubarak's predecessor, President Anwar Sadat, in 1981. In Libya, Qaddafi's security forces massacred 1,270 jailed Islamic prisoners in 1996, an incident that "became one of the rallying cries for the opposition movement that would eventually bring down the regime."[77] Popular anger at the economic and political policies of Arab regimes erupted first in Tunisia.

On December 17, 2010, Mohamed Bouazizi set himself on fire to protest his mistreatment by police. A police officer had slapped him and seized the goods from his pushcart. He was then beaten by police after he lodged a complaint.[78] His self-destructive act—he later died from his burns—ignited large-scale riots and protests across the country. The police killed twenty-three protesters during the first few weeks, but demonstrations still grew. President Zine al-Abidine ordered the army to crush the protests. But army leaders refused. Protesters called for a general strike, and the president and his family fled the country on January 14, 2011.[79] After the president left, leaders of the army, the regime, and dissident groups formed a transition government, which rewrote the constitution and held elections that brought a secular civilian government to power.[80]

The events in Tunisia galvanized young Egyptian activists, who gathered in Tahrir Square, in the heart of Cairo, to demand change.[81] President Hosni Mubarak ordered a crackdown, but the army balked, and protesters in the square chanted, "Al-shaab wal-gayscheed wahdah!" ("The people and the army are one.")[82] The demonstrations grew in size, the army withdrew its support for the regime, and the combined efforts of social movements and banned political parties such as the Muslim Brotherhood drove Mubarak from office. The military then organized an interim government that rewrote the constitution and held elections that brought Mohamed Morsi, a leader of the Muslim Brotherhood, to power as president.[83]

When riots and similar protests erupted in Benghazi, Libyan dictator Muammar Qaddafi did not equivocate. He launched an all-out military assault on his civilian opponents across the country. They took up arms and organized militias to defend themselves. Civil war ensued. For a time, Qaddafi's forces routed the poorly armed, poorly organized rebel forces. But attacks on the regime by US and NATO forces blunted the attack, destroyed Libyan planes and tanks, and degraded its military capabilities, which led to rebel success on the ground. The six-month civil war killed between thirty thousand and fifty thousand people, most of them civilians.[84] It ended when Qaddafi was captured, dragged from a culvert where he was hiding, beaten, sodomized, shot, and killed.[85]

Protests subsequently erupted in Gulf states, where the monarchies quickly suppressed them, and in Syria, where protest and violent repression led to an armed insurrection and a bloody, protracted civil war. Tens of thousands of civilians were killed in the fighting, and one hundred thousand refugees fled to neighboring countries.

DEMOCRATIZATION: EXPANDING CITIZENRIES, DECLINING VIOLENCE

The democratization of republics around the world during the late twentieth and early twenty-first centuries had two important consequences. First, democratization extended citizenship to people who had long been treated as *subjects* by fascist, capitalist, and communist dictatorships. Re-enfranchised citizens established constitutional governments based on popular sovereignty and used these institutions to make significant political change, though change was not everywhere the same.

In southern Europe, the fall of fascist regimes led to the election of socialist governments in Spain, Portugal, and Greece and those countries' entry into the European Union. In this context, democratization led to significant political and economic change.[86] Change was not nearly so dramatic in Latin America, where the conservative political parties that had ruled before the dictators took charge generally returned to power, in countries still burdened by debts that had been run up by dictators. In East Asia, dictatorships transformed themselves from military regimes to civilian political parties, which enabled them to retain power for many years before dissident political parties won power. The abrupt fall of communist regimes in eastern Europe and then the Soviet Union initially brought dissident social movements and opposition political parties to power, though former communist parties retained power in some of the post-Soviet republics. In eastern Europe, former communist parties now compete successfully with other conservative, nationalist, and religious parties for power, and dissident parties have *retreated*. In some of the post-Soviet republics, dissident social movements dislodged former communists from power in Georgia, Azerbaijan, and Ukraine during various "color revolutions" (a "rose" revolution in Georgia, a "tulip" revolution in Azerbaijan, and an "orange" revolution in Ukraine). The social movements responsible for the color revolutions promoted greater democratization, though battles between former communists and dissident groups have continued. However, in other post-Soviet republics, former communist political parties have returned to power and established conservative governments, as Vladimir Putin has done in Russia. Although democratization was a significant development, its meaning has been limited, restricted, and constrained in many republics.

Change in South Africa was more dramatic and extensive than most. Democratization resulted in the extension of citizenship to the black majority and brought Nelson Mandela and the African National Congress to power. Change in Indonesia was fairly extensive, but it was fairly modest in Turkey and in the Arab republics. It is unclear whether the Arab Spring will lead to the creation of conservative Islamic governments, which may enhance citizenship for men but also undermine it for women, or the revival of military regimes and dictatorships.

Of course, while democratization has everywhere expanded citizenries, it has also resulted in the exclusion of some residents—immigrants (and minors) almost everywhere, Russian-speaking residents in the Baltic republics, gypsies in some European republics, Chinese and Christian minorities in Indonesia and Burma, and so on. This has been a characteristic feature of the republics. Contemporary democratization expanded the size and shape of citizenries, but many residents were denied its benefits.

Democratization is a process, not a status. Many political scientists adopt a set of criteria to determine whether a state has met a "standard" of democracy that allows it to be certified as a "democracy." I take a different approach. The republics often allowed citizenries to participate in constitutional government. But citizenries were defined from the outset in fairly exclusive terms. Although waves of democratization have expanded these citizenries, they are nowhere wholly inclusive. As a result, the democratization of the republics is by no means complete.

The democratization of the republics substantially reduced violence within and among republics. It brought an end to the torture, murder, and dirty wars used by dictators to seize and retain power. The disintegration of Cold War spheres of influence brought an end to many of the conflicts along the fault lines between spheres and to many insurrections and civil wars. By and large, democratization was peacefully accomplished. Although democratization ignited violence in a few places—Yugoslavia, some of the former Soviet republics, Libya, Egypt, and Syria—it generally occurred without much bloodshed. Few observers predicted that democratization in South Africa could be achieved without considerable violence, but the process there was much less violent than most people expected. Changing political circumstances may have contributed to the surprising nonviolent character of change.

For years, dictators practiced violence because it *helped* them silence the multitude and retain power. But at a certain point, the continued use of violence *undermined* their authority and sped their demise. When crowds gathered in the main square, dictators were forced to ask themselves a series of questions: If we order the army to shoot, will the army obey? If they obey, will violence quiet our opponents or rouse them to fury? Will violence demonstrate our resolve and enhance our authority, or will it undermine our legitimacy, both at home and abroad? Moreover, if dictators hesitated, if they paused to consider these questions, they might be seen as "weak," which could compound their problems. If they answered any of these questions incorrectly, they could end up like Libyan dictator Muammar Qaddafi: dead in a ditch at the hands of a mob.

In general, dictators decided not to shoot, in part because factions in the army were prepared to mutiny or defect to the opposition. So dictators cut a deal: a quiet retirement, no reprisals, no public trials for murder and theft. Many dictators thereby escaped punishment for their crimes. But perhaps it was good that they did. It may have increased the likelihood of their leaving quietly rather than fighting it out, which might have crippled or corrupted the democratization process.

It probably helped, too, in that moment of decision during the uncertain period that accompanies any real transfer of power, that elites and the multitude could turn to the constitutional institutions and electoral mechanisms that *already* existed in these republics. Time and again, dictators and democrats dusted off old constitutions and used them as templates for change. The fact that republican institutions *already* existed probably eased conflicts and smoothed the way for relatively peaceful and legitimate transfers of power. As Nathan Brown observed, "Egyptians show[ed] a sophisticated understanding of their constitutional *past*" (italics added).[87] In Egypt, as in many other democratizing republics, this understanding of a constitutional *past* may have helped shape the peaceful realization of a more democratic *future*.

Chapter Six

The Expansion of Citizenship in the United States

When the Republic was first established, the architects extended citizenship to a small minority of people living in the United States. Because they awarded citizenship only to adult, white, Protestant, native-born males, only about 10 percent of the population could claim citizenship.[1] The architects assigned the vast majority of people to two socially subordinate categories. They gave some rights to "second-class" citizens or "denizens," a category that included white men without property, women, children, and immigrants, and they denied all rights to convicts, sailors, indentured servants, and slaves, who were made the "subjects" of public and private authorities.[2] The architects argued that denizens and subjects were incapable of exercising the rights and duties associated with citizenship and feared that the extension of citizenship to these groups would pose a threat to their own liberty, which consisted in part of dominion over wives, children, workers, servants, and slaves. So they *divided* civil society to prevent the disenfranchised multitude from seizing power and using it to exercise a "tyranny" over the ruling-class minority. "Creating a republic of virtuous equals turned out to require the rejection of others who were thereby deemed to be nonvirtuous," Wallerstein observes.[3] As a result, they created a pyramid-shaped civil society, divided horizontally into three separate tiers.

During the next 150 years, people struggled to become citizens and claim the liberty, equality, and solidarity associated with citizenship.[4] The ascent of adult white men without property, both native and foreign born, then of adult black men, and then of adult women, created a citizen majority for the first time in 1920. As these "ascendants" became citizens, the denizen and subject populations *contracted*. These developments changed the *shape* of civil society and inverted the pyramid. But they did not alter its *structure*, because the three-tiered social hierarchy, which consisted of citizens, denizens, and subjects, remained intact.

The expansion of the citizenry was a significant achievement, but it was complicated by several developments. Although some social groups became citizens and "ascended" during this period, others lost their status and "descended" into denizen or subject populations. People who were seen as threats to public safety (American Indians, royalists, Confederates, anarchists, socialists, communists, and Japanese Americans) or to public health (homosexuals, people with contagious diseases or mental disabilities) had their status revoked and were driven downward, at least for a time. The "descendants" either joined children and immigrants, who were treated as denizens throughout this period, or joined convicts, who were subjects, then as now. Although many of the descendants later ascended or returned to the citizenry, children, immigrants, and convicts have remained stuck in the same social space that they occupied two hundred years ago, which is why they might be described as the "remainders."

It turned out that social status in the Republic was not a permanent right but a contingent privilege that could be *revoked*. In this regard, social change in the United States resembled the children's board game Chutes and Ladders. In this game, players who land on a "ladder" square can climb up the ladder, improve their standing, and ascend to the top of the board, where the game ends. But if they land on a "chute" square, they are swept down to the bottom of the board, where they must start all over.

In this chapter and the next two, we examine the changing status or trajectories of different groups: the ascendants who climbed into the citizenry, the descendants who lost social status, at least for a time, and the remainders who experienced only minor changes in their status and who occupied the same place in the social hierarchy throughout this period.

By examining the trajectories of the ascendants, descendants, and remainders during the nineteenth and twentieth centuries, we can see how their movement changed the *shape* but not the *structure* of civil society in the United States. This will allow us to identify two key features of social and political change in the Republic. First, the ascent of some groups expanded the citizenry and extended the promise of liberty, equality, and solidarity to a majority of people in the United States. Second, the fact that many people lost status and descended in the social hierarchy while others were forced to remain in their assigned places meant that inequality persisted. As we will see, social change in the United States led to both growing liberty *and* persistent *in*equality.

Of course, it would be difficult here to recount the history of social change in all the other republics, where social groups—gypsies, untouchables, national minorities, indigenous groups, postcolonial immigrants— were assigned different places in the social structure and had different historical trajectories than their counterparts in the United States. So the discussion of social change here will serve as a proxy for the *kind* of changes that accompanied the expansion of citizenship in other republics around the world.

Keep in mind as we examine the trajectories of different groups in the United States that ascent and descent had different social consequences and changed the contours of civil society in different ways.

In general, ascent *divided* people who previously shared a *common* place in the social hierarchy. For example, in 1800, the vast majority of enslaved black men, women, and children in the United States shared a common status as *subjects*. When black slaves were emancipated and adult black men were enfranchised, *all* blacks ascended in the social hierarchy, but they rose to different *places*. Adult black men became citizens, but black women and children became denizens, though male children became citizens when they became adults. By raising *some* blacks higher than others, ascent *divided* blacks, who previously shared a common identity and a singular social status. As we will see, *differentiation* was a common by-product of ascent because citizenship was never extended to everyone in the same group, but only to some.

By contrast, descent had rather different social consequences. It generally homogenized people who previously possessed *different* identities and social statuses. For example, in 1800, diverse, indigenous, American Indian peoples lived in the new republic and across North America. These diverse "peoples" spoke different languages, practiced different customs, waged war with other tribes, whom they regarded as wholly different "peoples," and concluded separate treaties with foreign powers. But the officials of the new republic treated them collectively as "Indians" (the use of a collective pronoun to describe different groups was a symbolic expression of their legal homogenization) and forced them downward, as "Indians," into denizen and then subject populations. The collective treatment of Indians, royalists, Confederates, dissidents, and Japanese Americans, who comprised people with different social and political identities, resulted in their social-legal *homogenization*: very different peoples were all treated in the *same* way as denizens or subjects. The collective treatment of different people was a characteristic feature of descent.

To appreciate the complex and contingent character of social change in this period, it is important to examine the trajectories of different groups in relation to civil society as a whole. This allows us to see both what they had in common with other people and how they differed, which puts all of them in a different light.[5]

THE ASCENDANTS

During the nineteenth and early twentieth centuries, denizen and subject populations organized social movements and fought to obtain citizenship and suffrage in the United States. Their ascent had several important consequences. They made the citizenry more diverse in social terms. By expanding the citizenry, they reduced the size of denizen and subject populations, which changed the contours of civil society, and they created a citizen majority for the first time. To appreciate these developments, it is necessary to trace the ascent of adult white men, adult black men, and adult women.

When the architects created constitutional government, they did not immediately define "the people," determine who was a citizen, or say who could exercise suffrage and vote in the new republic. Instead, they allowed states to define citizenship and suffrage, and the different states drew up different sets of rules about each.

Most states reserved citizenship and suffrage for native-born, adult white men with property, a provision that excluded *most* adult white men. Legislatures in many states argued that men without property lacked the economic autonomy needed to make independent political decisions.[6] Further, John Adams argued that if men without property could vote, "an immediate revolution would ensue."[7]

Naturally, the adult white men who were excluded objected to their status as denizens and argued that they should be allowed to vote, in part because many of them had served in the military during revolutionary and postrevolutionary wars, and in part because they paid taxes, even if they did not own property. As taxpayers, they believed they should not be subjected to "taxation without representation."

Adult White Men

Between the Revolutionary War and the Civil War, most of the original thirteen states dropped property requirements and extended suffrage to adult, white, native-born men. Moreover, most of the states that joined the Union before the Civil War did not require voters to meet property requirements, though many states, new and old, imposed residency requirements on potential voters, some insisting that voters also be taxpayers.[8] By 1855, "there were few formal or explicit *economic* barriers to voting" for adult white men.[9]

Adult white men organized social movements to secure citizenship and suffrage. They did so slowly, on a state-by-state basis, a process that took more than sixty years. As they ascended, they asked some other groups to join them and worked to extend suffrage to adult white *foreign*-born men. We know relatively little about the social movements that fought for citizenship and suffrage for adult white men without property, both because they fought their battles separately in the states, not nationally, and because they consisted of diverse groups—veterans, farmers, artisans, and immigrants—who did not often collaborate but instead fought separately for citizenship on their own behalf.

In the early republic, Congress defined citizenship, while state legislatures defined suffrage and identified who might vote. In 1802, Congress "declared that any foreign-born [adult] white male who met a five-year residency requirement could become a citizen three years after declaring his intention to do so."[10] However, many states took a more inclusive view. Legislators who wanted to draw immigrants to western states offered suffrage as an incentive to attract foreign-born white men. Before the Civil War, Wyoming, Kansas, Minnesota, and Oregon allowed *foreign*-born immigrants to vote *before* they became citizens under US law, as long as they declared their intention to naturalize.[11] The courts affirmed "the right to suffrage to those who . . . identified their interests and feelings with the citizenry . . . though they may be neither native or adopted [naturalized] citizens."[12]

Although native-born adult white men invited naturalized and non-naturalized foreign-born adult white men to become citizens and vote, they denied suffrage to *some* white men. States abandoned *property* requirements, but they still barred native-born paupers, vagrants, and inmates, either of poor houses or "insane" asylums or prisons, from voting.[13] During this period, the percentage of adult white men who could vote doubled from about 30 percent of the white male population to about 60 percent, but a large number of native- and foreign-born white males did not become citizens or voters and remained in denizen or subject populations.[14] Moreover, the ascent of some native- and foreign-born adult white men did not include the vast majority of people still living as denizens and subjects in the Republic.

Adult Black Men

In 1800, the overwhelming majority of African American men, women, and children in the United States where held as slaves, deprived of any rights, and treated as the subjects of *private* authorities in America. A very small number of blacks who had never been enslaved, who had been freed by their owners, or who had won their freedom by serving in the army during the Revolutionary War lived as denizens in the North and the South. In a few northern states, legislators allowed some adult black freemen to vote until 1857, when the Supreme Court stripped freed blacks of citizenship in the infamous *Dred Scott* decision.[15]

A wide variety of social movements fought to end the slave trade, abolish slavery, and enfranchise adult black men. They included international groups that campaigned against the slave trade, women suffragettes who made common cause with abolitionists, plaintiffs and lawyers who sued for black rights, and black slaves who mutinied, organized revolts, ran away, fled to the sanctuary provided by Union troops, and fought for the Union and freedom during the war. During and after the Civil War, their collective efforts resulted in the abolition of slavery and the extension of citizenship and the franchise to adult black men. Although these developments contributed to the ascent of *all* African Americans, they also divided blacks and assigned them to new and different places in the social hierarchy.

The emancipation of slaves in 1863 and the abolition of slavery in 1865 raised blacks out of the subject population and into the denizen population, while the extension of citizenship and suffrage (the Civil Rights Act of 1866, the Fourteenth Amendment in 1868, and the Fifteenth Amendment in 1870) lifted adult black men into the citizenry. The advent of Jim Crow and segregationist practices in the South then denied citizenship and suffrage to adult black men and made them denizens, like black women and children in the North and South. In 1901, one Virginia legislator proclaimed, "I told the people of my country . . . that I intended . . . to disenfranchise every negro that I could disenfranchise under the Constitution of the United States, and as few white people as possible."[16] This approach worked effectively to make denizens of black citizens. In Louisiana, legislators reduced the number of black voters from 130,000 in 1896 to only 1,342 in 1904.[17] Federal courts allowed southern states to violate the Fourteenth and Fifteenth Amendments with impunity.[18] In 1883, in testimony before Congress, a black man from Georgia told a Senate committee: "We are in a majority here, but you may vote till your eyes drop out and your tongue drops out, and you can't count your colored men in . . . their [ballot] boxes; there's a hole gets in the bottom of the boxes . . . and lets out our votes."[19]

Southern legislators also adopted "draconian vagrancy laws (subjecting anyone without a job to possible arrest) as well as legislation prohibiting workers from quitting their jobs before their contracts expired" and allowed landowners to use debt as a mechanism to tie disadvantaged black sharecroppers to their lenders and prevent them from migrating.[20] This "counterrevolutionary terror" contributed to what Eric Foner described as a "compulsory system of free labor."[21]

Vagrancy laws "made children especially vulnerable" to white employers, who were permitted by law "to inflict such moderate corporeal chastisement as may be necessary and proper."[22] They were also used to force "idle" men, women, and children to sign onerous labor contracts with private white employers or work as convicts for public employers and their private subcontractors, a system that persisted "well into the 1960s."[23]

Southern legislators used the legal system to capture black adults and minors, imprison them, and then rent them out to work in chain gangs under the convict-leasing system. Further, they licensed public and private nonstate actors to lynch and terrorize blacks across the South. Both developments forced blacks back into a large, imprisoned, subject population in the South.

At the beginning of this period, blacks for the most part shared a common identity as slaves and occupied the same place in the social hierarchy as subjects. But at the end of the century, blacks occupied *different* places. Adult black men in the North had become citizens and practiced suffrage, while adult black men in the South had become denizens, a status shared by adult black women and children, and some black men, women, and children in the South had been (re)made the subjects of private and public authorities, no longer as slaves but as convicts.

Of course, while black men, women, and children in the South became denizens during the Jim Crow era, they did not occupy the same *place* in southern society. Black denizens were assigned different places in the category itself. So, for example, as heads of households, black men could sign binding labor contracts on behalf of women and children in the family,

giving them a measure of authority that women and children did not possess.[24] Developments during and after the Civil War differentiated blacks
and assigned them different places in public and private hierarchies. Age,
gender, and place came to play important new roles in determining the place
of blacks in what Barrington Moore called the "re-United States."[25]

Adult Women

In 1848, women gathered in Seneca Falls, New York, and announced that
they would fight to obtain citizenship and suffrage for adult women.[26] In the
"Declaration of Sentiments," Elizabeth Cady Stanton and Lucretia Mott
argued that men had denied women their "inalienable right to the elective
franchise," forced women to surrender their property and wages to their
husbands upon marriage, making women, "in the eye of the law, civilly
dead," and passed laws allowing husbands to deprive women of their liberty
"and to administer chastisement."[27] Because men had disenfranchised "one-
half of the people of this country," Stanton and Mott demanded that women
"have immediate admission to all the rights and privileges which belong to
them as citizens of the United States."[28]

Feminists filed suit to obtain constitutional rights and organized social
movements to obtain citizenship and suffrage for women. In parallel and
overlapping campaigns, they also fought to protect children, abolish slavery,
and prohibit alcohol. Many women advocated a zero-tolerance approach to
alcohol use to reduce male violence against women and children. During the
next seventy years, women worked to secure suffrage. During and after the
Civil War, women's groups lobbied the Republican-dominated Congress to
extend citizenship and suffrage both to adult women and adult black men.
Although Congress and the states extended citizenship and suffrage to adult
black men, they refused to extend them to women as well. "One question at a
time," Wendell Phillips said in defense of his decision. "This hour belongs to
the [adult] negro [male]."[29]

Women then asked the courts to recognize women as citizens under the
Fourteenth Amendment.[30] But the Supreme Court in 1875 rejected the suit
brought by Virginia and Francis Minor, a decision that prevented women
from using a legal strategy to obtain their rights.[31] As a result, feminists
pursued two separate political strategies.[32] Feminists who joined the
American Woman Suffrage Association fought for the right to vote on a
state-by-state basis, as adult white men without property had done, and persuaded legislatures in Wyoming, Utah, Idaho, and Colorado to extend wom-

en the vote during the 1880s and 1890s.[33] Meanwhile, feminists who participated in the National Woman Suffrage Association worked to persuade Congress to adopt a constitutional amendment and submit it to the states for ratification, as adult black men and their allies had done. Eventually, the two groups merged and worked to pass a constitutional amendment, with the help of radical feminists after the turn of the century, a collective effort that contributed to the ratification of the Nineteenth Amendment in 1920.[34]

The extension of suffrage to adult white women in the North and South and to adult black women in the North, but not in the South, marked an important turning point. For the first time, a *majority* of residents in the United States could claim citizenship and suffrage. Still, the ascent of adult women into the citizenry did not mean that they joined male citizens as equals. Although adult women became citizen-voters, they could not serve on juries in most states, which effectively prevented female defendants from being tried by juries of their peers.[35] Because women could serve in the military only in a limited capacity—primarily as nurses and noncombatants during and after World War II—few women could obtain the benefits and opportunities made available to male servicemen. The government provided male servicemen with the GI Bill, veteran's benefits, medical care, and preferential treatment for those who applied for civil service and post office jobs.[36] Although adult women ascended into the citizenry, they took a subordinate place within it.

WHY DID CITIZENSHIP EXPAND?

Why did citizenship expand? It expanded because disenfranchised social groups organized social movements to demand change and obtain the rights—citizenship and suffrage—that were reserved for some, not all. But while social groups took the initiative and fought to obtain these rights, citizens also voted to enfranchise previously disadvantaged groups. Why would citizens do that, particularly if it might weaken or compromise their own privilege, authority, and liberty? The historian Alexander Keyssar argues that citizens did so because disenfranchised denizens and subjects made effective, substantive, and principled claims for inclusion, because some citizens wanted to enlist them as allies in their battles with other citizen factions, and because political parties wanted to recruit them as voters.

During the nineteenth century, the adult white men without property, adult black men, and adult women who were assigned to denizen and subject populations argued that citizenship and suffrage should be extended to them because they performed military or wartime service for the government, or paid taxes, or both. Adult white men who served in the Revolutionary War argued that suffrage should be extended to "every man who buys his shot and bears his lot [in military service]."[37] During the Civil War, General William Tecumseh Sherman made a similar case for enfranchising adult black men, many of whom served in Union armies. "When the fight is over," Sherman said, "the hand that drops the musket cannot be denied the ballot."[38] Although women did not serve as soldiers, they participated in the Civil War and World War I as nurses. Their contribution to the war effort helped persuade President Woodrow Wilson to announce his support for women's suffrage in 1918 "as a war measure."[39]

Denizens also argued that they should be given suffrage because they paid taxes. "We are part of the People of the United States; citizens subject to all of its laws; taxed without representation, classed with animals, paupers, idiots and lunatics; governed without our consent; . . . deprived of trial by a jury of our peers," the feminist Phoebe Cousins argued in 1868.[40] "Taxation without representation is wrong," Abby Smith, a wealthy property owner, argued in 1869, when she announced that she and her seventy-six-year-old sister would refuse to pay taxes until they could vote. "Is it any more just to take a woman's property without her consent, than it is to take a man's property without his consent?"[41] These arguments, and similar ones made by adult white men and adult black men, were effective, Keyssar argues, because they laid claim to principles established by constitutional government in the United States.

Although denizens and subjects fought for citizenship and suffrage on their own, some citizens supported their efforts because they wanted allies to protect them from other denizens and subjects, whom they regarded as threats. "Why did voting members of the community sometimes elect to share their political power with others?" Keyssar asks. "In numerous cases, it was because they saw themselves as having a direct interest in enlarging the electorate."[42] In the South, slave owners (adult white men with property) wanted poor white men to vote so that they could enlarge southern electorates in federal elections, enlist them as allies to protect white property, and ensure "that poor whites would serve in militia patrols guarding against slave rebellions."[43] As Virginia senator Charles Morgan explained in 1829, "We ought to spread wide the foundation of our government, that all white men have a direct interest in its protection."[44]

After the Civil War, Republican voters in the North supported the extension of suffrage to adult black men because they saw them as allies against Democratic voters in the North and the South. And many adult male citizens wanted to enfranchise women to enlarge the native-born electorate against the growing number of naturalized immigrant voters. The feminist Olympia Born appealed to male citizens on this basis: "There are in the United States three times as many American-born women as the whole foreign population, men and women together, so that the votes of women will eventually be the only means of overcoming this foreign influence. . . . There is no possible safety for our . . . republican government, unless women are given the suffrage."[45]

Political parties sometimes supported the expansion of suffrage to increase their power at the polls. "Support for democratization stemmed in part from partisan self-interest," Keyssar argues.[46] The Democratic Party under Jackson reached out to "large numbers of propertyless men," Reconstruction Republicans demanded suffrage on behalf of freed black men who could "provide the Republican Party with an electoral basis in the South and make it possible for loyal governments to be elected in the once-rebellious states," and turn-of-the-century Republicans supported suffrage for women to increase their strength against immigrant voters, who typically voted for Democrats.[47]

Political parties that defended social inequality and worked to restrict the franchise to keep denizen and subject populations at bay argued that disenfranchised groups were "virtually represented" by responsible citizens. But they eventually supported the expansion of the citizenry because they wanted to neutralize demands for suffrage as a political issue and enlist *some* members of the new electorate.[48] Federalists eventually supported the extension of suffrage to white men without property, Democrats in the South were forced, as a condition for readmission to the Union, to ratify the Fourteenth and Fifteenth Amendments, which extend suffrage to adult black men, and Democrats under Wilson supported suffrage for women in part because they hoped to enroll southern white women and adult white immigrant women in the Democratic Party, a strategy that proved effective.[49] "Sensing correctly that [women's] suffrage was likely to triumph, that it would not necessarily damage their interests, and that their own constituents supported it, Democratic machine leaders in New York, Boston, Chicago, Cleveland and other cities joined hands with [feminist organizations] to promote suffrage reform," Keyssar observes.[50]

The ascent of social groups in the nineteenth and early twentieth centuries expanded the citizenry in the United States. By 1920, a majority of residents could count themselves as citizens. But the ascent of some groups was accompanied by the descent of others. To appreciate the complex character of social change in the Republic, we next examine why some groups fell and why other groups remained in their assigned social places during this period.

Chapter Seven

Persistent Inequalities

THE DESCENDANTS

The ascent of adult white men without property, adult black men, and adult women across most of the United States during the nineteenth and twentieth centuries created a citizen majority for the first time in the Republic in 1920. But the ascent of these groups was accompanied by the *descent* of others. When state officials and citizens viewed groups as a threat to public safety or a danger to public health, they revoked their status and forced them downward into denizen and subject populations or expelled them from the Republic.

State officials revoked or degraded the status of Indians, royalists, Confederates, radical dissidents, and Japanese Americans because they viewed these groups as threats to public safety, or what today might be called "national security." In some respects, they were casualties of war. State officials also revoked the status of people with contagious diseases (tuberculosis, typhoid, and leprosy) or with mental or physical disabilities (people regarded as insane, incompetent, or gay and lesbian) because they regarded them as threats to public health and subjected them to scrutiny or confinement by state and private authorities.

American Indians

Before the revolution, British officials "dealt with independent and conquered [American Indian] tribes on the fringes of the white settlements as *sovereign* political communities, negotiating with them as with foreign *na-*

tions" (italics added), like France or Spain.[1] In many respects, Indians possessed a status that was superior to white settlers, who were merely *subjects* of the king.[2] "The Indians, though living among the king's subjects . . . are a separate and distinct people from them, they are treated as such, they have a policy of their own, they make peace and war with any nation of Indians they think fit without control from the English."[3] Indian autonomy rankled white settlers, who complained, "I can in no manner consider the Mohegan Indians as a *separate* or *sovereign state*. . . . [Such a view] exposes his majesty and sovereignty to ridicule."[4]

When the Revolutionary War erupted, most Indians fought on the side of the British, largely because the British promised to protect Indian rights and land.[5] "The logic of nearly two hundred years of abrasive contact with colonizing Europeans compelled the choice most Indians made to support Britain," the historian Gary Nash observes, "since it was the *colonists* who most threatened Indian autonomy" (italics added).[6] But at war's end, the Indians, who had not been defeated on the battlefield, "emerged from the conflict with their independence decisively impaired."[7] During postwar negotiations, the British betrayed their promises to protect the Indians and ceded Indian lands from the Appalachians to the Mississippi to the new republic without the consent of Indian peoples.[8] US negotiators, led by John Quincy Adams, who regarded the Indians who fought with the British as traitors, refused to recognize the sovereignty of Indian tribes, arguing that they were "'subjects' of the United States rather than 'nations,' [and were] incapable of treating with a foreign power."[9] US officials demanded the surrender of Indian lands and rights as part of the peace agreement, and the British eventually agreed.[10] These developments degraded the rights and status of diverse and autonomous Indian tribes and reduced them collectively to denizens of the United States, a status comparable with resident aliens or unnaturalized immigrants, except, of course, that they were indigenous "aliens," not foreign "aliens."[11] One federal court ruled in 1823 that Indians were "of that class who are said by jurists not to be citizens, but perpetual inhabitants, with *diminutive* rights. They were considered an inferior race of people without the privileges of citizens, and under the perpetual protection and pupilage of the government" (italics added).[12] The Supreme Court later refused to treat Indians as people who deserved protection under the Constitution, arguing that Indians are "in a state of pupillage. Their relation to the United States resembles that of a ward to his guardian."[13]

As the Republic expanded to the West, white settlers and state officials increasingly viewed Indians as a threat to public safety, not only in lands west of the Appalachians but also east of the mountains, and demanded the removal of Indians there to lands west of the Mississippi.[14] Although state officials first discussed removing Indians in 1803, the War of 1812 and wars with the Creek in 1812–1814 and the Seminoles in 1817–1818 "gave new impetus to the removal policy," which was advanced by President Monroe in the 1820s and forcibly implemented by President Andrew Jackson after passage of the Indian Removal Act of 1830.[15] During the next twenty years, "three quarters of the 125,000 Native Americans living east of the Mississippi were 'removed' with the loss of one-fourth to one-third of all southern Native American lives."[16]

As a result, Indians descended from denizens to the subjects of US military authority and were forcibly deported to reservations, which the commissioner of Indian affairs described as a "legalized reformatory" for Indians, "a place where they must adopt non-Indian ways, 'peaceably if they will, forcibly if they must.'"[17]

The Supreme Court refused to consider Indians as "people" protected by the Constitution before the Civil War. After Congress and the states adopted the Fourteenth and Fifteenth Amendments, the court refused to extend its provisions to Indians, thereby denying Indians the right to either citizenship or suffrage, even though they were born in the United States. In the landmark 1884 decision in *Elk v. Wilkins*, the Supreme Court concluded that John Elk, an Indian born on tribal lands, could *not* claim citizenship under the Fourteenth Amendment or suffrage under the Fifteenth Amendment.[18]

Still, in the late nineteenth century, state governments and federal officials adopted policies that allowed adult Indian males to claim citizenship and suffrage if they abandoned their Indian identity, moved off the reservation, paid taxes, and assimilated, a development that essentially allowed Indians to "immigrate and naturalize," like foreign immigrants.[19]

Why did Indians, who descended from sovereign peoples to denizens and then subjects of state authority in the United States, fall so far? First, state officials and white settlers saw them as a military threat before and after the Revolutionary War. Although Indian military capacities diminished rapidly, sporadic and small-scale conflict kept the Indian military threat visible until late in the nineteenth century. State officials and citizens viewed Indian resistance as a betrayal, which deserved serious punishment, though state officials and private citizens routinely provoked Indian resistance by seizing Indian lands and "removing" Indian peoples.

Second, almost no one in the Republic defended or assisted Indians. No one organized a movement, comparable to the abolitionists, that objected to the mistreatment of Indian peoples, perhaps because white settlers viewed Indians not only as racially inferior but also as domestic "terrorists." Third, although Indians were collectively punished for the resistance of individual groups, they were enormously diverse and found it difficult to collaborate or unite against a common foe. Moreover, they did not generally seek citizenship and suffrage, but rather sovereignty as a political goal, which may have been an unrealistic or utopian aspiration in this context. Still, Indians filed lawsuits, organized social movements, and, during World Wars I and II, served in the army, which helped improve their social and legal status.

Royalists

Indians were not the only group regarded as a threat to public safety by republican officials during the Revolutionary War. Republicans viewed settlers who remained loyal to the British government as a threat to national security and took steps to degrade their status. First, Congress argued that because the Declaration of Independence created a sovereign nation, all residents of the Republic, with the exception of British officials, owed their allegiance to the Republic, as they would to any sovereign.[20] Anyone who refused to recognize sovereign republican authority or accept its currency, who remained loyal to Britain, or who gave aid and comfort to Britain's representatives would be guilty of treason and would be "deemed, published, and treated as an *enemy* of *his* country, and precluded from all trade or intercourse with the inhabitants of these colonies."[21] Although the architects of the Republic had argued that the social contract was *freely* chosen, citizens of the new republic would not be given any choice in the matter once the republic was formed. Ironically, the only people who could meaningfully choose to sign the social contract were *immigrants* who naturalized (or Indians who did the same).

Second, people regarded as traitors by state officials or by nonstate actors such as the Sons of Liberty could be assaulted, arrested, and hanged as traitors, and their property, both real property and slaves, could be confiscated and redistributed: "Loyalists were shot, hanged, beaten; rebel militia burned pro-British Indian towns and crops, killed Indians regardless of age or sex, and sold captives into slavery; slaves caught assisting the British faced whippings, hanging, even beheading. This relentless cruelty, as intended, intimidated many supporters of the British into remaining inactive."[22]

Authorities in the new republic revoked the royalists' status as subject of the king, made them citizens, and then immediately made them the subjects of government officials and nonstate authorities. These developments persuaded some royalists to submit, some to resist, and some to depart, migrating to Britain and other British colonies in the Americas. After the war, adult white men with property who had been royalists recovered their status as citizens, though they did not recover confiscated property.[23]

Confederates

The Confederates who took up arms against the Republic and seceded from the Union threatened public safety during and after the Civil War. After Union forces defeated Confederate armies and occupied the South, the Republicans in Congress revoked the citizenship and suffrage of adult southern white males and made them denizens, on par with blacks, who had been freed from slavery by the Emancipation Proclamation and the Thirteenth Amendment. On May 29, 1865, President Andrew Jackson issued an amnesty that restored citizenship to whites and suffrage to adult white males in the South, even if they had taken up arms against the Union, so long as they swore an oath of loyalty to the Republic (like immigrants and Indians who naturalized). He excluded from this amnesty a small group of Confederate army officers, government officials, and wealthy individuals with real property valued at more than $20,000, though these disenfranchised Confederates could seek individual pardons.[24]

But re-enfranchised white legislators quickly adopted "black codes" that restricted the rights of freed blacks—blacks were not permitted to vote, testify against whites in court, possess firearms or alcohol—and imposed coercive employment contracts and vagrancy laws that "were designed to reduce [free blacks] to a position little removed from slavery."[25] They also elected pardoned and unpardoned Confederate officers to the reconstituted state governments and to Congress, sending four Confederate generals to the House of Representatives and the former vice president of the Confederacy to the US Senate.[26]

In response to southern white intransigence, legal discrimination, and white violence against blacks—large-scale white riots in Memphis and New Orleans resulted "in a general massacre of innocent black bystanders"—the Republican supermajority in Congress refused to seat ex-Confederate legislators.[27] They then took a series of steps, known collectively as "Reconstruction." They extended citizenship to blacks and suffrage to adult black males (the Civil Rights Act of 1866, the Fourteenth Amendment of 1868, and the Fifteenth Amendment of 1870) and sought to protect these new rights with legislation designed to enforce their provisions in southern states (the Reconstruction Act of 1867 and Supplementary Reconstruction Act of 1867, and three enforcement acts in 1870 and 1871 that gave the president authority to deploy the military to enforce provisions of the Fourteenth and Fifteenth Amendments, provided federal supervision of registration and voting in federal elections, outlawed irregular militias such as the Ku Klux Klan, and "gave the president the right to suspend the writ of habeas corpus in cases of noncompliance with the law").[28] They reimposed martial law in southern states, insisted that southern states be readmitted only after they ratified the Fourteenth and Fifteenth Amendments, and extended suffrage to black male voters.[29]

The extension of suffrage to about one million adult black males in the South led to a coalition between newly enfranchised blacks and southern whites who opposed secession and remained loyal to the Union during the war, who rejected Confederate policies that had led to wartime disaster and economic ruin, or who embraced reform during Reconstruction.[30] This black-white coalition produced an electoral majority in many southern states that rewrote state constitutions, ratified the Fourteenth and Fifteenth Amendments, and obtained their state's readmission to the Union and representation in Congress.[31]

The Republican reconstruction of the Republic was short-lived. A number of developments contributed to its demise. Intransigent southern whites organized effective social movements outside the state, using irregular militias to murder, massacre, and intimidate black and white voters who supported Reconstruction.[32] White violence drove blacks from the polls, weakened the black-white coalition, and allowed ex-Confederates to win elections and return to power. They then used local, state, and national offices to adopt legislation to restrict black rights and enhance their own power, all the while keeping violent militias on call.

Meanwhile, Republicans in Congress grew weary of the Reconstruction effort. President Grant's attorney general admitted that the administration was "tired of the annual autumnal outbreaks [of violence] in the South," and adopted a "hands-off policy."[33] The disputed presidential election of 1876 led to the withdrawal of US troops from the South, which gave Democratic white legislators and violent nonstate actors a free hand to strip black men of citizenship and suffrage and use violence to subordinate them.[34] The US Supreme Court then ratified a slow-motion coup by whites who insisted that the recovery of citizenship and suffrage by adult white men be accompanied by the loss of citizenship and suffrage for adult black men.[35] As early as 1867, the court ruled that loyalty oaths were unconstitutional.[36] They subsequently ruled that the Civil Rights Act was unconstitutional and redefined the Fourteenth and Fifteenth Amendments in extremely narrow terms, which allowed states to revisit the meaning of citizenship and suffrage for blacks and also for *women* and *Indians*, and in 1896 sanctioned the segregationist black codes that whites adopted during the advent of post-Reconstruction Jim Crow.[37]

Although US officials disenfranchised Confederates and kept them from returning to power for a time, white denizens recovered their right to citizenship and suffrage while wresting it away from blacks after a protracted struggle, which led to the simultaneous ascent of adult white men and the descent of adult black men in the South.

Dissidents

During World War I, government officials treated dissidents who objected to the war as threats to public safety and adopted legislation that permitted authorities to jail citizens and deport immigrants identified with anarchist, socialist, or pacifist principles or organizations. Although the Immigration Act of 1891 allowed officials to prevent immigrant anarchists from entering the United States and deport anarchists who had not been naturalized, the Immigration Acts of 1917 and 1918 gave officials the authority to deport *any* resident alien on the grounds of "advocating or teaching the unlawful destruction of property, or advocating or teaching anarchy or the overthrow by force or violence of the Government of the United States" or on the grounds of belonging to an organization "that advocates or teaches the unlawful destruction of property."[38]

The Espionage Act of 1917 and the Sedition Act of 1918 allowed officials to prosecute *citizens* who objected to the war or who might "utter, print, write, or publish any disloyal, profane, scurrilous, or abusive language about the form of Government of the United States."[39] The government used it to jail Eugene Debs, the leader of the antiwar Socialist Party, and Bill Haywood, head of the antiwar International Workers of the World (IWW) for long prison terms, raid local offices across the country, make mass arrests, and destroy dissident political parties and trade unions.[40] At his trial, Debs told the jury, "I have been accused of obstructing the war. I admit it. Gentlemen, I abhor war. I would oppose it if I stood alone."[41] The Supreme Court unanimously upheld these convictions because the defendants represented a "clear and present danger" to the public safety and the security of the state.[42]

During the war, officials organized nationwide "slacker raids," detaining draft-age men in a search for draft evaders, and subjected conscientious objectors to brutal treatment in military prisons, sentencing some dissidents to long prison terms and seventeen people to death (the death sentences were not carried out) for refusing to obey military orders while in prison.[43] According to a report by the Bureau of Legal Advice, a contemporary of the American Civil Liberties Union, "The military authorities starved the objectors on bread and water, hanged them by their wrists, forced them to exercise and then drenched them in icy showers, and beat them with belts and broom handles."[44]

Government officials also licensed or allowed nonstate actors and unofficial surrogates to deploy violence and assault dissident groups. The American Legion attacked IWW locals (one attack in Centralia, Washington, led to a bloody confrontation that resulted in the deaths of several Legionnaires, the arrest of many "Wobblies," and the lynching murder of one) and also a rival veteran's organization, the World War Veterans.[45] The American Protective League conducted slacker raids and worked as a private investigative arm of the Justice Department, much like a neighborhood watch group, scrutinizing German aliens and reporting them to the police for infractions of wartime restrictions on their movements.[46] Meanwhile, the Ku Klux Klan attacked socialists, but mostly blacks, in the South.[47] The Wilson administration "refused to intervene, arguing that 'no facts have been presented to us which would justify federal action.'"[48]

After the war, in 1919, labor unions in Seattle launched a general strike, policemen in Boston walked out on strike, and labor unions in the coal and steel industry conducted industry-wide strikes. Socialists inspired by the Bolshevik Revolution in Russia and financed in part by the new Russian government organized a communist party that advocated revolution. An anarchist cell, probably led by Luigi Galleani, made a series of coordinated bomb attacks on dozens of government officials, including H. Mitchell Palmer, the US attorney general, in retaliation for the repression of anarchists during the war. The bomb attacks killed several people, a would-be assassin among them.[49]

Although postwar dissidents were diverse, ranging from nonviolent ship-yard workers in Seattle and conservative policemen to bomb-throwing an-archists, state officials viewed them all as radical threats to public safety and took aggressive measures to contain them. In Seattle, Mayor Ole Hanson, who argued that "every strike is a small revolution and a dress rehearsal for the big one," called out the troops and persuaded the American Federation of Labor to rein in the local unions.[50] In Massachusetts, Governor Calvin Cool-idge warned striking policemen that "there is no right to strike against the public safety by anybody, anywhere, any time."[51] He called in troops, re-placed striking cops, and fired the majority of them, breaking the strike. President Wilson described striking workers as "enemies of this country" and said in a State of the Union address that "there should be no leniency" toward those who "incite crime and insurrection under the guise of political evolu-tion."[52] He authorized the use of federal troops to quell strikes, issued injunc-tions against striking coal miners, and gave new investigative powers to the young J. Edgar Hoover, who, with A. Mitchell Palmer's assistance, orga-nized a series of raids on dissident groups.[53] Officials arrested and impris-oned dissident citizens and deported immigrant denizens. Emma Goldman and Alex Berkman, antiwar anarchists who had been imprisoned during the war, were deported to the Soviet Union on a ship with 247 others in 1919.[54]

Officials in many states moved to defend public safety by passing sedi-tion laws that made it a crime to criticize government officials or the republi-can form of government, organize labor unions, or display a red flag.[55] One woman, Anita Whitney, a social worker, suffragette, and socialist who joined the Communist Party, was sentenced under California's antisyndicalist legis-lation to one to fourteen years in San Quentin prison.[56] As a result of govern-ment attacks against dissidents and labor unions, union membership fell by one million between 1920 and 1922.[57] In Congress, the House refused to seat a representative from Wisconsin because he had been an antiwar socialist, and the New York State legislature denied seats to five socialist representa-tives from New York City, which effectively disenfranchised voters from their districts.[58]

During World War I and the Red Scare that followed, US officials ar-rested and deported denizen immigrants using administrative procedures rather than courts of law.[59] As a result, the number of immigrant denizens deported by US officials increased from 4,610 in 1914 to 6,409 in 1924, many of them for political reasons.[60] Most of the citizens who were jailed and denizen immigrants who were deported by US officials were conscientious objectors or antiwar pacifists, not bomb-throwing anarchists, and posed no real threat to public safety. But anarchist violence was used to justify retaliatory measures against nonviolent groups.

Japanese Americans

After the Japanese attack on Pearl Harbor in 1941, US officials detained, evacuated, and imprisoned most of the Japanese Americans living in the western United States, though not Hawaii, a development that led to the rapid descent of Japanese American citizens and denizens and made them the subjects of military authorities. Federal civilian and military leaders, western legislators, and journalists demanded that the federal government act against Japanese Americans because they presented an imminent threat to military operations, defense industries, and public safety. The judge advocate general, Major General Allen W. Guillon, warned that "Japanese inspired sabotage" by Japanese Americans living in the United States "cannot be temporized with. No half-way measures, based on considerations of economic disturbance, humanitarianism, or fear of retaliation will suffice."[61] John Dingell, a Democratic congressman from Michigan, urged "the forceful detention or imprisonment in a concentration camp of ten thousand alien Japanese in Hawaii" and another 150,000 in the United States (an exaggerated figure) and "held in a reprisal reserve," a view praised by newspaper columnists who advocated killing "100 victims selected out of our concentration camps" for "every hostage murdered by our enemies."[62] This vigilante lobby, a coalition of nativist anti-immigration groups, political parties, and military and government officials that acted on their own initiative and authority, urged President Roosevelt to strip Japanese Americans of their rights, evacuate them from the West Coast, and imprison them in "concentration camps," a term that fell into disfavor and was replaced by "internment camps."[63] Roosevelt agreed, signing Executive Order 9066 on February 19, 1942.[64] This decision led to the speedy incarceration of 120,000 Japanese Americans during the war.[65]

The Supreme Court ratified this policy on two occasions. In 1943, Chief Justice Harlan F. Stone wrote that the curfew imposed on Gordon Hirabayashi did not violate his civil rights but instead protected the government's power "to wage war successfully."[66] One year later, in 1944, the court upheld the incarceration of Fred T. Korematsu, rejecting the argument that racial prejudice played a role. As Justice Hugo Black wrote, "To cast this case into outlines of racial prejudice, without reference to the *real military dangers* which were presented, naively confuses the issue" (italics added).[67]

The decision to incarcerate Japanese Americans because they were seen as a threat to public safety was made *despite* the fact that the threat to national security was low to nonexistent. Military intelligence and FBI agents listed only a small number of Japanese Americans as a serious "threat."[68] Intelligence officers who engineered the burglary of the Japanese consulate in Los Angeles discovered that Japanese officials regarded Japanese Americans as "'cultural traitors' who could not be trusted with anything of importance" and "after careful investigations on both the West Coast and Hawaii, there was never a shred of evidence found of sabotage, subversive acts, spying, or fifth column activity on the part of [Japanese American immigrants or citizens]."[69] A 1981 report by the presidential Commission on the Wartime Relocation and Internment of Civilians concluded that the incarceration of Japanese Americans "was not justified by military necessity, and the decisions which followed from it . . . were not driven by analysis of military conditions. The broad historical causes which shaped these decisions were race prejudice, war hysteria, and a failure of leadership. . . . A grave injustice was done to American citizens and resident aliens of Japanese ancestry who, without individual review or any probative evidence against them, were excluded, removed and detained by the United States during World War II."[70] Yet guards at internment camps shot and killed unarmed inmates who protested conditions or tried to escape.[71]

The decision to relocate and imprison Japanese Americans resulted in the descent of different groups of Japanese Americans in different settings. Although Japanese Americans were collectively made "subjects," they consisted of three groups with different legal standing. First, 37 percent of Japanese Americans living in the United States (this excludes territories such as Hawaii) were foreign-born immigrants.[72] Unlike white immigrants from Europe, Japanese and other immigrants from Asia were barred from naturalizing and becoming citizens or exercising suffrage, so they lived as permanent denizens in the United States, or "aliens ineligible to citizenship." With the outbreak of war, they became "*enemy* aliens," who could, by law, be treated as subjects.[73] Second, the majority of Japanese Americans in the United States—79,642 in 1940, or 62.7 percent of the total—were born in the United States and were US citizens. These citizens consisted of two subgroups: adults who could vote and minors who could not, the latter being denizens. Despite their different legal standing, they were all treated like immigrant denizens and "deported," a forced relocation similar to the Indian "removal." US officials did not exempt children from the process, describing them as "volunteers" because "most minor children, it was assumed, would 'volunteer' to join their parents in the camps."[74] US authorities even swept orphanages for "infant children of partial Japanese ancestry" and removed them to the camps.[75]

Although they removed and imprisoned Japanese Americans living in a narrow, hundred-mile band along the Pacific West Coast, they excluded Japanese Americans living outside this "military zone."[76] In Hawaii, most of the 150,000 Japanese Americans were allowed to stay because their departure would have disrupted economic and military operations in the islands.[77]

US authorities imprisoned Japanese Americans in remote inland camps, though some officials secured the release of some inmates during the war. University of California president Robert Sproul obtained the release of 4,300 inmates so that they could study at colleges in the East; military authorities recruited thousands of Japanese American men to work as translators in the Pacific theater and later for combat infantry units that served in Europe; and business executives recruited ten thousand men and women to work on farms and in industry.[78] Perhaps most important, Mitsuye Endo obtained the release of many citizens like herself as the result of a case she took to the Supreme Court. The court granted her a writ of habeas corpus and restored her freedom because "whatever power the War Relocation Authority may have to detain other classes of citizens, it has no authority to [detain] citizens who are concededly loyal."[79]

THREATS TO PUBLIC HEALTH

State officials revoked the status of citizens and denizens who posed a real or imagined threat to public *safety*. State officials and nonstate actors also revoked the status of individuals and groups who threatened public *health*. Citizens and denizens with mental disabilities or infectious diseases or individuals identified as homosexuals had their rights revoked by state officials and private authorities, often without recourse to the legal system, and were committed, incarcerated, and confined in public and private asylums, fired from jobs, harassed by police, and denied entry into the United States or deported.

Mental Disabilities

In 1800, state officials generally identified mentally disabled citizens as "unfit" and denied them the right to vote.[80] They also divided citizens and denizens with mental disabilities into two groups: "lunatics" or the insane, which often included "epileptics" and female "hysterics," and "idiots." Because they viewed "lunatics" as a danger to themselves and others, they confined them in jails or allowed households to confine them, often in chains, in the basements or attics of private homes.[81] Individuals regarded as "idiots" were not generally confined, though they were sometimes consigned to poorhouses if their guardians were unwilling or unable to shelter them. This changed after 1820, when state authorities encouraged households to transfer lunatics and idiots to public or private congregate asylums.[82] State officials gave nonstate actors wide powers to revoke the rights of mentally disabled individuals and confine them in asylums without going through the legal system. Doctors, husbands, and fathers could commit patients, wives, children, and the elderly on their own authority.[83] As a result, "[Asylum managers] were comparatively free to confine the mentally ill [both dangerous and harmless] at their own discretion."[84]

During the nineteenth century, progressive reformers, social workers, police, and public health officials worked to institutionalize mentally disabled persons, which meant moving them out of private homes and confining them in public and private asylums. Initially, these new guardians believed that they might cure their inmates and eventually release them.[85] But they soon resigned themselves to a purely custodial role, which led to considerable abuse.[86] An 1857 report to the New York State Senate found that investigators "testified to the *whipping* of male and female idiots and lunatics, and of confining them in loathsome cells, and binding them with chains. . . . The committee found lunatics, both male and female, in a state of nudity. The cells were intolerably offensive, littered with the long accumulated filth of the occupants" (italics in the original).[87]

In the early twentieth century, state officials further undermined the status of inmates, passing laws that allowed public and private guardians, on their own authority, to forcibly sterilize inmates.[88] In 1927, the Supreme Court ruled in *Buck v. Bell* that officials in Virginia could forcibly sterilize Carrie Buck, a "feeble minded," unmarried inmate who had become pregnant.[89] Virginia officials "blamed her pregnancy on hereditary weakness—in particular on her feeblemindedness." Justice Oliver Wendell Holmes agreed that authorities could sterilize her without her consent because "three generations of imbeciles are enough."[90] This abusive practice became widespread. By 1968, when it ended, 65,000 Americans with mental disabilities had been forcibly sterilized.[91]

Contagious Diseases

During the nineteenth century, public health officials were given the authority to seize, vaccinate, quarantine, or confine individuals who contracted contagious diseases—smallpox, tuberculosis, leprosy, plague, and typhoid—if they posed a threat to public health.[92] Many states delegated police powers to public health officials, who could revoke the status of citizens, denizens, and subjects on their own authority, which deprived infected individuals of juridical relief.[93] The courts generally allowed public heath officials wide latitude.[94] In one famous case, public health officials in New York seized Mary Mallon, who was ridiculed in the press as "Typhoid Mary," after a number of people in households where she worked as a private cook had contracted typhoid and one had died.[95] Like many people exposed to typhoid, Mallon carried the bacteria but did not contract the disease. Scientists estimated that "carriers" made up about 3 percent of the total number of typhoid cases, which in 1900 amounted to about nine thousand in the United States.[96] Most carriers were simply monitored by health officials. Mallon, however, was confined. Health officials released her after a two-year confinement but then seized her again after she returned to work as a cook, which violated the terms of her probation, and exposed twenty-five others to the disease (two died). Mallon was then confined as an inmate on an island in the East River for the rest of her life (twenty-three years).[97]

Homosexuals

Local and state officials have long used sodomy laws to criminalize homosexual behavior and revoke the rights of gay and lesbian citizens and denizens. But in the early twentieth century, federal officials revoked the status of individuals based on their *identity* as homosexuals, an identity that government officials arbitrarily imposed on people whom they regarded as homosexuals, even if those people were not. As Margot Canaday observes in *The Straight State*, "The state's identification of certain sexual behaviors, gender traits, and emotional ties as grounds for exclusion [from entering the country or serving in the military] was a catalyst in the formation of homosexual identity," one that was imposed from above, not asserted from below. "The state . . . *constituted* homosexuality in the construction of a stratified citizenry."[98] It did so because immigration officials and military authorities came to regard homosexuals as a threat to public health, a kind of contagion that might affect the body politic. Immigration officials took the initiative and identified prospective immigrants as homosexuals if inspectors thought they exhibited homosexual traits, "gender inversion (mannishness in women and effeminacy in men) rather than sexual behavior per se."[99] Officials took it upon themselves to deny entry to immigrants who they thought exhibited these characteristics and deported immigrant denizens who had been arrested for homosexual practices.[100] They could act on their own authority because the courts gave immigration officials wide latitude, which deprived immigrants of access to the courts. In effect, immigration officials excluded homosexuals (real or imagined) from immigrating or naturalizing (much like Asian immigrants) without explicit legislation providing for their exclusion. "Federal awareness of sex perversion among immigrants preceded by several decades a reliable legal instrument to exclude or deport 'sodomites' or 'pederasts.' Indeed, not until the early 1950s did immigration law explicitly bar aliens alleged to be homosexual from entering or remaining in the county."[101]

Military authorities joined immigration officials during World War I, when military authorities came to view homosexuality as a "civilian disease" that could "infect" others.[102] So medical officers prevented conscripts whom they identified as homosexuals from serving and excluded, discharged, or jailed soldiers, sailors, and nurses who exhibited homosexual behavior or engaged in homosexual acts.[103] Exactly how zealous bureaucrats used *public* institutions to promote *private* political agendas is not well understood, though their presence in different state bureaucracies suggests that state officials have considerable autonomy to shape public policy (see the discussion of the state in chapter 2).

During World War II,

> the military inaugurated much more aggressive vice patrols. . . . Suspected homosexuals were sent to hospitals where they were interviewed by psychiatrists, observed by hospital staff, inventoried by the Red Cross, interrogated by military intelligence, and ultimately adjudicated by a board of officers. . . . They were able to ask all recruits point-blank if they were homosexual, strip them naked to look for feminine body traits (and expanded rectums), and pursue clues, such as occupational choices and teachers' impressions, for indications of effeminacy. Such techniques led the army to reject roughly five

thousand soldiers for homosexuality during World War II . . . a number that
dwarfed the tiny handful refused induction for similar reasons during World
War I.[104]

An additional five thousand soldiers and four thousand sailors were dishon-
orably discharged during World War II.[105]

Of course, people who were denied entry into the service or were dishon-
orably discharged from it were denied the benefits of military service and
often found it difficult to obtain jobs or housing in the civilian sector because
their discharges carried a negative social stigma.[106] One young soldier accused of lesbianism told a military review board in 1958: "I don't feel that I
am being treated like an American citizen. I would like to know why."[107]

After World War II, people identified as homosexuals were fired from
government jobs because officials thought that homosexuals were vulnerable
to blackmail by foreign agents, so they came to be regarded as a threat not
only to public health but also to public safety and national security.[108]

THE REMAINDERS

The ascent of white and black men and women expanded the citizenry in the
United States during the nineteenth and early twentieth centuries. But the
ascent of these groups was accompanied by the descent of other groups into
denizen and subject populations, at least for a time. The expansion of the
citizenry inverted the social pyramid and changed the contours of civil society. But the social hierarchy, the division of society into citizen, denizen, and
subject populations, remained intact. The structure of inequality endured
because minors and immigrants remained in their assigned place as denizens
and convicts remained as subjects throughout this period. It turned out that
the political liabilities associated with age, place of birth, and illegal activity
proved *more* durable than the liabilities associated with class, race, and gender. The latter ascended; the former remained behind.

For the most part, the "remainders," the minors, immigrants, and convicts
who were left behind, occupy the same places today that they did two hundred years ago. Still, their condition was not completely static. Let us examine both what changed for minors, immigrants, and convicts during the nineteenth and early twentieth centuries and what remained the same.

Minors

In 1800, adults assigned white minors to the denizen population and black minors to the subject population because they viewed minors as lacking the capacity to act on their own. Adult white males often demeaned other groups—women and slaves—by calling them "childlike," turning this youthful attribute into an epithet. State officials, then as now, treated parents, teachers, employers, and masters as the "guardians" of minors and gave them the authority to discipline and punish minors in public and private settings. [109] If parents died, abandoned their children, or failed to provide adequate supervision, state officials seized minors and confined them in jails or in public or private orphanages. [110] In the 1850s, local officials seized orphans in New York and Boston, put them on "orphan trains," shopped them around rural towns across the Midwest, and bound them over as indentured servants, more or less, to private households and employers, where they worked until they became adults. The New York Children's Aid Society, a private charitable agency, transported and "placed" about 125,000 orphans from New York to households across the Midwest between 1853 and 1925. [111] One observer notes that "the great majority of those who are applying for children . . . are looking for cheap help . . . [and] expect to make a handsome profit on the child's service . . . furnishing poor food, shoddy clothing, work the child beyond its strength . . . and sometimes treat it with personal cruelty." [112]

Although the legal *status* of minors has remained pretty much the same for the past two hundred years, four important developments changed the *condition* of denizen minors during the nineteenth and early twentieth centuries.

First, the decline of indentured servitude and the abolition of slavery improved the status of immigrant and slave children, as both subject populations became denizens. By one estimate, "more than half of all persons who came to the colonies south of New England were indentured servants, and most servants were [minors]." [113] In 1776, "about one in five children was a slave." [114] But while minors who were indentured servants and slaves improved their condition by the mid-nineteenth century, orphaned minors remained the subjects of public and private authorities, as they do today.

Second, the treatment of illegitimate children or "bastards" generally improved during the nineteenth century. In 1800, bastards, like orphans, were often seized by the state and placed out because they were defined by law as *filius nullius*, "the child and heir of no one, bearing no legally recognized relations with *either* parent. A bastard had no right to inheritance or maintenance."[115] Unwed mothers were often whipped as punishment for having illegitimate children, and unwed indentured women could have their terms of service extended if they had children, a practice that gave masters an incentive to impregnate servant girls so that they could extend the girls' indenture.[116] "Even when laws were adopted to prevent 'dissolute masters' from impregnating their maids . . . to increase the maid's term of service, they did not provide any punishment for the master," Scott Christianson notes.[117]

But starting in 1851, state officials gave mothers the right to claim their offspring as their heirs and to make economic claims on the biological father's income and inheritance and made it possible for fathers, relatives, and nonfamily members to adopt illegitimate children.[118] These developments brought an end to the treatment of bastards as subjects. The treatment of bastards improved largely because women organized social movements to improve the condition of mothers and their children, one of the parallel and overlapping campaigns organized by feminists in this period.

Third, starting in 1852, the introduction of compulsory education and truancy laws and later restrictions on child labor forced minors out of the workforce in most settings, though not on plantations or in households or on farms, and into schools, where they were closely supervised by teachers rather than employers or masters.[119] However, legislators in southern states, where employers in textile mills employed minors in large numbers, did not adopt compulsory education or restrictive child labor laws until the twentieth century.[120]

These developments had contradictory consequences for minors. On the one hand, compulsory education and restrictive child labor laws reduced the economic contribution minors made to household income, which likely reduced their status in households.[121] As feminists have argued, status in the household is related to the economic contribution made by its members. So when women increased their economic contribution to household incomes, their status and ability to make decisions in the household improved. The reverse is also true. On the other hand, compulsory education gave minors skills that likely increased the economic contribution they could make to their own households when they became adults and entered the workforce.

Still, the exit of minors from the workforce, where many performed informal or unsupervised work on the streets, and the entry of minors into the schools likely *reduced* the ability of minors to make their own decisions about work and education or conduct their own affairs without adult supervision. Like most minors during the nineteenth century, particularly boys, Tom

Sawyer and Huck Finn had few rights as denizens, but they were largely unsupervised by adults for much of their youth, which is why they enjoyed great adventures. In this respect, the liberties enjoyed by youths have probably diminished, not expanded, during the past two hundred years. About the only real liberty that male youths possessed during the nineteenth century was to enlist in the army or navy *before* they came of age. But this was a curious form of liberty because enlisting in the army meant surrendering their status as *denizens* and accepting a new status as *subjects* of adult military authorities. Still, "nearly 40 percent of the 'men' who fought in the Civil War enlisted before they had reached 21. In Illinois, boys as young as fifteen fought in the war, though their parents had to sign consent forms."[122] *The Red Badge of Courage* spoke to this experience.

Fourth, although state officials gave government and nonstate actors the authority to discipline and punish minors at school and at work, in the home or in the orphanage, throughout this period, as they still do today, the permissible level of violence used by state and nonstate actors has substantially declined.

The elimination of indentured servitude and slavery ended the considerable violence associated with coerced/enslaved labor. State officials gradually restricted the authority of public and private authorities to discipline and punish minors and, for the first time, revoked this authority if authorities exceeded socially acceptable limits, which were nonetheless severe by contemporary standards.[123]

In 1870, the Supreme Court ruled that the Fourteenth Amendment did not apply to women or minors, but it nonetheless restricted the ability of courts to confine minors in "reform schools" *without* being convicted of any crime.[124] The court then reversed itself in 1882 and allowed the practice to resume. It was not until 1967 that the court revisited its decision and "granted children in juvenile courts limited due process rights, including the right to notice, counsel, confrontation, cross-examination of witnesses, and the privilege against self-incrimination."[125]

In recent years, reformers have organized social movements to work on children's rights, though they have done less to improve the rights and/or status of children and have instead made it easier for state officials to move children from one set of guardians (their parents) to another set of guardians who work in state institutions (prisons) or are private subcontractors (foster parents). This activity resembles the efforts of nineteenth-century reformers who worked to move mentally disabled people from private homes to asylums (see the discussion earlier in this chapter).

Immigrants

When Europeans immigrated to the United States in 1800, they became denizens. The Naturalization Act of 1802 allowed adult white males who lived for five years in the Republic and declared their intention to become citizens two years after entry to be naturalized and become citizens. [126] Women immigrants remained denizens on a permanent basis, while indentured white male immigrants could not naturalize until they completed their indentures and residency-intention requirements.

State officials today still treat immigrants as denizens unless and until they naturalize and become citizens. They treat undocumented immigrants as denizens unless or until they are identified as illegal, at which point they can be jailed or deported as subjects. Although the status of denizen immigrants has remained more or less unchanged during the past two hundred years, several developments during the nineteenth and early twentieth centuries changed the ability of different immigrant groups to naturalize, become citizens, and exercise suffrage.

First, in the mid-nineteenth century, federal and state officials restricted the entry of immigrants from Asia (chiefly China, Japan, and the Philippines), limited their ability to naturalize, and took steps to prevent them from voting and owning land, which made Asian immigrants denizens on a permanent basis. The state officials who adopted these restrictive measures argued that these laws would prevent western states from becoming "the mercenary Mecca of the scum of Asia—a loathsome Chinese province."[127] Immigration officials made special efforts to prevent Asian women from entering the United States, joining resident immigrant communities, and having children who would become citizens (what anti-immigrant groups today might describe as "anchor babies"), despite the status of their parents as permanent denizens. The result for Chinese immigrants, who first arrived in the 1850s, was the creation of aging, predominantly male communities in urban "Chinatown" ghettos. Immigration officials allowed greater numbers of Japanese women to immigrate, though not to naturalize. As a result, Japanese immigrants created younger, mixed-gender communities with a growing number of native-born children who eventually claimed citizenship, a status that was interrupted by removal and incarceration during World War II.

Second, although state officials restricted the entry of Asian immigrants, they permitted the entry of European immigrants throughout the nineteenth century. "Between 1865 and World War I, nearly twenty-five million immigrants journeyed to the United States," and in 1914, about 12 percent of the population was foreign born.[128] Adult immigrant men could naturalize and vote, though women and girls could not.

During this period, the origin of European immigrants shifted to southern and eastern Europe. The entry of Catholics from southern Europe and Jews from eastern Europe changed the ethnic-religious character of denizen and citizen populations in the United States and transformed the political landscape in American cities, where large immigrant male populations elected politicians belonging to political "machines" to advance their interests. These developments persuaded native voters and state officials to restrict immigration before and after World War I and to extend suffrage to native-born women after the war, in part to counter the weight of immigrant voters (see chapter 6). The outbreak of World War I abruptly halted migration flows around the world. When the war ended, officials substantially reduced the entry of European immigrants, and the foreign-born population in the United States began a steady, decades-long decline.

Third, the extension of suffrage to native-born women in 1920 (though not to adult black women in the South) also opened the door of naturalization and suffrage to adult immigrant women. Both developments expanded the citizenry in America.

Soldiers and Convicts

In 1800, indentured servants and slaves were the subjects of private authorities, while soldiers, sailors, and convicts were the subjects of military or state authorities. During the nineteenth century, indentured servants were discharged and replaced with free wage workers, slaves were emancipated, and African Americans became citizens or denizens. Since then, most of the *subjects* in the Republic have been military personnel or convicts.[129]

Although the US military has long relied on volunteers and conscripts, both served a form of indenture for a term of service under military authority. Military officials can direct them to face death and injury on the battlefield and impose military discipline on them if they hesitate, resist, or refuse. The *status* of volunteers and conscripts in military service has not significantly changed since the Revolutionary War. Although the military now relies on volunteers to fill its ranks, Congress has kept the authority to draft citizens into the service and make them involuntary subjects of state officials.

For soldiers and sailors, battlefield conditions have not substantially changed during the past two hundred years. Soldiers, then as now, face lethal disease, disfiguring and crippling injury, psychic trauma, and sudden death on the battlefield, whether at Bunker Hill, Gettysburg, Iwo Jima, or Kandahar. But while battlefields are still lethal environments for American soldiers, their chances of surviving battlefield encounters have improved. The introduction of helmets and body armor, vaccines and penicillin, the rapid evacuation and prompt medical treatment of battlefield casualties, and the deployment of armored vehicles and advanced weapons systems that can provide both battlefield security and superiority have reduced casualty rates. Today, combatants can survive encounters that would have killed their predecessors. Moreover, the savage military discipline—flogging and other corporal punishments—regularly imposed on nineteenth-century soldiers and sailors has eased, though physical violence and emotional stress are still deployed by military authorities and their subordinates.

Conditions have also improved for military personnel while they are in the service and after they complete it. Housing, education, and health care for military personnel and their dependents have improved at forts and bases, and Congress has provided substantial postservice benefits, subsidies, and preferences to veterans.

Convicts

The status of convicts as the subjects of state authority has remained unchanged for the past two hundred years. Convicts were, and still are, deprived of the rights available to citizens and denizens and can be deprived of their lives and executed by public officials. But while their *status* has not substantially changed, several developments have altered the *condition* of convicts during the nineteenth and twentieth centuries.

First, in 1800, after convicts completed their sentences, state officials generally *restored* their previous status as citizens or denizens. In some states, officials denied them suffrage and disenfranchised citizens convicted for infamous crimes, though they defined "infamous" in very different ways.[130] During the nineteenth century, a growing number of states disenfranchised ex-convicts for a growing number of crimes. This process accelerated in the South after Reconstruction, where state officials disenfranchised ex-convicts for misdemeanors, laws targeted primarily at African

By insisting that constitutional government be divided—into separate branches and into separate states and political parties—the architects made it extremely difficult for the multitude to establish unfettered control over the state, even during times of war and economic crisis.

Second, the division of civil society into three parts (citizen, denizen, and subject) and the intricate, complex, and contingent division of people in each status category by class, race, gender, age, place of origin, and myriad other social distinctions (whether people in these categories had mental disabilities or physical ailments, whether they were bastards or orphans, whether their crimes were petty misdemeanors or grand felonies, etc.) effectively divided people in civil society and in the new citizen majority. This made it extremely difficult for the multitude, the "99 percent" in contemporary usage, to combine effectively or use its collective capacity to establish a transformative majority. Moreover, a *divided* society became *more* divided over time, in part because the ascent of some groups resulted in social *differentiation*, not *homogenization*.

Third, when people from denizen and subject populations became citizens, they often used their power not to transform the state and civil society, as the architects feared, but to defend the status quo. Scholars have debated why they have done so, but there are two plausible reasons why they defended the status quo instead of assaulting it.

First, new citizens obtained important benefits from the state, the right to vote and to enjoy the rights associated with liberty, equality, and solidarity chief among them. They also obtained other important economic benefits from the state: free land, veterans' benefits, pensions, social security, unemployment benefits, tax benefits for homebuyers, and so on. Should it be surprising that newly empowered citizens would fight to defend these benefits and the republic that provided them?[138]

Recall, too, that adult white men, black men, and women were allowed to become citizens because political parties wanted to enlist them as partisan voters who might increase the parties' political strength. By and large, newly enfranchised voters returned the favor and supported the parties that admitted them: adult white men without property supported the Democratic Party during the antebellum period; adult blacks supported the Republican Party during Reconstruction (and did so until the 1960s); and women split, with native-born white and black women in the North and West supporting the Republican Party and immigrant white women in the urban North and native-born white women in the South supporting the Democratic Party.

THE EXPANSION OF CITIZENSHIP AND
THE DECLINE OF VIOLENCE

As the citizenry expanded, the level of violence in public institutions and private settings declined. This was a significant and unexpected development.

In 1800, state officials and nonstate actors routinely inflicted violence on denizens and subjects. In public institutions, military officers flogged soldiers and sailors, jailers flogged convicts, and schoolteachers were allowed to whip, cane, and beat their students. In private settings, nonstate actors were authorized to inflict violence on denizens and subjects. Husbands beat their wives, parents beat their children, masters beat apprentices and servants, plantation owners beat slaves, teamsters beat draft animals. Of course, adult white men committed *most* of this violence. And the violence that men, in public and private settings, routinely visited on their victims was ferocious, savage, and humiliating. Surgeons who examined black men enlisting in the Union army found that half of the applicants "presented evidence of flogging or injuries from other forms of punishment" and "one man showed the marks of over a thousand lashes."[139] The men who practiced violence were given a free hand to punish and discipline their inferiors. Law and custom did little to stay their hands. Of course, the law did not license them to kill or maim their victims, but legal authorities, judges, and juries rarely punished them if they did.[140]

But during the next 150 years, a number of developments contributed to the decline of violence practiced by male authorities in public and private settings. Violence declined because citizens, denizens, and subjects organized social movements that demanded an end to violence against subordinate groups and insisted that the authority to use violence, both by public officials and, importantly, by nonstate actors, be restricted. Myra Glenn's important book, *Campaigns against Corporal Punishment*, a study of early antiviolence campaigns in the 1830s, examines the role that women played in parallel and overlapping social movements.[141]

First, Congress abolished the slave trade in 1806. This reduced, though it did not end, the violence associated with the capture of slaves in Africa and their transport on ships to the Americas during the lethal "middle passage."[142] The abolition of the slave trade may also have had an important impact on white slave-owner violence in the United States. Curtailing the supply of captured slaves may have driven up the price of slaves in the

United States, and this may have restrained owner violence because slaves may have become too valuable to kill or maim, though evidence for this is mixed and owners still inflicted terrible cruelties on slaves after the slave trade ended.[143]

Emancipation and the abolition of slavery in the United States brought an end to the ubiquitous, routine, and savage violence inflicted by white slave owners on black men, women, and children. However, the end of Reconstruction and the rise of Jim Crow led to renewed violence against blacks, black men in particular, by state officials and nonstate actors. Historians such as David Oshinsky have argued that the convict-leasing camps and prisons like Parchman Farm were, for the inmates, "worse than slavery."[144] Because convicts cost nothing and could be replaced, white overseers had no *economic* reason to restrain violent behavior. Still, the violence of white officials during Jim Crow was directed at a much smaller percentage of the black population than during the antebellum period, and some southern states abolished convict leasing and eliminated flogging: Tennessee in 1895, Georgia in 1909, Arkansas in 1913, and Alabama, Florida, and North Carolina in 1923.[145]

The murderous violence inflicted by unofficial lynch mobs nonetheless continued. Mobs tortured, mutilated, shot, hanged, burned, and dismembered their victims. But while white violence was inflicted on a relatively small percentage of the black population and was primarily aimed at adult black males, lynch-mob terror hung over the entire black population like a thundercloud.[146]

Outside the South, public campaigns against flogging and other kinds of corporal punishment curbed the violence inflicted against sailors, convicts, students, women, children, and horses by state officials and nonstate actors. In 1850, Congress abolished flogging in the navy over the objections of southern representatives, who saw it correctly as a repudiation of the violence that white owners inflicted on slaves.[147] Southern representatives tried to have flogging reinstated and attacked the "sickly sentimentality" and "hyperphilanthropy" that was "rife" in the North.[148] One southern representative declared that "the campaign against naval flogging represented another radical 'ism' for the North, 'similar to socialism . . . fourierism . . . [and] abolitionism.'"[149]

Prison reformers persuaded legislatures and wardens to curb or eliminate flogging in the prisons. In Sing Sing, the average number of lashes inflicted on prisoners fell from 1,121 in 1843 to 38 in 1847.[150] Officials also curbed the practice in state-run mental asylums. Legislators in Massachusetts prohibited all forms of corporal punishment in the state's prisons, though they permitted solitary confinement to continue.[151]

During the late 1840s, "school committees and administrators increasingly regulated and restricted a teacher's traditional right to punish [students in public schools]," and rules requiring teachers to record all cases of punishment "precipitated a decline in the amount of school room punishment."[152]

The entry of women into the classrooms as teachers—"by 1860 women constituted a majority of teachers in New England schools"—and the decline of male teachers also contributed to the decline in classroom violence.[153]

In public institutions, the historian Myra Glenn argues, "the extant evidence demonstrates two crucial facts: 1) there was a significant decline in the actual use of corporal punishment during the antebellum period, especially during the latter half of the 1840s; 2) parents, teachers, naval and prison officers increasingly experimented with a range of disciplinary techniques that were psychologically, if not physically, punitive."[154]

In private settings, women used different means to curb male violence. They organized temperance movements to curb the violence triggered by alcohol use and abuse, demanded suffrage so that they could legislate against male violence, and sued men for cruelty in divorce courts.[155] Elizabeth Cady Stanton urged legislators "to grant wives divorces from physically abusive husbands, arguing that women lived in legalized slavery."[156] Legislators heeded these calls and made "extreme" or "intolerable" cruelty grounds for divorce in Connecticut, Pennsylvania, Ohio, Indiana, and Illinois.[157] Women then sued for divorce on these grounds. Between 1860 and 1878, the Bureau of Statistics found that of the 7,233 divorced granted, "2,949 were for cruelty, 375 for extreme cruelty, and 233 for cruel and abusive treatment."[158] Divorce enabled women to escape from violence in private settings. Did the threat of suits for divorce curb or restrain male violence? It is difficult to tell. But it certainly restricted *socially acceptable* levels of violence, which may have helped curb violence. Of course, male violence has declined slowly. So, too, have legal sanctions against private male violence. "There was no legal concept of marital rape in American states until the mid-1970s," and it was not until 1992 that the Supreme Court ruled "that it would no longer recognize the power of husbands over the bodies of their wives. That is the moment when coverture, as a living legal principle, died."[159]

Women's efforts to curb male violence against women also helped curb adult violence against minors. Efforts to curb violence against children in the home lagged behind efforts to curb violence against children in the schools, against adult women in the home, or against horses on the street. The *New York Times* reported that the first complaint lodged against a parent for the abuse of a child was filed only in 1874, by the Association for the Prevention of Cruelty to *Animals*.

Although violence declined between 1800 and 1945, its level remained high by contemporary standards. Still, two important social changes had occurred. First, the permissible and actual level of violence practiced by male, state, and nonstate actors substantially declined in most, though not all, settings. Second, the authority of nonstate actors declined relative to state officials. Both of these developments were significant achievements, and both were closely associated with the expansion of citizenship in the United States.

Chapter Eight

The Further Expansion of Citizenship

By 1950, a majority of residents in the United States and other democratic republics in western Europe and Japan claimed citizenship and suffrage. But states still consigned large groups of people to denizen and subject populations and treated women, who had obtained suffrage, as "second-class" citizens in many respects. In the United States, adult blacks in the South and youth across America rejected their treatment as denizens and fought to claim their "civil rights" as citizens, while women and homosexuals struggled to upgrade their status as "second-class" citizens and become "first-class" citizens in the Republic. This chapter examines how blacks, youth, women, and homosexuals claimed citizenship and changed its meaning in the United States during the second half of the twentieth century.

BLACK DENIZENS, MIGRATION, AND THE STRUGGLE FOR CIVIL RIGHTS

In the Jim Crow South, whites treated adult black men and women as denizens, even though the Fourteenth and Fifteenth Amendments extended citizenship and suffrage to adult black men and the Nineteenth Amendment extended it to adult black women. Blacks resisted the onset of Jim Crow in different ways. During the 1870s, Henry Adams and Benjamin Singleton urged blacks to leave the South and organized a mass exodus to Kansas. They persuaded tens of thousands of blacks to escape as "refugees from poverty and terrorism, breaking with a way of life they found increasingly unbearable. . . . What united them was the belief that 'anywhere is better than here.'"[1]

But during the late nineteenth and early twentieth centuries, blacks found it difficult to leave the South. White public officials and nonstate actors used violence, incarceration, lynch mobs, torture, and murder to keep blacks in their "place."[2] In the South, "place" was both a geographical location and a social status. It meant making black tenant sharecroppers dependent on white rural farm proprietors and tying them to the land, and it meant making sure that blacks did not rise above or escape from their assigned social status. During the black exodus to Kansas, "armed whites closed the river and threatened to sink all boats carrying black migrants. . . . One migrant who had returned from Kansas to get his family was seized by whites, who cut off his hands and threw them in his wife's lap, saying, 'Now go to Kansas and work.'"[3]

Black migration was discouraged not only by southern whites but also by northern whites, who often proved unwelcoming to black migrants.[4] But this changed during World War I. The growing demand for workers in northern industries and the end of immigrant labor flows from Europe prompted northern employers to recruit southern black workers, who were eager to escape growing white violence in the South (white lynch-mob violence grew during the period before the war, according to most observers).[5] Between 1915 and 1918, 750,000 blacks left the South and moved north.[6] During the "Great Migration" that followed, one million blacks fled the South during the 1920s, another million during the 1930s, and one million more during World War II, nearly four million in all.[7] Although some scholars have argued that economic demand drew blacks north, blacks migrated not only when demand was strong—during World War I and World War II—but also when it was *weak* or nonexistent, during the Great Depression (1929–1941). This suggests that blacks migrated not only for economic but also for social and political reasons.[8] By migrating north, adult black men and women could obtain citizenship and suffrage, which was unavailable to them in the South, and escape the endemic violence deployed by state and nonstate actors in the South.[9] These were powerful incentives to leave. According to Johnson and Campbell, "Both blacks and whites mentioned lynchings as one of the most important causes of outmigration of blacks from the South during World War I," and a study of migration "indicated that mistreatment by police resulted in almost as many persons leaving the South as did lynchings. . . . In many respects, the migration took on the character of a *mass movement*" (italics added).[10] Isabel Wilkerson agrees, arguing that "it was the first big step the nation's servant class ever took without asking."[11]

Black migrants used their feet to obtain the vote. "The slogan down here is: To hell with the South," a Texarkana resident observed in 1917. "The Negro loves the South, but he does not love the white man's South," a Vicksburg resident insisted.[12] One black man who reflected on his decision to move north recounted, "I just begin to feel like a man. . . . My children are sitting in the same school with whites and I don't have to be humble to no one. I have registered [to vote and] will vote in the next election and there isn't any yes Sir and no Sir. It's all yes and no, Sam and Bill."[13]

Southern whites obstructed the black exodus. "Police arrested blacks in railroad stations as vagrants, they hauled passengers off northern-bound trains, they imposed heavy fines on labor [recruiters] and they sought to suppress black newspapers [that] advertised the . . . opportunities awaiting blacks in a free North."[14]

Of course, northern whites did not always welcome black migrants. During World War II, some white communities failed to accommodate black migrants in a nondiscriminatory fashion, resulting in four major race riots, "one each in Harlem and Los Angeles and two in Detroit," where twenty-five blacks and nine whites were killed during a riot on June 20, 1943.[15]

Black migration had several important consequences. First, black migration secured citizenship and suffrage for nearly four million adult black men and women, which contributed to a dramatic expansion of the citizenry years before the passage of the Civil Rights Act of 1964. As many blacks claimed citizenship by migrating (about four million) as were freed from slavery by the Thirteenth Amendment (about four million).[16] Second, migration weakened white authority, both public and private, in the Jim Crow South and may have reduced white violence against blacks (the pace of lynchings slowed after 1920). Third, the expansion of the black citizenry in the North made it possible for black *citizens* and organizations—the NAACP, independent black newspapers, and trade unions—to assist black *denizens* in the South and provide them with legal and financial resources when they launched "civil rights" campaigns during the 1950s.

World War II

Although black men and women in the North claimed citizenship and suffrage, black men were allowed to serve in the military only in restricted duties or in segregated units and were barred from serving in some branches.

In 1940, the Marine Corps and Army Air Corps barred black men, the US Navy allowed blacks to serve only as "messmen," and the US Army enrolled only 3,640 blacks in segregated units.[17] The Red Cross refused to accept black blood donations "on the score that white men in service would refuse plasma if they knew it came from Negro veins," and local draft boards across the country refused to induct blacks and, by 1943, had passed over more than three hundred thousand qualified men, a development that antagonized whites, who viewed this practice as a form of favoritism, and insulted blacks, who saw it as discriminatory.[18] As one black college student observed, "The Army jim-crows us. The Navy lets us serve only as messmen. The Red Cross refuses our blood. Employers and labor unions shut us out. Lynchings continue. We are disenfranchised, jim-crowed, spat upon. What more could Hitler do than that?"[19]

In 1941, Asa Philip Randolph, leader of the all-black Brotherhood of Sleeping Car Porters, organized a march on Washington to protest the exclusion of blacks from war industries and the military. The threat of protest persuaded President Roosevelt to open wartime industries to black workers and allow black men to serve in the military, though only in segregated units. By the end of the war, one million black men had been inducted, and some served in segregated combat naval, air, and ground units.[20]

After the war, Randolph and black servicemen pressed for an end to segregation in the military. In 1948, Randolph organized a campaign to persuade black youth to refuse to register for the draft. Blacks were in no mood "to shoulder a gun for democracy abroad so long as they were denied democracy here at home," Randolph told President Truman.[21] If Truman refused to desegregate the services, Randolph announced, black men would refuse to serve.[22] In a poll conducted by the NAACP, 71 percent of black college students "were sympathetic to civil disobedience against the draft."[23] Truman, who had been "outraged at the murder of dozens of black veterans" by whites in the South and thought that desegregation of the military might win black votes in the upcoming presidential election, agreed to take action.[24] On July 26, 1948, Truman issued Executive Order 9981, which announced a policy to desegregate the military "as rapidly as possible."[25] Black voters then gave Truman the margin of victory in a very close election.[26]

Although the military did not fully integrate black men into the service until 1954, the integration of the military not only gave millions of black GIs access to the significant benefits that service provided—access to health care, pensions, job opportunities, financial aid for education and housing—it altered the institutional relations between the federal government and southern white communities, where many US military bases were located.[27] The integration of the military in the early 1950s put pressure on local communities to alter segregationist practices in housing, marriage, employment, education, and transportation. Local commanders could put local communities or businesses "off-limits" to servicemen, white or black, if they discriminated against black servicemen. In 1963, Secretary of Defense Robert S. McNamara directed all local commanders to foster "equal treatment for servicemen and their dependents both off and on military installations," a development that prompted southern congressmen to complain that the policy was "economic blackmail in its rawest form" and a "direct invasion of local affairs."[28]

Civil Rights and Citizenship

Black citizens in the North supported organizations such as the NAACP, which mounted legal challenges to segregation and the treatment of black denizens in the South.[29] Although NAACP lawyers persuaded the Supreme Court to overturn some segregationist laws—the all-white primary and segregation on interstate buses—they decided in 1950 to abandon a piecemeal approach and challenge the doctrine of separate but equal education, which they regarded as a central pillar of Jim Crow.[30] They then organized black citizens in the North and black denizens led by Rev. Joseph Armstrong DeLaine in Clarendon, South Carolina, to file suits against segregated education in their communities, which by "tapping into the aspirations of black communities . . . [helped] create a sustainable, organized struggle for first-class citizenship rights."[31] This collaboration brought the collective suit—*Brown v. Board of Education*—to the Supreme Court in December 1952. According to one Supreme Court justice, the court was not then prepared to invalidate school segregation and the assumptions behind *Plessy v. Ferguson*, which in 1896 allowed whites to construct Jim Crow, and would have voted five to four to reject the NAACP's suit.[32] But a majority in June 1953 voted to have the case reargued, which delayed their decision, and in September, Chief Justice Vinson suddenly died. Justice Felix Frankfurter remarked that Vinson's death was "the first indication I have ever had that there *is* a God."[33] President Eisenhower then appointed California governor Earl Warren, a Republican, to replace Vinson. Warren presided over the rearguments in December 1953, joined a majority of the court who opposed segregation, and persuaded the remaining pro-segregationist justices on the court to join the majority and issue a unanimous opinion that ended school segregation and abolished its legal rationale in 1954.[34] The twenty adults and forty-six children who brought suit in Clarendon, South Carolina, paid a terrible price for their one-time participation in this legal social movement.[35] They were fired from their jobs and driven from their homes by threats and white violence.[36] Local whites, with one exception, subsequently abandoned the local public schools rather than integrate.[37]

Although the Supreme Court ruling changed the law of the land, it did little to change conditions on the ground. To change that, black denizens took steps of their own. On December 1, 1955, Rosa Parks refused to sit in a segregated section of the bus in Montgomery, Alabama, and was arrested for breaking local law.[38] Two local ministers, the Reverends Ralph Abernathy and Dr. Martin Luther King Jr., then used their pulpits to rouse members of their congregations to challenge the public authorities and private vigilantes who defended segregation.[39] During the next five years, black denizens based in religious communities and led by religious leaders and groups such as the Southern Christian Leadership Conference (SCLC) in the South and supported by black citizens and secular organizations such as the NAACP in the North fought for civil rights in the South.[40] They won some campaigns, in part because they challenged local authorities and institutions, not national authorities and centralized institutions, and they lost other campaigns. But these limited gains prompted white officials and nonstate actors to organize a "massive resistance" to civil rights movements and Supreme Court rulings. Nearly 250,000 whites joined the White Citizens' Council in the two years after the *Brown* decision.[41] During the rest of the 1950s, determined and violent white resistance limited the gains made by local civil rights groups.

Then, in February 1960, four black youths sat down at a whites-only lunch counter at Woolworth's in Greensboro, North Carolina, and asked to be served.[42] Thousands of other black and white youths organized protests across the South. During the next year, "over 50,000 people participated in one demonstration or another in 100 cities and over 3,600 demonstrators spent time in jail."[43] Black youths from the South and white youths from the North, who were recruited from secular colleges and religious communities, created a wider mass movement that simultaneously challenged local authorities across the South. They challenged segregationist laws and voter restrictions, which allowed whites to disenfranchise blacks.[44] The voter-registration drive organized by youths through the Student Nonviolent Coordinating Committee (SNCC) and Congress for Racial Equality (CORE) triggered a violent white response, which eventually prompted federal government intervention and passage of the Civil Rights Act of 1964 and the Voting Rights Act of 1965.[45] These measures finally redeemed the promises made by the Fourteenth and Fifteenth Amendments, which had been suspended for decades by southern whites, Supreme Court rulings, and the collaboration of federal officials and leaders of both political parties.

Migration, executive orders, litigation, and protests by blacks and whites, young and old, from the North and in the South all contributed to the expansion of citizenship in the United States between 1915 and 1965. Black migration to the North enabled nearly four million black adults to claim citizenship and suffrage; the passage of the 1964 Civil Rights Act and 1965 Voting Rights Act extended suffrage to between three and five million black adults in the South.[46] It is noteworthy that about as many blacks obtained citizenship by *migrating* north as obtained citizenship by *fighting* for their civil rights in the South. However, the black and white youths who participated in the civil rights movement during the early 1960s did not immediately obtain suffrage. As a group, youths eighteen to twenty-one obtained suffrage only with the passage of the Twenty-Sixth Amendment in 1971, as we will see below.

Civil rights movements—migration, litigation, protest, executive action, and legislation—expanded the citizenry in the United States, broadened citizenship's meaning, and extended its benefits not only to blacks but also to women and to other minorities. By abolishing laws that permitted segregation or discrimination in employment, housing, and education in the South and, importantly, also in the North, civil rights movements extended benefits to *other* groups—Chinese, Japanese, Filipino, Hispanic, and American Indians—and helped them improve their social status.[47]

DENIZEN YOUTHS REVOLT

During the 1960s, youths in America challenged adult authority—state officials, parents, and their surrogates—and demanded an end to the treatment of youths as *denizens*, who were denied suffrage and adult rights and opportunities, and as *subjects*, who could be conscripted by military authorities and sent to war without their consent. Scholars have generally dismissed or minimized the contribution that denizen youths made to social change in the 1960s and 1970s. They have done so for two reasons. First, youths often joined adult organizations. Black youths in the South joined the civil rights movement led by the SCLC, white youths joined Students for a Democratic

Society (SDS), which was organized by adults in the League for Industrial Democracy, and young women joined the National Organization of *Women* (not "Girls"—adult women objected to being treated like minors, or "girls"). By submerging themselves, for a time, in adult movements and organizations, the contributions made by youths were less visible than they might have been. Of course, youths soon advanced their own issues, developed new and separate identities, and organized groups of their own. Black youths organized the Student Nonviolent Coordinating Committee and later the Black Panther Party, white youths organized the free speech movement and developed SDS into an autonomous organization for youths after its young leaders described the parent organization as "a musty relic of a bygone past," and young women organized Redstockings, consciousness-raising groups, and the Boston Women's Health Collective.[48]

Second, adult scholars and many activist youths dismissed the idea that "youths" were capable of agency, regarded them as a "privileged" group (not a denizenry), and argued that "oppressed" groups defined by race, class, or gender were the only groups capable of making "real" or "revolutionary" change. For example, Columbia University professor Zbigniew Brzezinski described dissident youths as "historically irrelevant," incapable of making "a true revolution."[49] Political scientists John H. Scharr and Sheldon Wolin agreed, arguing that while youths "achieved a distinctive status for themselves" and advanced "many modes of action . . . —civil rights work, community organizing, on-campus organizing, anti-draft unions, faculty organizing, political action as guerrilla theater, even electoral politics—*none* offered a decisive lever of change."[50] American historian Henry Steele Commager expressed frustration with the "exasperating combination of logic and irrationality" of youths and blamed it on their position of *privilege* in society: "Never was a generation so pampered."[51] Many scholars agreed with Commager's depiction of youths as "the members of the privileged class," which meant that youths could have no legitimate political goals of their own.[52] This view was held not only by adult authorities but also by many youths in the black, student left, and women's movements. As Alice Echols observed, many youths "shared the conviction that authentic radicalism could not emerge among middle-class white students from college campuses."[53]

Fortunately, youths were not persuaded by these condescending and ageist arguments. As SDS president Gregory Calvert argued in 1967, "We must stop apologizing for being students or for organizing students. No individual, no group, no class is genuinely engaged in a revolutionary movement unless their struggle is a struggle for their *own* liberation."[54] Although many adults and youth activists viewed youths as a privileged group that was incapable of making change, as spoiled "rebels without a cause," the fact is that youths altered the social status of denizen and subject youth populations and contributed to significant social changes during the 1960s and 1970s, developments that led to a vast expansion of citizenship and suffrage in the United States.

Rebel youths first found a cause in the civil rights movement. In 1960, black students conducted sit-ins across the South and joined the civil rights movement, which had been organized by adult black denizens in the South (SCLC) and adult black citizens in the North (NAACP). When black and white youths from the South and the North, who shared a *common* status as denizens in both places, joined the civil rights movement, they infused it with new energy. They created, for the first time, a mass movement capable of making simultaneous change across the South. Youths soon created their own organizations (SNCC) and identified new issues and tactics (sit-ins, freedom rides, voter registration) that changed the shape and character of the civil rights movement, which was at a low ebb in 1960.[55] They forged a new identity, as "black," not "Negro" or "colored," and demanded not only "civil rights" but also "Black Power," a development that divided the movement, more or less, along both generational (youths vs. adults) and racial (black vs. white) lines.[56]

Although black youths found a cause first, white youths who participated in the civil rights movement then demanded civil rights for students at American universities, which had been transformed by a large influx of baby-boom youth.[57] In 1964, "seventeen-year olds became the largest single age group in the country [and] for the next seven years—that is until 1971— the seventeen-year-old group [was] larger every year than it was the year before."[58] Many of these youths were students, and by 1968, seven million attended college.[59] Youths became increasingly aware of their growing numbers and their status as denizens and subjects.

As students, youths lived in sex-segregated dorms under the supervision of adult authorities who acted as parental surrogates (in loco parentis) for the minors in their care, what one youthful critic called "the Big Daddy Complex."[60] Young men and women were denied adult rights—the right to vote and to exercise free speech or freedom of assembly—on campus, and consensual sexual activity was treated as "illicit" or illegal.[61]

148 Chapter 8

In 1964, students in the free speech movement at the University of California at Berkeley challenged adult authority and demanded that students be given adult civil rights.[62] As FSM spokesman Mario Savio explained, "Last summer I went to Mississippi to struggle there for civil rights. This fall I am engaged in another phase of the same struggle, this time in Berkeley. The two battlefields may seem quite different to some observers, but . . . the same rights are at stake in both places—the right to participate as citizens in democratic society and the right to due process of law."[63] Denizen youths in colleges and high schools across the country subsequently demanded the rights of citizens.

The following year, in 1965, President Lyndon Johnson increased the number of US troops in Vietnam by ten times, from 25,000 in January to 200,000 by November, and later increased the number of troops to 400,000 by 1967.[64] Because male youths could be conscripted and made the subjects of military authority and because the military relied heavily on conscripts to fight the war in Vietnam, the escalation of the war raised new issues for youths, both student and nonstudent alike.[65] Youths in SDS organized anti-war "teach-ins" and mass marches against military training on campus (ROTC) and against the war, while other groups urged youths to refuse induction, burn or return their draft cards, or leave the country to evade conscription.[66] Two youths, Catholic Roger La Porte and Quaker Norman Morrison, set themselves on fire and died of their injuries to protest the war.[67]

By demanding civil rights and campaigning against the war and conscription, youths in the New Left, which was made up of diverse national and local political organizations such as SDS, advanced a set of political issues that grew out of their status as denizens and subjects. At the same time, in 1965, the year that the Rolling Stones' song "(I Can't Get No) Satisfaction" was the number-one selling record, hippie dropouts and marginally employed youths in San Francisco, a group that one observer described as "lumpen beatniks," mounted a "cultural revolution" against what President Johnson called "the Great Society."[68] As the editors of the *Berkeley Barb*, an underground newspaper, explained, "We [countercultural hippies] have gone AWOL from the Great American Army that is our society. . . . We [came] to the conclusion that our society was corrupt, vile, and heinous, and that to obey any of its dictates, any of its concepts, was to doom us eventually to a living death, killing others as we died."[69]

Countercultural youths advocated a different kind of "politics." As the activist Jerry Rubin explained, "Our politics is our music, our smell, our skin, our hair, our warm naked bodies, our drugs, our energy, our underground papers, our vision."[70]

By advocating "sex, drugs, and rock and roll," countercultural activists, who had close ties with the bohemian Beat subculture of the 1950s, invited youths across America to join their cause.[71] As the feminist historian Alice Echols observed, "More [youths] passed through 'love ghettos' like Haight-Ashbury, a working-class, international neighborhood [in San Francisco] than took part in Students for a Democratic Society, the leading New Left group of the 1960s. Seventy-five thousand kids spent their summer vacation in the Haight during the 1967 'Summer of Love.'"[72]

The New Left and the counterculture both challenged adult authority, which contributed to widespread social conflicts between youths and adults. Youths battled adult state officials, parents, and their surrogates (teachers) about foreign policy, mandatory military service, sex before marriage, length of hair, style of clothes, drug use, and popular music. These public and intimate battles were bitter and protracted, leading to a yawning "generation gap," and the singer Bob Dylan warned adults, parents, and authorities, "Your sons and your daughters are beyond your command."[73]

The youth revolt not only led to intergenerational conflict, it led to conflict between different youths—male and female, black and white. Male youths, who were subject to conscription, dominated the antiwar political organizations of the New Left. Male youths typically treated female youths as menials in the antiwar movement. "We were usually relegated to positions of typists, office clerks, janitors and flunkeys in [New Left organizations]," Linda Gordon and Ann Popkin observed. "Our opinions were seldom asked for and rarely heard."[74] Female youths were offended by male activists who advanced the slogan, "Women say 'yes' [to sex] to guys who say 'no' [to the draft]."[75] Male youths also dominated the counterculture and its ad hoc organizations, such as rock groups, communes, and underground papers, and the notion of women as groupies and casual sex partners. "Hippies treat their women like squaws," Grateful Dead drummer Danny Rifkin admitted.[76]

During the late 1960s, female youths objected to what Robin Morgan denounced as the "ejaculatory politics" of men in the New Left.[77] "The processes and priorities of the male Left alienated us," Gordon and Popkin wrote, "and we began to come together as women to try to understand and change our situation."[78] The male-dominated counterculture and its music, what some women derisively described as "cock rock," an idiom in which "men always seem to end up on top," angered many female youths.[79] The Rolling Stones' song "'Under My Thumb,' a revenge song filled with hatred for women, made me feel crazy," a *Rat* staff writer reported. "For some reason, the Beatles' 'rather see you dead little girl than see you with another man' pops into my head . . . but to catalogue the anti-woman songs alone would make up almost a complete history of rock."[80]

Alienated by the behavior of male youths, women decamped from New Left and counterculture movements and joined adult feminist organizations, such as NOW, or organized "women's liberation" movements, which were designed primarily for feminist youths.

The division of youths by gender in the New Left and counterculture was accompanied by the division of youths by race during the late 1960s. In 1966, Stokely Carmichael and the leaders of SNCC announced, "If we are to proceed toward true liberation, we must cut ourselves off from white people" and pursue "black self-determination," by force if necessary.[81]

Conflicts between and within denizen youths led, in the late 1960s, to the fragmentation of youth movements and the decline of many civil rights, countercultural, women's, and black organizations. Still, despite these diffi-culties, the revolt of denizen youths contributed to three important develop-ments in the 1970s. First, in 1971, Congress and then a majority of states adopted the Twenty-Sixth Amendment, which extended citizenship and suf-frage to youths between eighteen and twenty-one. "The ratification process was by far the most rapid in the history of the republic," which suggests that adult authorities from both parties were eager and determined to address the challenge mounted by denizen youths.[82] The Twenty-Sixth Amendment en-franchised twenty-five million youth, the largest expansion of the citizenry since suffrage was extended to twenty-eight million women in 1920.[83]

The extension of citizenship and suffrage to youths brought an end to their supervision by adult surrogates in public and private colleges, which meant that students could exercise their civil rights on college campuses and other public settings, as the leaders of the free speech movement had de-manded.

Second, the US government in 1975 withdrew its troops, many of them conscript youths, from Vietnam and ended the war, which had been the primary focus of the antiwar New Left during the 1960s.

Third, the US government in 1975 suspended conscription and introduced voluntary military service, which met New Left demands for an end to conscription. These two developments transformed US foreign and military policy and changed the composition and social character of US armed forces.

Youths contributed to changes associated with the civil rights movement and the women's movement, as we will see below. Countercultural youths changed relations between adults and youths and transformed social-cultural values and practices. Curiously, the decriminalization of marijuana, which was first advocated by countercultural youths in the 1960s, has proceeded apace. It is now supported by a majority of the population, and marijuana use has been legalized in a growing number of states. This suggests that counter-culture youths contributed to significant and *ongoing* social change.

SECOND- AND THIRD-CLASS CITIZENS: WOMEN, GAYS, AND LESBIANS

Although the Nineteenth Amendment extended suffrage to adult white women and to adult black women in the North, women remained "second-class citizens" in many respects. In the 1950s and 1960s, women voters were barred from jury duty, and their participation in the military was restricted by law.[84] Restrictions on military service meant that few women could obtain the benefits and job preferences extended to servicemen. Professional schools restricted the entry of women into graduate schools and the legal and medical professions. Public employers refused to allow women to work as law enforcement officers or firefighters. Private employers segregated male and female workers into sex-stereotyped jobs. Public and private employers typically fired women if they became pregnant or married or, in the case of flight attendants, turned thirty.[85] State authorities restricted women's access to contraceptive devices and to abortion, even if it threatened their life, made it difficult for them to divorce their husbands without criminal grounds, and demanded that women provide witnesses to verify complaints of rape in court.[86]

The second-class status of adult women highlights the fact that status categories—citizen, denizen, subject—are not homogeneous. Instead, they are divided into complex, intersecting, and overlapping hierarchies. Although this chapter has described how denizens—blacks in the South and youths across the United States—fought to obtain citizenship and suffrage, it is important to note that some *citizens*, particularly women and gays and lesbians, also fought to improve their status. Their efforts expanded and deepened the meaning of citizenship, making it more homogeneous.

During the 1950s and 1960s, denizens and citizens fought for civil rights and the re-extension of suffrage to adult blacks in the South, which led to the passage of the 1964 Civil Rights Act and the 1965 Voting Rights Act. Although these laws elevated the status of black denizens in the South, they also improved the status of citizens, the adult women who were covered by new civil rights legislation. Originally, the Civil Rights Act prohibited discrimination in employment based on *race*. But a southern congressman, Howard Smith, added language to bar discrimination based on sex, evidently with an eye to killing the bill. "I offered it as a joke," Smith admitted.[87] But this language was eventually included in the final legislation, a development that provided real gains not only for adult black *denizens* but also for adult female *citizens*.[88]

Youths also challenged their status as denizens. Their efforts led to the speedy ratification of the Twenty-Sixth Amendment, which then extended suffrage to twenty-five million youths, half of them women.

Although female youths participated in the civil rights, antiwar, and countercultural movements that challenged the status of denizens in the United States, many women were alienated by male practices and politics. In the late 1960s, they joined organizations established by adult women, such as NOW, or created groups that introduced a new set of issues and tactics to feminism and made "women's liberation" a mass movement, much as black youths in SNCC had done in the civil rights movement and white youths in SDS had done in the New Left. Young women in New York Radical Women organized "consciousness-raising groups" that explored the connection between women's personal and political lives, arguing that "the personal is the political"; women in the Boston Women's Health Book Collective wrote *Our Bodies, Ourselves*, a book that changed the way women practiced health care; women in the National Abortion Rights Action League (NARAL) demanded changes in abortion laws, and women in a collective called "Jane" provided abortions to eleven thousand women between 1969 and 1973, before abortion was legalized by the Supreme Court in *Roe v. Wade*.[89]

The efforts made by women denizens and citizens in the 1960s and 1970s generally expanded and improved the meaning of citizenship for women. Although they did not secure ratification of the 1972 Equal Rights Amendment, women successfully eliminated many of the restrictions imposed on female citizens (the right to serve on juries or in the military), their rights as employees of public institutions and private firms (access to most jobs, athletic programs, and professions, regardless of their status as mothers or wives, irrespective of their age or disability), and their access to contraception and abortion (the Supreme Court provided women with access to contraception in *Griswold v. Connecticut* in 1965 and to abortion in *Roe v. Wade* in 1973).[90]

In the mid-twentieth century, gay men and lesbian women could, like adult women, claim citizenship and suffrage in the United States. But if they identified themselves as homosexuals or were identified by government officials, immigration officers, military authorities, police officers, private employers, psychiatrists, public health officials, or spouses as homosexuals, even if they were mistaken, gays and lesbians could be discharged from the military and government employment, fired from private jobs, divorced for cause, denied custody of their children, arrested and imprisoned, and, if they were immigrants, stripped of their status and deported. Officials of public and private institutions could revoke or restrict the rights of gay and lesbian citizens, reducing them to denizens or subjects, because they viewed homosexuality as a threat to public health and safety, essentially as a dangerous and contagious disease (see chapter 7).[91]

Gay men in the 1950s organized the Mattachine Society and lesbian women organized the Daughters of Bilitis to discuss ways to challenge laws that criminalized homosexuals. But they operated more like secret societies than public political organizations.[92] The covert and separate character of gay and lesbian groups was due in part to the fact that in many states it was illegal for gays and lesbians even to gather in public or in bars. Still, gays and lesbians met in gay-friendly bars despite the risk of arrest and exposure.[93] As Del Martin and Phyllis Lyon observe, gays and lesbians were "isolated and separated—and scared."[94]

This changed in the 1960s. Gays and lesbians participated covertly in the civil rights, antiwar, and feminist movements and more overtly in the counterculture. The gay poet Allen Ginsberg was a prominent member of the Beats and the counterculture; Janis Joplin, an advocate of diverse sexual identities, bragged that she "slept with thousands of men and a few hundred women."[95]

Leaders of the civil rights movement kept gay activists such as Bayard Rustin at arm's length but did not disown them. Leaders of the New Left were notoriously hostile to gays, and Betty Friedan purged lesbians from NOW because she "worried that if the enemies of the movement succeeded in equating feminism with lesbianism, they'd discredit the drive for women's rights."[96] Alienated by Friedan, many lesbians left NOW in 1970 and organized independent lesbian organizations such as the Furies and the Gay Liberation Front.[97]

Meanwhile, gay men rioted when police raided the Stonewall Inn, a gay bar in New York's Greenwich Village, on June 28, 1969, and in the summer of 1970 held the first large public demonstration defending gay civil rights.[98] Gay and lesbian organizations subsequently mounted public and legal challenges to restrictions on citizenship, persuaded legislatures and the courts to decriminalize homosexual behavior, prevented public and private employers from denying jobs to homosexuals, and convinced public health officials and psychiatrists to stop treating homosexuality as a disease, even though the spread of AIDS in the 1980s threatened to restigmatize homosexuality as a contagion.[99] Moreover, these organizations persuaded a majority of Americans to support same-sex marriage, and gays and lesbians now serve openly in the military.[100] Although gays and lesbians still do not possess all the rights of other citizens, the "chutes" or "trapdoors" that were used to speed their descent into denizen and subject populations have largely been closed.

THE NEXT WAVE?

An estimated eleven million undocumented or "illegal" immigrants reside in the United States. Although they live as denizens, they can be treated as subjects—arrested and deported—if they are identified as immigrants by authorities. Anti-immigrant movements have demanded that US borders be sealed to block illegal immigration, asked federal, state, and local authorities to identify and deport resident immigrants, and encouraged immigrants to "self-deport" voluntarily.[101] But the anti-immigrant position of social movements and their political allies in the Republican Party made it difficult for Republican presidential candidates in 2008 and 2012 to win votes from legal Hispanic voters, who make up a growing percentage of the population and an important voting bloc in key electoral states. Social movements organized by Hispanics, the Catholic Church (30 percent of congressional representatives identify themselves as Catholic), factions of the Republican Party led by President George W. Bush and his brother, former governor Jeb Bush, and leaders of the Democratic Party have campaigned on behalf of resident immigrants and proposed legislation that would reform immigration law and provide a path to naturalization, citizenship, and suffrage for many immigrants. If these movements were to succeed, and it is by no means certain that they will, the citizenry would undergo its first big expansion since youths were allowed to vote in 1971.[102]

THE EXPANSION OF CITIZENSHIP AND
THE DECLINE OF VIOLENCE

In 1920, twenty-eight million adult women in the United States claimed citizenship and suffrage. During the years that followed, four million adult blacks left the South and claimed suffrage in the North. Another four million adult blacks in the South reclaimed suffrage in 1964 and 1965. In 1971, the Twenty-Sixth Amendment extended suffrage to twenty-five million youths. Women, gays, and lesbians subsequently improved their rights as citizens. The expansion of citizenship and suffrage significantly reduced the violence deployed by state officials and nonstate actors in the United States. As Piven and Cloward observed:

> In the South, the deepest meaning of the winning of democratic political rights [was] that the historical primacy of terror as a means of social control has been substantially diminished. The reduction of terror in everyday life of a people is always in itself an important gain. . . . But now, with the winning of formal political rights, the reliance on terror—on police violence, on the lynch mob, on arbitrary imprisonment—has greatly diminished as the method of controlling blacks.[103]

The extension of citizenship and suffrage also contributed to the decline of violence, particularly by *nonstate* actors, against youth, women, gays, and lesbians. The legal authority given to parents and their surrogates to use violence as a way to "discipline" youths and minors has been substantially restricted or revoked. The ability of husbands to abuse, beat, and rape their wives has been restrained. State officials have adopted laws that prosecute and punish the perpetrators of violence, and nonstate actors provide safe shelter and legal services in "crisis centers" for women and children who have been abused. The routine use of violence by police against gays and lesbians in "vice raids" has been curtailed, and gay-bashing attacks have been criminalized. These are significant achievements, though violence by state officials and nonstate actors continues. Still, this kind of violence is no longer seen as legitimate, which is itself an important development.

Chapter Nine

Social Movements and Global Social Change

During the past two hundred years, social movements advanced, assisted, and resisted global social and political change. Their struggles resulted both in "change" (greater liberty and equality for most people) *and* "continuity" (persistent inequality for many people). To appreciate this kind of change, the reader needs to keep two contradictory developments (equality and inequality) in mind at the same time and recognize that they are joined together in a social relation that changes over time. Moreover, changing social relations are a product of social forces, the result of struggles by diverse "social movements."

The German philosopher Friedrich Hegel described this as "dialectical" thinking, while Karl Marx described it as "historical materialism." The American sociologist C. Wright Mills called it "the sociological imagination" because he wanted readers to imagine both their individual lives and the social world around them at the same time. Some readers might ask, "Which is it?" (Change *or* continuity?) The answer here is that it is both, together, at the same time.

Looking back at global political developments during the past two hundred years, it is evident that three types of social movements, broadly defined, shaped change. Aspiring social movements advanced change ("liberty, equality, and fraternity"), altruistic movements assisted change, and restrictionist movements resisted change.

At the bottom, change was driven forward by the multitude, by the people who lived as subjects in dynastic states and colonial settings, by denizens and

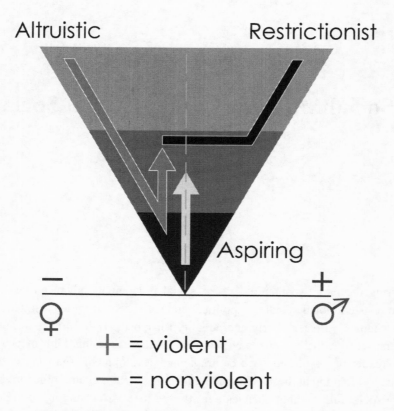

Social Movements: Violence and Gender

subjects in the republics. They fought to claim what French republicans called the "rights of man" or what we might call "human rights" and to exercise popular sovereignty and constitutional government in republican states. As we have seen, they created independent republics all over the world, democratized the republics, and expanded citizenries within them. They were responsible for the *ascent* of slaves, women, and youth. They did not always succeed, which is why it is appropriate to describe them as "aspiring" social movements.

It is clear that aspiring movements did not act alone. In many colonial and postcolonial settings, aspirants did not have the legal standing, political capacity, or financial means necessary to act effectively on their own. They needed help. Fortunately, people who had the social capacity and financial means to aid subaltern groups came to their aid. It is appropriate to describe them as "altruistic" movements, even though they sometimes provided aid for selfish reasons. They were responsible for helping aspirants ascend, and they helped aspirants succeed over the long run more often than not.

Social change was also shaped by people who rejected popular sovereignty, championed oligarchy, and defended *in*equality. They fought to defend property and their own liberty, which consisted in part of dominion over others. They resisted the ascent of denizen and subject populations, forced others (American Indians, blacks in the South, Japanese Americans, homosexuals) to descend, and locked others (convicts, children, immigrants) in place. By fighting to preserve political, economic, and social structures of *in*equality, they have been a force for continuity, not change. Because they sought to restrict or reserve liberty for a few, not extend it to the many, it is appropriate to describe them as "restrictionist" social movements.

The field is oriented in this way to illustrate the social-political character of different types of movements. Aspiring social movements typically enlisted denizens and subjects. They fought to claim human rights and ascend in the social hierarchy. Altruistic movements typically enlisted citizens and denizens to assist subaltern groups and help them ascend. Restrictionist movements typically organized high-echelon groups—aristocratic or bourgeois "subjects" in dynastic states, "citizens" in republics—to prevent, obstruct, and delay the ascent of subaltern denizens and subjects.

These three types of social movements define the boundaries of a field or arena where social movements meet and struggle to define the direction and meaning of social change. Although this model identifies three major types of social movements that make change, movements may combine features of different types, and they may change their character over time. So, for example, the women's movements that fought both for suffrage (aspiring) and abolition (altruistic) might be located on this map as "aspiring-altruistic"; women's groups that worked to alleviate poverty (altruistic) by promoting population control (restrictionist) might be described as "altruistic-restrictionist"; and women's movements that fought for democratization in an Islamic republic (aspiring) but supported the imposition of Sharia law (restrictionist) might be identified as "aspiring-restrictionist."

Moreover, movements that made change often changed as a result of struggle and engagement with other movements. Aspiring movements sometimes became restrictionist after they won power. The adult white men who obtained suffrage during the early nineteenth century then created movements that worked to deny citizenship and suffrage to blacks, women, and immigrants. This model is designed so that the types and trajectories of social movements might be mapped across the field over time.

The field might also be divided or bisected to describe the relation between different types of movements and violence and also gender. Writing this book, I was struck by social movements' relation to violence and gender (see the chart).

Some aspiring movements promoted or adopted violent strategies for change (+), while others eschewed violence and advocated nonviolent strategies for change (−). The aspiring movements that advocated violence were led and organized almost exclusively by men, such as Mao Zedong, who famously argued that political power grows out of the barrel of a gun. But aspiring movements that adopted nonviolent approaches included women, such as Elizabeth Cady Stanton, Rosa Parks, and Betty Friedan, and also men, such as Mohandas Gandhi and Dr. Martin Luther King Jr. Women rarely participated in or led violent aspiring movements.

Altruistic movements typically advocated nonviolent strategies, though on rare occasions, altruists such as John Brown took up arms to free slaves. Restrictionist movements have often advocated violence, though they often insist that it be deployed on their behalf by state officials or that they be licensed to use force on their own initiative, either in groups or as individuals. Historically, state officials and the nonstate actors who were authorized to use violence were male. The association between restrictionist movements and male violence has been quite strong.

In broad terms, we know that social movements were responsible for shaping the direction, pace, and meaning of global social and political change during the past two hundred years. But we do not know very much about how their collective *interaction* shaped change. Social movements need to be examined together, not just alone.

The model advanced here is designed to provide a comprehensive and inclusive historical approach to the study of social movements and social change. It is not designed as a proprietary operating system but as an open-source application that might be freely adopted, tested, and modified by scholars in different disciplines, to people who have *already* contributed to its development and design. This approach is imbued with the work of many others, which the references acknowledge but do not adequately celebrate. Scholars and students are invited to carry forward the work begun by others.

For scholars who might download this application, let me describe some of its important features. First, while I have identified three *different* "types" of social movements, they share much in common as "social movements." I argue that they all include a broad range of actors (individuals, social networks, bureaucratic organizations, and political parties) who engage in a wide range of activities (litigating, going on hunger strikes, migrating, joining clubs, forming bands, patronizing clubs and bars, throwing stones and running riot, organizing rebellions and armed insurrections, and campaigning for office and passing legislation) to claim or shape human rights (liberty, equality, and the solidarity found in community) and create political institutions (constitutional government based on popular sovereignty in a republic) that can help them realize these goals.

Second, I examine the three different types of social movements—aspiring, altruistic, and restrictionist—and look at some of the issues and problems specific to each. Third, I describe how this approach draws on the work of scholars in different fields and how it differs from many contemporary treatments of social change and social movements.

Although aspiring, altruistic, and restrictionist movements differ in important ways, they share some common features as social movements. They all include a broad range of actors who engage in diverse activities or repertoires to obtain or deny human rights. Of course, these actors may engage in activities that fail to make or prevent change. But even if they fail, they may contribute to the production and maintenance of existing social relations. That is, although they may aspire to change, they may become a force for continuity.

Many scholars have examined "collective behavior," "social movements," and "political parties." In doing do, they have focused on "groups" of people, either informal groups and social networks or organized groups and bureaucracies. Sociologists have examined collective behavior and social movements, while political scientists have studied political parties. Because many sociologists look only at social groups, they have often neglected the role that individuals have played in making social change. But it is clear from our previous discussion that individuals have contributed to global social change. Accordingly, they should be included in a discussion of the forces that make social change, even if they act only as a "movement of one." Any effort to understand global social change should examine the contribution made by individuals, social networks, organizations, and political parties. Moreover, we should examine the different kinds of activities or repertoires that people use to make change. A "repertoire" is an activity that is adopted by others, a practice that can, in some circumstances, contribute to change.

INDIVIDUALS

As we have seen, individuals have adopted different strategies to make social change. Litigation has been one important tactic used by individuals to advance or restrict change. Indeed, lawsuits and legal battles played key roles in the expansion of citizenship in the United States. For instance, the 1958 lawsuit filed by Richard and Mildred Loving, an interracial couple who were arrested in Virginia for violating the state's law against interracial marriage (the "Racial Integrity Act"), eventually persuaded the Supreme Court to strike down segregation laws in sixteen states and allow interracial couples to marry.[1]

Of course, individuals have also sued to *prevent* or *reverse* change. Abigail Fisher, a young white woman who was refused admission to the University of Texas, recently sued to end the university's affirmative action and diversity policies. This gave the Supreme Court the opportunity to revisit its 2003 decision in *Grutter v. Bollinger* that "allowed public universities to take account of race as part of a 'holistic review.'"[2] Win or lose, individual litigants have shaped social change, not only for themselves but for others, which means that they engaged in a social act as a social movement of one.

In India, Anna Hazare conducted a hunger strike in 2011 to force the government to pass anticorruption legislation, an individual repertoire with a long history in India and elsewhere, which persuaded others to demand change.[3] "We have come here to make change," Suman Wadhwa said, explaining why she joined a demonstration supporting Hazare in New Delhi. "If we had not come today, we would have felt that we didn't contribute to the freedom struggle."[4]

Individuals used migration to make change. By changing their *geographical* place, individual migrants changed their *social* position. Individual slaves fled the South to find freedom in the North or in Canada. Blacks who migrated north during the Jim Crow era became citizens who could exercise suffrage. During the 1960s, alienated youth fled the heartland and flocked to San Francisco's Haight-Ashbury, which provided a countercultural community for hippies. In the 1970s, gay youth fled punishing intolerance in conservative communities and migrated to San Francisco's Castro District and to

New York's Greenwich Village to find places where they could openly express their sexual identities.

Although scholars have not generally treated migration as a social movement repertoire, individual migrants, deserters, fugitives, and refugees not only changed their social position, they also contributed to social change. The flight of individual slaves challenged slave-owner authority over fugitive slaves in the North and contributed to the Civil War. The flight of individual whites from inner cities to the suburbs and from public to private or home schools changed race relations, education, and the urban landscape in the United States. The exodus of political dissidents from East Germany in 1989 led to the collapse of the communist regime.

Today, individual actors, who are often described as "pioneers" or "crusaders," have developed diverse strategies for making change, often from their home, alone. John Tanton runs an anti-immigrant crusade out of his home in northern Michigan, while Ralph Isenberg, a Texas businessman, assists immigrants by conducting one-on-one meetings over his webcam.[5] In Ireland, 50 percent of taxpayers, on an individual basis, have refused to pay a new property tax that is part of the government's austerity plan.[6] In Switzerland, Matthias Pohm started a one-man "Anti PowerPoint Party" that won enough support to qualify for parliamentary elections, a strategy that was subsequently adopted by other one-member parties in Europe.[7]

Of course, individuals have also adopted violent repertoires to make change. In Tunisia, Mohamed Bouazizi, a street vendor, set himself on fire to protest his mistreatment by police and later died.[8] His suicidal protest ignited widespread antigovernment protests and persuaded other individuals to adopt this repertoire and immolate themselves, a development that led to the fall of the dictatorship and elections for a democratic government. This self-destructive act, which was earlier practiced by protesters in Vietnam and the United States during the 1960s, had been adopted more recently by Buddhist monks and livestock herders who oppose Chinese Communist rule in Tibet and by Moshe Silman, an Israeli man who set himself on fire to protest social injustice.[9] As Emile Durkheim argues in *Suicide*, it is important to appreciate the public, *social* character of private, *individual* acts.

Individual protesters have also directed violence against others. During the late nineteenth and early twentieth centuries, individual anarchists who believed that dramatic acts of violence, what they called "the propaganda of the deed," would inspire others to revolt assassinated the czar of Russia (1881), the president of France (1894), the empress of Austria (1898), the

king of Italy (1900), the president of the United States (1901), and the archduke of Austria (1914). The archduke's murder by Gavrilo Princip triggered
the outbreak of World War I, which contributed to revolutions in Ireland and
Russia and the demise of the Austro-Hungarian, German, and Ottoman Empires after the war.[10]

Individuals used violence not only to promote change but to prevent it.
The assassins who killed Mohandas Gandhi and Martin Luther King Jr. were
determined to abort change. Moreover, an individual act of violence might be
treated as a kind of social movement repertoire if it is a *social* act, if it is
directed at a subaltern group or class of people—women and girls, blacks,
gypsies or other minorities, gays and lesbians—and is used to keep group
members in their place and deny them liberty, equality, and community. The
law now recognizes that individual acts of violence are *social acts* if they are
hate crimes, if they are motivated by social animosity against a group and not
the individual victim alone. Bullying, hazing, and anonymous poison-pen
letters are all repertoires of individuals who engage in social acts of violence
against subaltern groups.

Feminists have long argued that "individual" male violence against wom-
en and girls is a social act, an uncoordinated social movement of individuals
acting alone but with a common purpose, like the turn-of-the-century anarchists. Of course, rape is used as a repertoire of male social networks in
fraternities and in the military and by organized social movements in warlord
militias and armies. The fact that one in five women in the United States has
reported being the victim of male sexual assault supports the idea that rape
and sexual assault might be regarded as a repertoire of restrictionist male
social movements, used to keep women and girls in a subordinate social
status.[11]

The young women and girls who commit suicide to protest arranged
marriages or who run away from abusive homes and seek shelter in crisis
centers are using the repertoires available to them as individual actors. Adult
males who practice "honor" killing, permit the mutilation of their wife's,
daughter's, and relative's genitals, or murder a daughter-in-law for failing to
bear their son a male heir commit individual crimes that are part of culturally
available social repertoires. The women and girls who defy adult male authority and speak out against it—such as Malala Yousafzai, the fourteen-
year-old Pakistani girl who defended the education of girls and was shot in
2012 by Taliban assassins, or Naama Margolese, the eight-year-old Israeli
girl who stood up to ultra-Orthodox men and boys "who spat on her, insulted

her, and called her a prostitute because her modest dress did not adhere exactly to their more rigorous dress code"—are engaged in a struggle about the direction and meaning of social change, even though they act as individuals, on their own.[12]

Although individuals make change, it is often difficult to treat them singly, in isolation, because they belong to households, small groups, and *social networks* that are embedded in communities. What should we make of the "107 Tunisians [who] tried to kill themselves by self-immolation in the first six months after [Mohamed] Bouazizi's death"? Of the monks and nuns who burned themselves in Tibet? Of the women in Saudi Arabia who took to the wheel and drove their cars in defiance of the law?[13] These individuals were likely connected to social networks embedded in particular communities. Much the same is true of migrants. Demographers now treat migration less as the product of individual choice and more as the product of collective decisions made by households and informal social networks based in local communities. Long before Facebook, people joined with relatives, friends, and associates to engage in activities that contributed to social change.

SOCIAL NETWORKS

Like individuals, people who belong to social networks engage in diverse activities to promote change. They file class-action suits, migrate in groups, and participate in a range of nonviolent and violent activities. For example, parents who oppose the vaccination of young children use social networks to organize "pox parties" so that they can expose their children to other children who have chicken pox as a way to acquire an immunity to the disease.[14] They also organize relatively spontaneous or ad hoc groups or "mobs" that engage in peaceful and violent "riots."

Although scholars have long studied violent mobs, the "kiss-ins" staged by peaceful mobs of college students supporting education reform in Chile, the "dance-athons" performed in the streets by mobs of dissidents opposed to the Assad dictatorship in Syria, and the "swim-in" performed by mobs of Israeli and Arab youth on the beaches of Tel Aviv to promote Arab-Israeli unity all illustrate the nonviolent, though demonstrative or "riotous," character of peaceful mobs organized by social networks on an ad hoc basis.[15] These kinds of riots are not new. The feasts and fetes that French republicans organized to challenge dynastic rule in 1848 were early expressions of this behavior.

There is a large literature on violent mobs and riotous behavior. For many years, sociologists treated this kind of "collective behavior" unsympathetically, as a form of deviant behavior. Charles Tilly then persuaded many of his colleagues to treat this collective behavior more sympathetically, as a form of "contentious politics."

But several things might be said about mobs, violent and nonviolent riots, and social change. First, mobs are typically rooted in social networks that are embedded in local communities. Second, they were organized *first* by dominant social groups who deployed them against subaltern groups. The historian Paul Gilje persuasively argues that during the nineteenth and twentieth centuries, adult white males joined mobs that rioted against blacks, immigrants, political dissidents, and striking workers.[16] They rioted to protect their status and forestall change, and they did so without fear of legal consequence. The white male vigilantes who joined lynch mobs and race riots— anti-Chinese and -Filipino riots, the male riot against female suffragettes during President Wilson's inaugural parade, the 1921 riot against blacks in Tulsa, Oklahoma, and the zoot suit riots against Hispanic youths in Los Angeles during World War II—used them to terrorize subordinate social groups. They got away with violence because state officials turned a blind eye or even joined them. Subaltern groups also rioted, though much less frequently. Gilje argues that this pattern changed after World War II. White riots declined and riots by subaltern groups increased, reaching a peak during the 1960s, when most of the rioters were drawn from urban minority populations. Unlike the period before the war, when state officials often allowed nonstate actors to riot, state officials after the war sent in the police and national guard to quell riots by subaltern groups.[17] These developments have not been adequately addressed or explained in the collective behavior literature. Riots by adult white males may have declined because state officials grew increasingly reluctant to license violence by nonstate actors and instead used the police to control minority populations, though police violence in urban ghettos often triggered the riots by urban minorities, as occurred during the Watts and later Rodney King riots.

Third, mobs provided participants with a kind of anonymity, which enabled people to engage in illegal behavior and make forceful demands for change without penalty. People found that they could act effectively in a mob, either because state officials found it difficult to identify participants in a mob and charge them individually or because state officials allowed citi-

zens or nonstate actors to commit violence against denizen and subject populations.

During the nineteenth and early twentieth centuries, it was often illegal
for denizen or subject populations to meet in groups, join formal organizations, or demonstrate in public. (Recall that it was illegal in the 1960s for
homosexuals even to meet for a drink in a bar, much less hold a parade on the
public streets.) If they did, state officials and nonstate actors could assault
them. By gathering in mobs and engaging in spontaneous demonstrations,
subaltern groups could use the anonymity and collective security provided by
the mob to challenge authority and then disperse so that they might fight
again some other day. During the Great Mutinies of 1797, striking British
sailors purposely avoided creating a union or formal organization because
they wanted to prevent authorities from identifying participants and then
immediately hanging them as mutineers.[18] More recently, the Arab dissidents who gathered in public squares in Tunisia, Libya, Egypt, Iran, and
Syria joined mass rallies because the crowd allowed them to participate
anonymously and provided them with some protection from assault by the
police and the regime's hired thugs. They avoided joining dissident *organizations* because membership in an organization would make it easier for
state officials to identify them and send the secret police to seize them in the
night. The organizers of the "Occupy" movement here in the United States
encouraged mob behavior for the same reasons.

BUREAUCRATIC ORGANIZATIONS

People acted on their own, as individuals, and in social networks in diverse
ways to make, assist, and resist change. But they also created bureaucratic
organizations to shape change. Bureaucratic organizations differed from social networks in two important respects. First, they allowed actors to create
organizations run by experts, in a hierarchical division of labor, according to
a set of formal rules or practices, to achieve specific goals. Second, they
allowed actors to pursue these goals over long periods of time. Bureaucratic
organizations made it possible for actors to undertake difficult projects—
make a revolution against dynastic authority, overthrow a dictator, extend
suffrage to women—that might take years to achieve. Women fought for
seventy years to obtain suffrage in the United States. The women who first
initiated this campaign did not live to see its conclusion. But the organizations they created made it possible to recruit members, raise money, and

adopt tactics that contributed to long-term, strategic success. The men who organized communist parties in Russia and China and the nationalist parties in Ireland and India created organizations that struggled for decades to achieve their ambitious goals. Bureaucratic organizations made it possible to work for large-scale change over long periods of time.

Arrighi, Hopkins, and Wallerstein argue that the discovery of bureaucratic organization by social movements in 1848 was "the great innovation in the technology of rebellion," an invention that helped "prepare the ground politically for fundamental social change."[19] Other social movement scholars, such as Charles Tilly and Sidney Tarrow, agree that bureaucratic organization was a key innovation, though they argue that this technology was first invented earlier, in the late eighteenth century.

Of course, dynastic rulers, dictators, and citizens often viewed the bureaucratic organizations capable of making large-scale change—labor unions, socialist parties, abolitionist organizations—as a threat and outlawed them. In response, social movement actors created *clandestine* organizations to avoid the risks associated with forming public organizations and membership lists. When gays organized in the 1950s, they did so in clandestine fashion because authorities treated *any* gathering of homosexuals as criminal.[20] When a coworker and I organized a labor union at an environmental organization in 1984, we did so in secret to prevent detection by management and avoid being fired, going "public" only when we obtained membership cards from everyone in the bargaining unit and secured the protection of the National Labor Relations Board.[21] Of course, when actors advocated violence as part of their strategy to make change, as communists did in Russia and the United States, as the Ku Klux Klan did in the United States, as Sinn Fein did in Ireland, and as the Muslim Brotherhood did in Egypt—they organized clandestine organizations both to protect themselves from state authorities and to conceal their real power and numbers from public view.

Capture

Social change actors often found it difficult to create effective bureaucratic organizations. They faced a series of daunting problems: how to recruit members, particularly if they had to do so in secret, select able leaders, raise money, and adopt effective tactics that contributed to long-term goals. Many leaders—Lenin, Mao, Gandhi—devoted considerable attention to bureaucratic practices and organization-building strategies. To solve some of these issues, Lenin and Mao advanced the idea that organization building was best done by a small group of determined men, what the political scientist Robert Michels called an "oligarchy."

As an alternative to building organizations from scratch, many activists decided instead to "capture" an *existing* bureaucracy and make it their own. Like the factions that seized state power and created dictatorships in many of the new republics, activists often captured existing organizations and used them to advance change on their behalf. During the 1940s and 1950s, communists and also mobsters in the United States fought to take over union locals and bend them to their separate purposes. Communists wanted to build a political base in working-class organizations; mobsters wanted to siphon off union dues to enrich themselves and finance casino construction in Las Vegas. But "capture" need not be seen only as a sinister or cynical process.

Martin Luther King Jr. and Ralph Abernathy mobilized the members of faith-based organizations and used their churches to recruit members, raise money, and engage in courageous activities designed to challenge segregation and end the violence used to sustain it. Later, fundamentalist clergy organized members of evangelical churches to campaign against abortion, homosexuals, and the integration and/or secularization of public schools. Different groups or factions have tried to capture local Catholic churches and use them to make social change. Cesar Chavez persuaded some local Catholic priests to mobilize congregants to participate in union building, the group Mothers of East Los Angeles worked with priests to develop antipoverty programs in Los Angeles, the Sisters of St. Francis waged campaigns against corporate behavior on behalf of children, farmworkers, and consumers, while activist bishops mobilized parishioners to campaign against abortion, health care, and gay marriage.[22]

Exit

The actors who created or captured bureaucratic organizations to make, assist, or resist change often disagreed about how best to achieve their goals. They disagreed about who should participate as members, what relation members should have to elected or self-appointed leaders, how best to spend their money, and what kind of tactics and strategies might be most effective. Ideological and pragmatic disagreements over these and many other issues persuaded dissidents to form factions that often decided to exit these organizations and create new ones of their own, which might compete with or complement parent organizations. They were also sometimes ejected, or "purged," if they failed to adhere to their leader's agenda. Some leaders, like

Lenin and Mao, were adept at using purges to expel rivals. William F. Buckley, a leader of the conservative movement in the United States, purged anti-
Semites, racists, and John Birchers, who threatened to turn the Right into
"crackpot alley," so that he could create a conservative "New Right" with
broader public appeal.[23]

Does the exit of factions from activist organizations increase their effectiveness or weaken it? Social movement scholars and activists have long
debated this question. For example, many scholars argue that factional fighting (exit and subexit) among leftist organizations during the 1920s contributed to the rise of fascism; that the breakup in 1968 of SDS, which itself was
the product of capture by the Progressive Labor faction and the exit of the
Weatherman faction, led to the demise of the New Left and the rise of the
New Right. Some feminist and gay scholars have challenged this account,
arguing that the exit of factions from SDS and also from NOW created a
diverse set of organizations that were stronger as a group than a single,
oligarchic organization.

This debate raises a larger question. If bureaucratic organizations are
subject to Michels's "iron law of oligarchy," in part because many activists
advance the primacy of disciplined cadres to enhance their effectiveness,
why do they regularly fail? How can they be captured by factions? Why do
they permit the exit of factions that may weaken them or create organizations
that compete with them?

Looking back at social change, it is clear that bureaucratic organizations
that have become oligarchies have been vulnerable both to capture by faction
and to exit by faction. What does that say about Michels's view that oligarchy was both inevitable and efficient?

Although some movements discovered that the creation of oligarchic bureaucracies, such as that of communist parties, were "effective" in some
respects, they proved "ineffective" in other ways, which undermined their
authority. The fall of dictators who organized fearsome oligarchies and the
inability of organizational behemoths to cope with challengers and change
suggests that scholars should reexamine their assumptions about both the
"inevitability" of Michels's iron law of oligarchy and the purported "effectiveness" of oligarchies.

POLITICAL PARTIES

The architects of republican government did not provide a constitutional role for political parties. As Frances Fox Piven observes, "The framers were famously leery of mass parties and the prospect of majority rule they represented, and the elaborate division of powers in the national government, along with the resulting fragmentation of popular constituencies, was designed to *thwart* such parties" (italics added).[24] Nonetheless, they invited citizens to exercise popular sovereignty, and citizens did so, in part by organizing political parties, which first appeared during the Second Congress (1791–1793).[25] In a sense, political parties were among the *first* social movements created by citizens in the republics. Although bureaucratic social movement organizations might be thought of as "*non*governmental organizations" (NGOs), political parties were designed as social movements that *participated* in government (as quasi-governmental organizations, or QGOs), which allowed citizens to obtain power and economic benefits from the state.[26]

Political parties can play a role that other social movement organizations cannot. Political parties might be thought of as social movements that citizens embedded in the state. Of course, this gave citizens, with access to embedded social movements, an advantage over social movements that did not have the same access to the state. Although sociologists often restrict the study of social movements to NGOs and political scientists restrict themselves to the study of political parties or QGOs, any serious effort to understand social movements should include both.

Of course, citizens are not the only ones to organize political parties. Subaltern groups have long organized political parties of their own. Denizens and subjects organized political parties to lay claim to the idea that they *should* be able to exercise popular sovereignty, wield political power, and obtain economic benefits from the state. Socialist, nationalist, feminist, and religious groups created "political parties" and invited delegates to attend party "congresses," where they might debate issues and pass resolutions on behalf of "the people." The activists who organized the Indian National Congress, the African National Congress, Sinn Fein, the Muslim League, and socialist and communist parties all did so to create the kind of social movement that might claim to represent the people, embed itself in the state, and use their position, as the central intermediate and intermediary structure between society and government—to make, assist, or resist change.

Political parties, like social movement organizations, have been subject both to capture by faction and exit by faction, which has affected their ability to shape change. Still, while citizens, denizens, and subjects created social movements that managed to embed themselves in the state, this embeddedness has not necessarily allowed them to make, assist, or resist the kind of change they imagined. "First of all, state structures are embedded . . . in the interstate system, and their degree of autonomy is strictly limited," Wallerstein has argued. As a result, whatever their ideological goals or commitment to change, they quickly discovered that "control of the machinery of a state . . . affords less real power in practice than it does in theory."[27] In retrospect, Wallerstein argues that social movements might view the seizure of power as a tactical, not a strategic, goal and should be prepared to relinquish power and maneuver politically, as Antonio Gramsci recommended, "since it is in the process of movement, of mobilization, that the really constructive power of movements lies."[28]

Scholars have debated why this might be so. Some have argued that Michels's "iron law of oligarchy" undermines or cripples a political party's determination to make change and instead makes it cling to power, which results in continuity, not change.[29] The argument here has been that constitutional government in the republics is an operating system that is extremely difficult to use to promote social change. This is not simply a product of the division of government in the republics but a consequence of the division of the interstate system into multiple states. Even if actors make change in one republic, it is difficult for them to make change in all. Still, despite these difficulties, they have managed to make change, which resulted in the decline of dynastic states, the demise of many dictatorships in the republics, and the expansion of citizenries within them. Political parties have played important roles in these developments, which is why they should be included in a discussion of social movements and social change.

LIBERTY, EQUALITY, AND SOLIDARITY

Since the French and American Revolutions, social movements have fought over the social meaning of "liberty, equality, and fraternity." Because "fraternity" has a gender-identified connotation, it might better be described as the "solidarity" that community can provide. Although scholars have examined movement efforts to achieve liberty and equality, they have said less about solidarity, except for the solidarity provided by labor unions and political parties. They might pay more attention to the solidarity provided by voluntary and cultural communities.

During the 1960s, countercultural and gay youth hitchhiked to neighborhoods such as Haight-Ashbury, the Castro, Telegraph Avenue, and Greenwich Village. They met on the streets, in flops, bars, and clubs to find kindred spirits and create communities that provided the kind of solidarity and support that hometowns across America refused to provide. They panhandled, made music, made love, grew their hair long, and thumbed their nose at straight culture, fashioning a different one, one of their own, in the process.[30]

They were not the only ones. Today, ex-Marines gather in cemeteries where their comrades are buried and hoist a beer in their memory; Somali, Cameroonian, Khmer, and other political refugees in the United States grow native foods in community gardens across the country; white supremacists in the United States and neo-Nazis in Germany organize rock bands—Blue Eyed Devils, Intimidation, and End Apathy—that use music to recruit youths and promote their views; in Russia, a female punk-rock band named Pussy Riot sang antigovernment songs from the altar of a cathedral in Moscow, a performance that resulted in their arrest and imprisonment for "inciting religious hatred"; Confederate reenactors in Alabama shot their muskets and sang "Dixie" in front of the state capitol to celebrate the 150th anniversary of the Confederacy, or the "War for Southern Independence," as they prefer, while Prussian reenactors in Potsdam commemorated Frederick the Great's three-hundredth birthday and praised the Prussian values of the "enlightened despot."[31]

During the nineteenth century, aspiring, altruistic, and restrictionist movements organized not only trade unions and political parties but also cultural organizations designed to promote solidarity among their members: Shriners, Knights of Columbus, Loyal Order of Moose, the Sierra Club, Veterans of Foreign Wars, Big Brothers, the YMCA, Girl Scouts, Hadassah, the Community Chest, the American Civil Liberties Union, and the Ku Klux Klan.[32]

The individuals, social networks, organizations, and political parties that participated in social movements provided solidarity by creating real, face-to-face communities *and* virtual, or imagined, communities, to borrow Benedict Anderson's term. (He coined the term "imagined communities" to describe how people created large secular and religious communities composed of people—Christians and Muslims, Italians and Americans—who did not know one another or meet face to face.)[33]

Social movements created real and imagined communities—in bars, in neighborhoods, on the Internet, in churches, and in republics—for two reasons. First, they built communities to protect themselves from the rapid social change (anomie) that is a characteristic feature of capitalist development on a world scale and from the dominant social groups that deprived them of liberty, equality, and solidarity.[34]

Second, they built communities to forge the social networks and social identities, what political scientist Robert Putnam calls "social capital," that made it possible for these movements to make, assist, and resist change.[35] "Fraternity, as the French democrats intended it, was another name for what I call 'social capital.'"[36] So, for example, African American slaves and African American denizens found sanctuary (in both the literal and figurative sense) in black churches, one of the only places where they might safely and legally gather in public. During the 1950s and 1960s, black churches provided the economic resources and bonds of affection, trust, and solidarity that parishioners needed in order to mount public protests during the civil rights era. Because social movements created economic, political, and cultural communities, both material and immaterial, that they needed in order to make, assist, or advance change, they should be included in a discussion of aspiring, altruistic, and restrictionist social movements.

Chapter Ten

Aspiring Social Movements

Subjects, denizens, and citizens have rejected the social inequalities imposed on them by dynastic states and new republics, embraced the promise of liberty, equality, and solidarity, and organized social movements to change their circumstances. The upward thrust of aspiring social movements has propelled social change around the world during the past two hundred years. Aspiring movements created republics in postcolonial states, democratized the republics, and expanded citizenries within them. These developments reduced interstate violence and world war, curbed state violence against subject populations, and constrained violence by nonstate actors. Of course, aspiring movements were not wholly responsible for these developments. Altruistic and restrictionist movements also played important roles. But the struggles waged by aspiring individuals, social networks, organizations, and political parties drove global social change.

RISE OF THE REPUBLICS

Subjects in the colonies of dynastic states fought to create constitutional governments based on popular sovereignty in republican states. But they appealed to different kinds of social identities when they mobilized denizen and subject populations. For example, Sinn Fein and the Indian National Congress organized people along secular, ethnic lines.[1] By contrast, both the Zionist movement, which created a Jewish state in Palestine, and the Muslim League, which created a Muslim state in postcolonial India, organized along ethnic religious lines.[2] Meanwhile, socialist and communist parties in dynastic states and their colonies and in the new republics appealed to secular, class-based identities. Still, whether they used status- or class-based identities to enlist recruits, aspiring movements all fought to establish republican forms of government: the Republic of Ireland; the Islamic Republic of Pakistan; the People's Republic of China.

DEMOCRATIZATION OF THE REPUBLICS

In many of the new republics, factions captured state power and established dictatorships, which undermined or destroyed popular sovereignty and reduced citizens to subjects of state authority. Eventually, aspiring movements overthrew many dictatorships and democratized the republics. Individual dissidents, such as Vaclav Havel in Czechoslovakia, and members of social networks, such as the Mothers of the Plaza de Mayo in Argentina, challenged government authorities. Others fled singly or in groups from East Germany and by boat from Cuba and Vietnam to escape the state's jurisdiction and become denizens or citizens in more democratic republics. People gathered illegally in public squares—in Buenos Aires, Leipzig, Seoul, and Cairo—to demand change. In Poland, workers organized Solidarity, a dissident union, to challenge government authority and Soviet military occupation. In South Africa, the African National Congress waged strikes by workers and students to challenge apartheid. Although they were not everywhere successful and dictators remain entrenched in China, North Korea, and Iran, aspiring movements democratized perhaps forty republics during the past forty years.

In some places, secular and religious ethnonational movements fought not only to democratize the republics but also to divide power and create separate republics of their own, a development that led to both the democratization and division of the Soviet Union, Yugoslavia, Czechoslovakia, Ethiopia, and Sudan. In Canada, Scotland, Belgium, Spain, Italy, Sri Lanka, Burma, and other states, ethnoreligious movements have emerged to demand the division of the republic so that states can be provided for minority populations. If they succeed in seceding, they will contribute to the further proliferation of republics, though not necessarily to the democratization of successor states.[3]

EXPANSION OF CITIZENRIES

Around the world, denizens and subjects in republics and in dynastic states and their colonies aspired to citizenship and suffrage. Alone and in groups, they created aspiring social movements to obtain these rights. The ascent of different groups slowly expanded citizenries in the republics.

In the United States, aspiring groups adopted different approaches to change. In the early nineteenth century, adult white men without property organized as taxpayers and veterans in relatively small groups to demand suffrage from legislators in separate states. They did not approach the federal government as a group to seek change. Feminists first adopted the same strategy, lobbying legislators in individual states to grant women suffrage, though unlike white men, they organized large organizations based on a shared identity as women. But they later abandoned the strategy of obtaining suffrage from state legislatures when it became apparent that they would fail to achieve universal suffrage for women and decided to ask Congress and the president to introduce a constitutional amendment on their behalf, which eventually paid off.

By contrast, the emancipation of black slaves (men and women, young and old) and the extension of suffrage to adult black men was the product of federal executive action and constitutional amendments introduced by Republicans in Congress. Aspiring slaves and free blacks helped prompt federal action by challenging southern white claims to possess blacks as slaves and reclaim them as "fugitives" in the North. The determination of blacks to escape from bondage, rise in revolt, challenge white authority in court, support Union forces during the Civil War, and serve in uniform on the battlefield persuaded the federal government to act.

During Jim Crow, aspiring blacks in the South relied primarily on their own initiative to obtain citizenship and suffrage by moving north in large numbers, particularly after World War I. In the North, adult black men obtained suffrage and, after 1920, adult black women found it, too. During the 1950s, black denizens in the South organized aspiring social movements that challenged local and state authority, rather like white men without property and early suffragettes. But when these efforts proved insufficient, black denizens, like the later suffragettes, demanded federal action, which resulted in the passage of legislation that reinforced the Fourteenth and Fifteenth Amendments.

During the 1960s, aspiring denizen youths organized local and national organizations to challenge adult political and cultural authority. They migrated in large numbers, like blacks during Jim Crow, conducted sit-ins, like black denizens in the South, created large national organizations to challenge conscription and the federal government's conduct of the Vietnam War, and organized alternative cultures and communities that challenged adult author-ity in households, institutions, and public settings. Their determined efforts persuaded the federal government and the states to extend suffrage to youths, end conscription, and withdraw from Vietnam in a fairly short period of time (1963–1975).

Of course, while some groups ascended, others were forced down into subaltern positions as denizens or subjects or were forced into exile. Except for exiles, many of the descendants—American Indians, Confederates, Asian immigrants, Japanese Americans, and homosexuals—eventually (re)as-cended, though the process took a very long time for American Indians and is still incomplete.

Other aspiring groups have had less success. Minors remain as denizens, much as they did two centuries ago, though they are now organized, as individuals and in groups, to claim rights denied to them by adult authorities. Martha Payne, a nine-year-old girl in Scotland, recently started a global movement that urged minors to protest the poor quality of school lunches; students at a premier public school in New York challenged the school's dress-code policy by wearing prohibited fashions; and Jose Luis Zelaya, an illegal immigrant, ran for student body president at Texas A&M to rally support for denizen and subject youths.[4]

Like denizen youths, convicts who protest their status as subjects of the state (and sometimes private) prison authority have found it extremely diffi-cult to improve their status. Still, they aspire and persist. Inmates in Califor-nia prisons conducted a three-week hunger strike in 2011 to protest condi-tions, an extremely difficult thing to coordinate, given their conditions; while youths who were convicted of crimes after being tried as adults have sued to end this practice.[5] But aspiring movements' efforts to improve the subject status of the six million convicts in America—more than were incarcerated in Soviet gulags—have not resulted in substantial change.[6] Still, the denizens and subjects who participate in aspiring social movements are a force for change, even if they do not succeed.

STRATEGIC CHOICES AND DECISIONS

Aspiring, altruistic, and restrictionist movements all made important deci-sions about their social identities (in gender, ethnic, age, class, and religious terms), organizational forms (as individuals and in social networks, organiza-tions, and political parties), tactical repertoires (litigation, hunger strike, migration, riot, protest, insurrection, referendum, election, and legislation), and political goals (to define the meaning of liberty, equality, and solidarity). But because aspiring social movements were typically made up of denizens and subjects who have tried to *make* social change, they have had to make a series of strategic decisions or choices about how *best* to make change.

For many years, scholars who studied riots and other forms of collective behavior regarded participants as *"irrational"* actors, swayed by the mob. This view was criticized by Tilly and others, who argued that participants in social movements were *"rational"* actors who could make rational *"choices,"* a theory that draws on the assumptions made by economists about actors in the marketplace. I think this is a false distinction based on poor assumptions. Political actors often lack the information necessary to make informed decisions, so it is difficult to determine whether the action based on this information is "rational" or "irrational." Moreover, they often make decisions under duress, so it is difficult to assert that they are freely making a "choice."

It is important to recognize that the strategic decisions made by aspiring movements have not always been "rational choices." Many scholars treat members of social movements as "rational" actors. But this assumes that they can, like consumers, make choices freely and that they possess the information (given by the market) they need to make rational choices. But this is an unwarranted assumption. As denizens and subjects, their decisions were often made under *duress*. A slave's decision to run away may or may not have been "rational." After all, it often ended in capture or death. But it was nonetheless "understandable."

Denizens and subjects also acted without adequate information that might have allowed them to *weigh* the risks and assess the costs and benefits of their action. So they often acted without knowing the outcome, in part because their success depended on the actions and reactions of others. They acted in concert, often without hesitation or question, because their bonds of affection or solidarity *compelled* them to act. They acted with conviction, with a certainty that was unwarranted by the facts and undeterred by the odds. Think, for example, of Simon Bolivar, Mohandas Gandhi, Elizabeth Cady Stanton, and Rosa Parks. They acted with a determination to seize a chance or turn the odds in their favor. They acted on the basis of principle, even when adherence to principle might get them assaulted or killed. They acted on behalf of others, knowing that they might not themselves benefit from their action. And they reflected on the decisions they made and reexamined their assumptions, tactics, and goals. Although they may not have discovered how best to make change, they learned different ways to make things better.

Of course, many denizens and subjects acted with resignation. They kept their heads down and their mouths shut. They stood on the sidelines, watched in silence, and walked through their lives as if in a slumber. Aspiring movements the world over recognized this problem and tried to change this behavior, urging denizens and subjects to "awake," arise, or, as the Jamaican singer Bob Marley put it, "Get up, stand up, stand up for your rights."[7]

When denizens and subjects in aspiring movements debated how best to make social change, they had to make decisions (or choices) about four related issues.

First, they argued about whether it was best to act in a legal, public fashion or in an illegal, clandestine manner. For example, aspiring socialist movements in Europe debated whether they should organize legal, public political parties, such as the German Social Democrats, and participate in elections or organize an illegal, clandestine party, such as Lenin's Bolshevik Party in Russia. To some extent, their answer to this question depended on whether they *could* act legally, in public, without fear of arrest. Some split the difference. In Ireland, nationalists organized a public political party that ran in elections but also a secret, oath-bound clandestine brotherhood, the Irish Republican Army, that plotted rebellion.[8]

Of course, an aspiring movement's decision to act in a legal, public manner did not necessarily prevent state officials and nonstate actors from treating them as criminals and conspirators. Participants in the American civil rights movement and in the anticolonial movements demanding *swaraj*, or independence, in India engaged in legal, public behavior but were nonetheless regularly assaulted, jailed, and killed.

Second, they debated whether it was best to create small-scale, democratic organizations in which participants would make tactical and strategic decisions or large-scale bureaucratic organizations and political parties in which professionals or elites would make the important decisions. During the 1980s, antinuclear activists in the United States debated whether change was best made by a network of small grassroots groups based in local communities, a position advanced by members of the "Freeze" (they wanted to "freeze" the number of nuclear weapons possessed by the superpowers), or by a professionally run, national organization based in Washington, DC (SANE). This question has long divided aspiring social movements. In this case, activists decided to combine forces and merge the two wings into a single umbrella organization (SANE/Freeze), which persuaded Congress to adopt a nonbinding "freeze" resolution.[9]

Third, they debated whether it was best to change economic-social-cultural practices or obtain state power and its economic and political resources. During the nineteenth century, Mikhail Bakunin, Prince Peter Kropotkin, and other anarchists in the First International argued that it was best to *destroy* the state, which they regarded as a capitalist institution, and replace it with voluntary nongovernmental organizations such as the Red Cross. Karl Marx and other socialists argued that it was best to *seize* the state, establish a dictatorship of the proletariat (the seizure of power by a faction), and then use the state and its resources to build socialism and prepare the economic and social conditions necessary for a transition to communism.[10] Conflict over this issue led to the dissolution of the First International and the creation of a Second International, where socialists debated whether it was best to obtain power by winning elections, as social democrats such as Karl Kautsky argued, or seize it by force, as Vladimir Lenin and the Bolsheviks maintained.[11] In one form or another, debates about whether to adopt peaceful or violent measures have divided almost every other aspiring movement around the world.

Fourth, aspiring social movements debated whether it was best to adopt nonviolent practices or use violence to make change. In the nineteenth century, the social democrats pursued peaceful strategies while the Bolsheviks and the anarchists chose violence; Gandhi and anticolonial nationalists in India practiced nonviolence while Mao and the Chinese communists argued that power grew out of the barrel of a gun; Martin Luther King Jr. adopted nonviolence while Malcolm X, Stokely Carmichael, and Huey Newton chose violence and "armed self-defense."

Of course, the decisions that aspiring movements made about violence shaped other strategic decisions. The decision to use violence persuaded many of them that it would be sensible or necessary to adopt a clandestine approach, create a tightly held organization run by expert professionals and disciplined cadres, and use violence to make significant, large-scale, "revolutionary" change, such as seizing state power and using its resources to benefit "the people" and themselves.

This decision also had important gender consequences. Men often proved willing to engage in violence, and some, like Frantz Fanon and Mao, celebrated violence. But women were extremely reluctant to participate in violent movements, largely because they were often victimized by male violence and did not regard it as something they should embrace. They believed that male violence, whatever its source, diminished women's liberty and compromised gender equality.

By contrast, when aspiring movements rejected violence and adopted nonviolent approaches to change, they were inclined to take a legal, public approach, adopt democratic organizational practices, and work to change social-cultural practices, particularly the reduction of violence by male state authorities and nonstate actors. Not surprisingly, women found it easier to participate in these kinds of movements than in movements where small, self-selected groups of determined men advocated "revolutionary" violence.

As a result of making decisions about these strategic issues, aspiring social movements divided into two groups, more or less: (1) nonviolent movements that operated legally in public, practiced democratic forms of decision making, sought social-cultural change, and encouraged men and women to participate; and (2) violent movements that operated in a clandestine manner, practiced oligarchic forms of decision making, sought state power, and invited men to participate, practices that tended to exclude women from active or leadership roles (see the chart in chapter 9).

Of course, the strategic decisions that aspiring groups made often changed over time. In the 1950s, homosexuals in the United States organized clandestine groups, largely because homosexuals were subject to arrest and exposure if they gathered in groups or acted as homosexuals in public. But in the 1970s, gay youths urged homosexuals to abandon clandestine politics, "come out of the closet," embrace a new public identity as "gay," and engage in legal, public politics. The first gay pride parades were designed by organizers to change not only homosexual identities but also the strategic approach of gay and lesbian activists.[12]

Aspiring movements also changed their views about violence. The Zionist movement in Palestine and the Muslim League in India for many years advocated nonviolent strategies for change. But in the late 1930s, as the Holocaust threatened and Arab resistance to Jewish immigration in Palestine grew, Zionists took up arms, creating both regular and irregular, clandestine forces to defend Jewish settlers and attack their opponents (Jewish irregulars assassinated a senior British official in Cairo in 1944).[13] In the mid-1940s, the Muslim League adopted the partition of India and the creation of a separate Muslim state in postcolonial India and announced that it would use violence to achieve it. As Muslim League leader Ali Jinnah explained: "Never have we in the whole history of the League done anything except by [nonviolent] constitutional methods and by constitutionalism. But now we are obligated and forced into this position. This day we bid goodbye to constitutional methods. . . . Today, we have forged a pistol [violent direct action] and are in a position to use it."[14]

By contrast, the Irish Republican Army and the ETA, a violent Basque separatist movement, abruptly abandoned violence as a strategy after years of waging clandestine, irregular wars against state authorities and civilian populations.[15] Some convicted ETA assassins recently met with relatives of their victims to apologize for their actions.[16]

In all of these cases, the decision to adopt or abandon violence had important consequences for these movements, which scholars might usefully explore. Unfortunately, many social movement scholars have argued that violence is a "more effective" strategy for social movements than nonviolence.

IS VIOLENCE A MORE EFFECTIVE STRATEGY?

In *The Strategy of Social Protest*, the sociologist William Gamson famously argues that the social movements that used violence were more effective than "challengers" that adopted *non*violence: "Unruly groups, those that use violence, strikes, and other constraints, have better than average success."[17] Although he asserts that violence "is commonly thought to be self-defeating," he argues instead that groups that used violence "won new advantages."[18]

But Gamson reached this conclusion by making a number of questionable assumptions and adopting a number of dubious methodological procedures. First, he excluded from his study of social movements any "groups whose members are neither American citizens nor striving for such citizenship."[19] As a result of this decision, he excluded from his study any groups from denizen and subject populations who, until 1920, made up a *majority* of the population in America. So he drew his analysis of five hundred to six hundred groups during the nineteenth and early twentieth centuries from a nonrepresentative sample, a sample that represented only a *minority* of the population. Second, he randomly selected "a small sample" of groups in the survey, fifty-three in all, to examine in detail and then "ripped each from its historical context," arguing that "each challenge had a thousand unique features that have been studiously *ignored*" (italics added).[20]

Using this approach, Gamson made a series of dubious decisions. He ignored the fact that the results were based on a minority of social movements representing a minority of the population, that this minority had a unique, privileged status as citizens in the republic, that this minority, made up only of men until 1920, were often given license by state authorities to use violence against subaltern populations (owners were licensed to use the Pinkerton Agency against striking workers; vigilante groups were given the authority to attack black denizens in the South, etc.), and they were often "effective," or got what they wanted, when they deployed violence. Given Gamson's selective and purposely ahistorical methodological approach, it should not be surprising to find that "challengers," really adult white male citizenries that deployed violence against subaltern populations during the antebellum and Jim Crow period, had "better than average success" at achieving their goals.

Gamson himself expressed second thoughts about his findings. He admitted that he was not quite "ready to conclude that violence basically works."[21] He speculated that violence "worked" both because violence in his sample was typically used by "large groups" who attacked "small ones," a version of "might makes right," and because large-group violence was "tacitly condoned by large parts of the audience [state authorities and members of the white community]."[22] Just so. He knew something was wrong, but his methodological strategy prevented him from seeing why violence might have been "effective" for dominant adult white citizenries in this period.

Gamson did not find that violence was a more effective strategy for social movements *generally*. His skewed sample and ahistorical methodology made it impossible for him to test this assertion or reach a different conclusion. He could find only that violence was an effective strategy for a particular group of social movements (adult white male citizens) during a particular historical period (slavery and Jim Crow). Although he claimed to be studying "challengers," Gamson was not looking at aspiring social movements but primarily at *restrictionist* movements that regularly deployed violence against denizen and subject populations during this period, as we have seen.

Still, it is important to ask, was violence a more effective strategy for aspiring social movements than nonviolence? Although the answer to this question depends on the historical circumstances, the answer is: probably not. I say this for several reasons.

First, aspiring movements have long argued about the efficacy of violence, which suggests there is no consensus on this issue, and scholars should take this lack of consensus seriously. At the very least, their reliance on Gamson's answer to this question ought to be reexamined.

Second, the answer depends on the historical circumstances and the objects of change. The aspiring movements that fought to democratize the republics and expand citizenries within them were predominantly *non*violent. They typically used litigation, migration, and legal protest to make change. They chose nonviolent strategies because they were vulnerable to attack by state authorities and nonstate actors. Aspiring movements that used violence often incited an even more violent response. They also chose nonviolent strategies because they could mobilize both men and women, whereas violent strategies made it extremely difficult to recruit women. Nonviolent strategies made it possible for aspiring movements to create broad-based, multigendered constituencies rather than the small groups "of angry men" depicted in *Les Misérables*.

There are some exceptions to this general pattern. The adult white men without property and black slaves fought violently to achieve citizenship and suffrage. But it was their role as *soldiers*—white men without property during the American Revolution, War of 1812, and wars with Indians; black slaves as Union soldiers during the Civil War and black citizens from the North and black denizens from the South in segregated units during World War II—that helped secure citizenship and suffrage. In both cases, white and black violence was deployed on behalf of the state, not against it, and they appealed for justice as veterans, not rebels. [23]

Third, in colonial settings, aspiring movements often took up arms to throw off dynastic rule and establish new republics. Aspiring republican movements used violence in the United States, France, Haiti, and across Latin America during the nineteenth century and made violent revolutions in Ireland, Russia, China, and Vietnam during the first half of the twentieth century. Their success is cited by many scholars and activists as proof that violence is an effective, perhaps the only, strategy that aspiring movements can use in colonial settings. But even this assumption needs to be reexamined. After 1945, aspiring movements used violence less frequently, and nonviolent strategies proved effective. Decolonization after 1945 was largely a peaceful process, and most of the new republics in Africa, the Middle East, and South and East Asia were established without violent revolution. As the historian John Gallagher has argued, "[There were] no Dublin Post Offices [in most colonial settings]." [24] Of course, aspiring movements waged violent insurrections in China, Vietnam, Algeria, and elsewhere. But the movements that used violence to create new republics frequently also used violence to establish *dictatorships* and subjugate domestic citizenries, which calls into question their claim that violence was a necessary and effective strategy for social change. In this context, it is difficult to argue that violence for aspiring social movements was an effective, long-term strategy for social change, though there might be some justification for violence by aspiring movements in some colonial settings where dynastic states resisted decolonization by force. In some contexts, violence may not have been much of a choice but a necessity imposed by others who were determined to use violence to prevent change. Aspiring movement violence in Haiti certainly fits this bill. Unfortunately, the use of violence by aspiring groups in Haiti has been used to defend violence in other settings, where it may have been less necessary. Although the proponents of violence were always quick to claim that it was necessary, that it was forced on them, they did not always exhaust or explore nonviolent alternatives.

Although aspiring social movements made decisions about how best to make change, they did not do so alone. They were often assisted by altruistic movements. It is to these movements that we now turn.

Chapter Eleven

Altruistic Social Movements

Altruistic social movements organized on behalf of subaltern groups and *assisted* global social change. They assisted subaltern groups because denizens and subjects often could not legally act on their own behalf and because aspiring movements often lacked the legal, economic, and political resources needed for acting effectively.[1] Altruistic movements provided resources to aspiring movements and fought with them to obtain rights and resources from dynastic and republican states. Altruistic movements objected to the violence inflicted on denizens and subjects by state officials and nonstate actors and worked with nonviolent aspiring groups to reduce violence in public and private settings and elevate the rule of law over arbitrary violence by state officials and their proxies. Although aspiring movements have been the driving force of global social change during the past two hundred years, altruistic movements have helped make it possible for aspiring movements to make change more often than not.

Historically, altruistic movements from "above" helped people from "below" make change. They filed lawsuits on behalf of American Indians (*Elk v. Wilkins*), African Americans (*Dred Scott*, *Brown*), Japanese Americans (*Ex Parte Endo*, *Korematsu v. United States*), women (*Griswold*, *Roe v. Wade*), children, immigrants, people with mental and physical disabilities, drug users, convicts, and death-row inmates.[2]

They organized movements to assist migrants and refugees. Conductors on the Underground Railroad helped blacks escape slavery, traveler's aid societies helped immigrants settle in the United States, Casa del Migrante assists Mexican immigrants to the United States, and churches in the "sanctuary movement" shelter economic migrants and political refugees, both legal and illegal.[3]

Altruistic male citizens supported suffrage for denizen women in the United States and around the world. Male citizens and female denizens fought first to end the slave trade and then to abolish slavery in dynastic states and slaveholding republics. White college students from the North registered adult black voters in the Jim Crow South. College students in the United States campaigned to release trafficked women from brothels and child soldiers from gangster armies.[4]

Consumer activists in the North promoted fair-trade coffee and bananas on behalf of small farmers and rural cooperatives in the South.[5] Pro-democracy activists from Scandinavia dropped small toy teddy bears from an airplane over Minsk to protest dictatorship in Belarus.[6] Gene Sharp, an American intellectual, distributed his manual on how to topple a dictatorship to activists in dictatorships around the world.[7] "I Paid a Bribe" organizers exposed corrupt government practices in India.[8] Interventions by altruistic activists prompted government officials in Russia and Israel to restrict the charitable activities of foreign and domestic nongovernmental organizations.[9]

Amnesty International, Movements.org, Human Rights Watch, and the Joint Mobil Group in Chechnya monitored the violations of human rights by governments and nonstate actors, while Oxfam, the Red Cross, and Doctors without Borders provided food, shelter, and medical care for the victims of war and natural disaster.[10] Philanthropic foundations—Carnegie, Rockefeller, Gates, Soros, and Atlantic—provided funds for altruistic and aspiring movements in the United States and around the world. Philanthropy has not been restricted to the rich. In 1907, Emily Bissell organized the sale of Christmas Seals to working-class and poor people to fund a campaign against tuberculosis, which ravaged the poor.[11] More recently, Muhammad Yunus organized the Grameen Bank in Bangladesh so that poor people could themselves fund the work of other poor people.

PROVIDING RESOURCES, REDUCING VIOLENCE

Altruistic movements assisted aspiring movements and worked on behalf of denizens and subjects who may not have had the legal standing, political capacity, or financial means to act effectively on their own. Altruistic movements provided resources to assist disadvantaged subaltern groups and protect them from violence by state and nonstate actors in public and private settings. Their efforts transformed the policies and practices of dynastic and republican states.

For most of the past two hundred years, between 1800 and 1940, dynastic and republican states refused to provide economic resources or "welfare" to the urban poor, the displaced or landless farmer, the unemployed worker, the widow and her children, the abandoned child and the orphan, the mentally or physically disabled, the elderly or infirm, the derelict male or fallen female. However, altruistic movements and eleemosynary or charitable institutions, as they were once called, stepped in and provided disadvantaged subaltern groups with resources that state officials refused to provide.[12] For example, because the US government refused to provide contraceptives or abortions to women and girls, Margaret Sanger and two other nurses opened a birth-control clinic in 1916 to provide these services, fought with the government for the right to provide them, which resulted in their arrest and imprisonment (Ethel Byrne, Sanger's sister, nearly died from a hunger strike while in jail), and later founded the American Birth Control League, the organizational predecessor of Planned Parenthood, which later also provided abortions.[13] Although state officials (and Republican presidents) for a time supported these efforts, they later turned against them, refusing to provide state resources for women and girls who wanted abortions and threatening to defund Planned Parenthood, which provides birth control and other health services for one in five American women.[14]

Altruistic movements such as Planned Parenthood have fought to provide resources from public and private sources to assist people who have few resources.

Since the early nineteenth century, altruistic movements provided resources to people whom state officials refused to service, providing homes for indigents, orphans, pregnant girls and homeless men, asylums for the insane, and shelters for battered women. Moreover, they fought to obtain state resources for unserved populations and persuaded state and local officials to assume responsibility for their care and provide funds to assist these and other groups. Their collective efforts resulted in an important shift during the 1930s.

Before the Great Depression, private altruistic and charitable institutions provided resources to disadvantaged subaltern groups.[15] During the 1930s, local, state, and federal officials assumed greater responsibility for assisting these groups and used *public* resources to do so. (State officials had always provided public resources to rich and advantaged citizens.)

The extension of suffrage to women was likely responsible for this shift. Women provided the electoral support needed by Roosevelt and the Democratic Party to allocate public resources for the first time, in a big way, to subaltern groups. Is it possible to imagine the passage of "welfare" programs—unemployment insurance, Aid to Families with Dependent Children, social security, Medicare, farm subsidy and crop insurance programs—*without* suffrage for women? I think not. The rise of the "welfare state," which really describes the distribution of public resources to subaltern groups for the first time, was largely a product first of women's participation in altruistic movements and private charitable institutions and then of their participation in electoral politics as citizen voters, developments that scholars have neglected or ignored.[16]

Early on, state officials deployed violence and delegated the authority to use violence to nonstate actors. They still do. The soldiers, convicts, students, wives, children, workers, servants, and slaves who were victimized by nonstate actors could not legally or easily object to public and private violence. Altruistic movements fought to protect the victims of violence both because they could not defend themselves without risking further violence and because state officials would not defend them from nonstate actors who used violence on their own authority. For example, during the 1830s and 1840s, altruistic movements demanded that state officials and private authorities abandon the flogging or beating of soldiers, students, convicts, wives, children, servants, slaves, and also horses and other animals (see chapter 7).

Altruistic movements also stepped in to protect people from other dangers. They campaigned to protect travelers from boiler explosions on steamboats, which resulted in one of the first acts of "protective" state regulation, from dangerous drugs and hazardous foods, from the fires that menaced poor families in tenements and workers in factories, and from the floods, fires, earthquakes, and drought that ruined people without insurance and sometimes people *with* insurance (many insurance companies went bankrupt from losses incurred in the 1906 earthquake in San Francisco and Hurricane Katrina in New Orleans).

Altruistic movements not only intervened to protect the victims of violence and disaster, they campaigned to restrict the violence wielded by state officials and to revoke the authority given to nonstate actors, which allowed employers to hire Pinkertons to shoot striking workers, allowed whites to lynch black men, women, and children, allowed husbands to beat their wives, and permitted teamsters to flog their horses. Of course, in recent years, non-state actors have fought to reclaim their ability to use violence on their own authority, persuading state officials to adopt concealed-carry and stand-your-ground laws. But efforts by altruistic movements to reduce violence have contributed to the consolidation of legitimate physical force by the state, a process that is still incomplete.

MOTIVATIONS: PRINCIPLES, ALTRUISM, AND SELF-INTEREST

Altruistic movements *acted* on behalf of others. Of this there is no doubt. But they assisted subaltern groups and challenged the state for different *reasons*. First, many believed that liberty, equality, and solidarity were principles that should be extended to others, not only to themselves. Abolitionists believed that slavery violated democratic principles and undermined the liberty not only of slaves but also of free men and women. They believed in the rule of law and justice for all. Because religious and secular laws have much in common, many altruistic movements in the United States drew their partici-pants from faith-based religious (Quakers, Protestants, Catholics, and Jews) and secular legal (the NAACP and the ACLU) communities.

Second, they believed in helping others. They reached out to other groups and built relations based on cooperation, mutual respect, and solidarity. Adam Smith argued that while capitalism was driven by self-interest, it also relied on a spirit of giving: "How selfish so ever man may be supposed, there are evidently some principles in his nature, which interest him in the fortune of others, and render their happiness necessary to him, though he derives nothing from it except the pleasure of seeing it."[17] This could be said of almost every parent.

Many natural scientists now think that altruism, cooperation, and equality were key to the success of *Homo sapiens* and the emergence of human communities. David Sloan Wilson, an evolutionary theorist, "sees the onset of humanity's cooperative, fair-and-square spirit as one of the major transi-tions in the history of life on earth, moments when individual organism or selection units band together and stake their future fitness on each other. . . . A major transition occurs when you have a mechanism for suppressing fit-ness differences and establishing equality within groups, so it is no longer possible to succeed at the expense of your group." Wilson argues, "It is a rare event, and it's hard to get started, but when it does you can quickly dominate the earth. [Human evolution] clearly falls into this paradigm."[18]

Sometimes, altruism grows out of a shared experience. Women in the 1830s supported efforts to curb male violence against others (children, servants, students, slaves, and horses) because they, *too*, were victims of male violence. Altruistic movements often fought for others because they identified with them, an identification based on their own experience.

Third, altruistic movements took action because they were motivated by different kinds of self-interest. The adult white men with property who voted to extend suffrage to adult white men *without* property did so in part because they sought to obtain political advantage in an enlarged electorate. As we have seen, the Jackson Democrats thought a wider franchise would increase their political power, and the Whigs followed suit because they did not want their opposition to this populist measure to disadvantage them politically. They both adopted altruism in their self-interest, as did the Republicans who extended adult suffrage to adult black men and the Democrats and Republicans who extended it to women and to youth.

Guilt has motivated some altruistic movements, particularly the wealthy industrialists who financed philanthropic foundations (Carnegie, Rockefeller, Ford, Gates, Soros). Philanthropy has eased the conscience of cutthroat capitalists, helped them remake their public image, and secured tax benefits for themselves and their heirs.

Altruistic movements have acted because they wanted to change subaltern groups and, with messianic zeal, remake them in their own image. Religious and secular groups have tried to convert others to their faiths and political ideologies and tried to make others more like themselves, a self-centered, narcissistic aspiration.

Finally, altruistic movements acted because they *feared* subaltern groups or viewed them as a threat. They worried that if they did not assist subaltern groups, those groups might rise up in anger and destroy everything. Recall that slave owners in the South helped poor whites obtain suffrage because they wanted poor whites to "serve in militia patrols guarding against slave rebellions."[19] In this case, help for whites was motivated by fear of blacks. Fear of immigrants likewise persuaded many adult male citizens to support women's suffrage and help women get the vote. In short, greed, guilt, narcissism, and fear have persuaded some altruistic movements to act on behalf of others. Still, whatever their motives, they nonetheless managed to assist and make change. As *New York Times* columnist David Brooks wryly observes,

"Many Americans go to the developing world to serve others. A smaller percentage actually end up being useful."[20]

PROBLEMS WITH ALTRUISTIC MOVEMENTS

Activists in aspiring social movements and many social movement scholars view altruistic movements with skepticism. Generally, they have criticized altruistic movements for three reasons. First, they argue that altruistic movements have not promoted social *change* but only *reform*, which has strengthened capitalist states. Second, they maintain that people make change only when they act on their *own* behalf, when they exercise their capacity for "self-determination." Third, they argue that the misguided attempt to help others may actually make things worse.

In the *Communist Manifesto*, Karl Marx argued that altruistic movements, what he called "bourgeois socialists," did not promote change but instead promoted reform, which strengthened the capitalist state and bourgeois society: "Philanthropists, humanitarians, improvers of the working class, organizers of charity, members of societies for the prevention of cruelty to animals, temperance fanatics, [and] hole-and-corner reformers of every imaginable kind [are] desirous of redressing social grievances in order to secure *the continued existence of bourgeois society*" (italics added).[21] Marx allowed that a "small section of the ruling class cuts itself adrift and joins the revolutionary class," and he welcomed them into the proletarian fold, but he rejected assistance from reformist do-gooders.[22]

Immanuel Wallerstein agreed with Marx, arguing that "liberals" and other altruistic groups advanced reform, not change. As Macaulay argued, in defense of the 1832 Reform Bill, "Reform, that you may preserve [the social order and the state]."[23] Although liberal reformers and altruistic movements campaigned to improve the condition of others, they deflected, deferred, or deterred demands by aspiring movements for real, substantive change. For Wallerstein, the expansion of citizenship and other reforms were designed "to tame the dangerous classes—in particular the urban proletariat—by incorporating them into the system politically, but in such a way that would not upset the basic economic, political, and cultural systems of [Great Britain and France]."[24]

Of course, many altruistic movements contributed to reform, not to the transformation of the capitalist world-system, as Wallerstein suggested. Many helped to secure "the continued existence of bourgeois society," as

Marx maintained. But this was not always the case. The altruistic abolitionists who fought successfully to end the slave trade and abolish slavery in dynastic and republican states transformed the capitalist system. For centuries, slavery fueled economic development in the capitalist world-economy and enriched slaveholding European empires and republican states in the Americas. The end of the slave trade and the abolition of slavery changed the character of economic development in the capitalist world-economy, eliminated the slaveholding gentry as a key faction of ruling classes, and so transformed the character of bourgeois society and made it possible for slaves to ascend and become denizens and citizens.

Marx dismissed altruistic reformers such as the "members of the society for the prevention of cruelty to animals." But recall that activists who fought against animal cruelty also fought to restrict male violence against women and children, sailors and slaves, servants and students. These were not inconsequential reforms. They contributed both to a secular decline in male violence and to new relations between state officials and male nonstate actors. At the urging of altruistic movements against violence, state officials rescinded the authority, given by the state to male nonstate actors, to use violence against subaltern groups (people and animals) on their own initiative. In light of these developments, Marx and Wallerstein's characterizations of altruistic movements might be reconsidered.

It is true, of course, that state officials allowed or encouraged altruistic movements to ameliorate the conditions of subaltern populations and so "tame the dangerous classes," strengthen the state, and secure the continued existence of "bourgeois society." For example, US officials licensed the Red Cross to act as the first responder in emergencies and disasters across the United States. But the failure of the Red Cross to assist victims of Hurricane Katrina had the opposite effect: it failed to tame the dangerous masses, who looted New Orleans, and undermined the legitimacy of the Bush administration and the state.[25]

Second, activists and scholars have argued that aspiring movements can make real or effective change only by acting on their own behalf, by exercising their capacity for self-determination, not by relying on altruistic movements to help them. In 1966, Stokely Carmichael, the president of SNCC, argued that white participation in the civil rights movement was based on the assumption, by whites, that "the Negro is somehow incapable of liberating himself. . . . Shouldn't people be able to organize themselves?"[26] Although white participation might be well intentioned, Carmichael argued that it crip pled black initiative, subordinated black interests to white interests, and made change more difficult. To prevent whites from having an "intimidating effect" on blacks and prevent them from subverting "our true search and struggle for self-determination," Carmichael argued that blacks "must cut ourselves off from white people" and "form our own institutions, credit unions, co-ops, political parties, write our own histories."[27] This approach, which drew heavily on the arguments made earlier by Malcolm X and the Nation of Islam, persuaded activists in many other aspiring movements in the United States and around the world—women's, youth, gay and lesbian—to abandon collaborative alliances with other altruistic and aspiring movements and instead exercise their self-determination and pursue social change on their own.

As we have seen, millions of blacks in the South exercised their capacity for self-determination and migrated to the North after World War I to obtain citizenship and suffrage. They did so without much encouragement or assistance from altruistic whites, without much assistance from anyone but themselves. They mobilized the meager resources available to them, seized the political opportunities that existed, and, by pursuing their self-determination, made change, much as Carmichael advocated. But this kind of self-determination was difficult for many denizen and subject groups to practice. Generally, citizens have a considerable capacity for self-determination (if by self-determination we mean self-reliance, which is how Carmichael used the term). Their liberty as citizens made it easier for them to mobilize resources and seize the political opportunities provided by popular sovereignty and constitutional government than denizens and subjects, who are typically deprived of economic means and legal, political opportunities to improve their status. As a result, denizens and subjects often sought or accepted assistance from altruistic groups and made principled or tactical alliances with them to increase their social weight and political clout. Alliances and collaborations between aspiring and altruistic movements made it possible for many movements to make change. Would they have been able to do so alone, as Carmichael suggested, if they relied only on their capacity for "self-determination?" Perhaps. But many of the aspiring social movements that successfully made change forged alliances with different ethnic groups (the nationalist approach) or different classes (the socialist, internationalist approach) and collaborated with altruistic movements that included people with higher social status.

For example, the civil rights movement brought together people from different racial, class, gender, geographic, age, and status groups in a collaborative struggle. Collectively, they brought an end to Jim Crow and the violence associated with it and (re)secured citizenship and suffrage for four million black adults in the South. By contrast, the groups that advocated black "self-determination" and, importantly, also armed "self-defense"—the Nation of Islam, SNCC after 1965, and the Black Panther Party (which Carmichael joined)—enjoyed considerably less political success. Still, while it is impossible to imagine the election of Barack Obama without the civil rights movement, it is also impossible to imagine rap music without the movement for "Black Power." It may be that black power contributed more to cultural change in the black community—promoting a new identity and solidarity in the community—than to political change, though the two were related.

Carmichael's critique of white altruism was joined by a critique of nonviolence. In the civil rights movement, the two were closely linked. By attacking white altruism, Carmichael made it easier to jettison black and white nonviolence and promote black violence as an alternative political strategy. In his "Declaration of War," Carmichael advocated "revolutionary warfare" to protect black people from attack by "the missionaries, the money, and the marines," and said that "we have no alternative but to fight . . . black people have got to fight, got to fight, got to fight."[28] He went on to say that if black people "become a threat [to our struggle], we off them. We off them. . . . We're talking about being the executioners of the executioners."[29]

Given the history of black movements that emphasized self-reliance, not collaboration, in the years after 1965, there is good reason to be skeptical of Carmichael's claims that people should make change *only* on their own behalf or that violence is a *necessary* or effective instrument of change. Unfortunately, many aspiring movements in the 1970s adopted the view that self-determination was the best way to make change, that violence might sometimes be "necessary," and that they should not collaborate with altruistic movements, which typically shun violence. As a result, many aspiring movements pursued change separately, on their own, which weakened them at a time when New Right restrictionist movements emerged to deter, deflect, and reverse change.

Third, activists and scholars argued that altruistic movements' efforts to assist others actually made things worse.[30] During the 1990s, critics of humanitarian organizations that provided food, resources, and health care to victims of war and natural disaster in Africa, Asia, and the Americas argued that because altruistic movements did not understand or appreciate local political, economic, social or cultural realities, they adopted policies and practices that *undermined* the ability of victims to regain their independence and made them dependent and despondent.[31] In *The Road to Hell*, Michael Maren describes relief organizations as "mercenaries" and argues that "their work is pointless or counterproductive."[32] In Zaire, De Waal argues, "it was the disaster relief agencies that were out of control."[33]

Altruistic movements have promoted and assisted real change, advanced reforms that strengthened the state, and took ill-advised or inappropriate steps that made things worse for the people they were trying to help. But much the same could be said of aspiring movements, whose members also adopted poor strategies and ineffective tactics based on faulty assumptions and poor information and whose failures set back their causes for decades.

Many of the aspiring movements that seized state power advanced dictatorship, practiced ruthless forms of capital accumulation and economic development, and failed to transform the capitalist character of the state or the world-economy as a whole. Although a large number of "antisystemic" movements "have come to power in a large number of states," Wallerstein admits that "post-revolutionary regimes continue[d] to function as part of the social division of labor of historical capitalism."[34] The seizure of state power was an "unfulfilled revolution" because, while "changes in state structures have altered the politics of accumulation, [they] have not yet been able to end them."[35] Indeed, Wallerstein argues that aspiring socialist movements failed to make substantive change and suggests that the anarchists may have been right when they argued that state power should be destroyed, not seized.[36]

But keep in mind that all social movements risk failure and that failure can exact a heavy toll on movement participants and others. Failure can embolden opponents, strengthen the forces of reaction, and incur the wrath of state officials. Still, because people who organize movements operate in environments where information about the consequences of action is poor and incomplete, it may be better to risk failure than to do nothing at all. In the long run, both aspiring and altruistic movements have succeeded more often than not, and their collective efforts have contributed to significant social change.

Chapter Twelve

Restrictionist Social Movements

Restrictionist movements fought to resist and reverse social change. They opposed the creation of constitutional government based on popular sovereignty in the republics, installed dictators in the republics, and resisted the expansion of citizenries in the republics. They viewed these developments as a threat to their own liberty, which consisted, in part, of dominion over others in both public and private settings. They enlisted state officials to obstruct change and persuaded them to authorize nonstate actors to use violence against subaltern groups. Restrictionist movements have routinely used or threatened violence to protect their own liberty and deny it to others. When state officials refused to license their violence, they persuaded their peers to give them informal legal immunity from prosecution by refusing to convict them for their crimes in court, which allowed them to commit violence with impunity.

For the most part, sociologists have excluded restrictionist movements, or what Sidney Tarrow called "the ugly movements," from the study of social movements.[1] For Tarrow, the ugly movements are "rooted in ethnic and nationalist claims, religious fanaticism, and racism."[2] Because many scholars *define* social movements as antiauthoritarian challengers, they exclude *pro*authoritarian or restrictionist movements.

According to Alberto Melucci, a social movement "breaks the rules of the game . . . [and] questions the legitimacy of power," while Frances Fox Piven argues that social movements not only challenge authority but disrupt the patterns of daily life, "a pattern of ongoing and institutionalized cooperation [with state authorities, who depend] on their continuing contributions [to maintain their legitimacy]."[3] William Gamson defines social movements as "challenging groups" that target social authorities and persuade them to change their practices and policies.[4] Doug McAdam agrees that social movements are "challenging groups" or "insurgents" who seek to make modest reforms or radical changes in economic, political, or social institutions.[5] Sidney Tarrow defines social movements as "collective challenges, based on common purposes and social solidarities in sustained interaction with elites, opponents and [state] authorities," though Suzanne Staggenborg notes that "not all social movements target the state" but also "other types of authorities, such as business owners or religious leaders."[6] She goes on to say that "movement scholars have generally regarded movements as *challengers* that are, at least in part, *outsiders* with regard to established power structures," though they have typically excluded political parties and interest groups, whom they regard as "insiders" or defenders of established power structures.[7] From this perspective, insiders who defend authority should not be treated as social movements, though some scholars concede that they may constitute a countermovement, which suggests that they have no real autonomy or agency but exist only to counter a *real* social movement, one that possesses agency and autonomy.[8]

Social movement scholars have excluded restrictionist movements because these movements seek to preserve authority, defend inequality, and deny state power or political rights to subaltern challengers. For example, Paul Street and Anthony D. Maggio insist that the Tea Party "is *not a social movement*, but rather a loose conglomeration of partisan interest groups set on returning the Republican Party to power." The authors argue that the Tea Party "is not an 'uprising' against a corrupt political system or against the established order," which might define it as a social movement, but is intead "a reactionary, top-down manifestation of the system . . . a classic, rightwing and fundamentally Republican epitome of what . . . Christopher Hitchens once called . . . 'the manipulation of populism by elitism.'"[9]

Theda Skocpol and Vanessa Williams disagree, arguing that the Tea Party *is* a social movement, both because it has a grassroots component that consists of about two hundred thousand "angry, conservative-minded citizens who have formed vital local and regional groups" and because it has an antigovernment rhetoric, rooted in opposition to the election of President Barack Obama, that makes it an "antiauthoritarian" challenger like other social movements.[10]

I take a different view. Restrictionist movements should be included in the study of social movements for several reasons. First, restrictionist movements have shaped the pace, direction, and meaning of global social change during the past two hundred years, and they continue to do so. The Southern Poverty Law Center, which has studied racist, antigovernment "hate groups" in the United States for the past thirty years, found that the number of grass-roots groups and armed militias has grown from 602 in 2000 to 1,018 in 2012. Second, they possess the agency and autonomy needed to resist change in both public and private settings. Although some are supported by state officials and nongovernment authorities, many restrictionists organize and act independently and are beholden to no one but themselves. Third, many of the antiauthoritarian challengers identified by sociologists as members of "real" social movements have themselves become pro-authoritarian restrictionists. This development, which is quite common, suggests that social movements be defined not by their opposition to authority but by their relation to social change. Their efforts delayed, compromised, and deflected social change and ensured the survival of social inequality.

RESISTING CHANGE

Restrictionists fought to preserve dynastic states and prevent the creation of constitutional government based on popular sovereignty in republican states. They included the royalists who opposed republican government in the American colonies and their American Indian and African American allies; the whites and mulattoes who fought to suppress the slave rebellion in Haiti and enlisted the French, British, and Spanish Empires in their counterinsurgency campaigns; the dynastic rulers and military cadres that crushed republican uprisings across Europe in 1848; the antirepublican fascists who defeated anarchist and socialist republicans during the Spanish Civil War and crushed socialist and communist movements in Italy and Germany before World War II; and the Taliban and al-Qaida, who fought to overthrow republican governments in Afghanistan and Pakistan and establish retrograde dynastic states based on a narrow definition of Islamic law.

Restrictionists seized power and established dictatorships in many republics and then fought to prevent democratization in these states. They included the caudillos who established dictatorships in postcolonial republics across Latin America; the white minority that organized an apartheid regime in South Africa; the communist parties that took power in the Soviet Union,

China, North Korea, Vietnam, Cuba, postwar states in eastern Europe, and postcolonial states in Asia and Africa; the dictators who seized power with US assistance or consent in Europe, East Asia, Latin America, Africa, and the Middle East during the Cold War; and the dictators who seized power in postcommunist states across the former Soviet Union and fought to prevent the spread of the "color revolutions."

Restrictionists resisted the expansion of citizenries within the republics and revoked or reduced the status of citizens, denizens, and subjects when they could. In the United States, restrictionists deprived American Indians of their sovereignty and forcibly relocated them to reservations in the West; slaveholders and secessionists fought to keep slaves, retrieve escaped slaves, and expand slavery to new territories outside the South; during Jim Crow, whites in the South deprived black men of citizenship and suffrage and made them denizens and subjects; anti-immigrant groups restricted the entry of Asian immigrants and worked to expel immigrants whom they viewed as a threat to public health or safety; men refused to extend suffrage to their mothers, sisters, wives, and daughters; men treated women and children as chattel and beat them at will; and teachers defended the right to administer corporal punishment in public and private schools.

In recent years, restrictionist movements have worked to restrict or revoke the rights of citizens, denizens, and subjects in a variety of ways.

Suppressing Citizens, Denizens, and Subjects

Restrictionists complaining of "voter fraud" have introduced legislation in different states that requires voters to "show photo ID at the polls or to prove their U.S. citizenship. Same-day voter registration would be ended in some places, strict new limits would make it harder to mount voter-registration drives, and early voting has been cut back."[11] They have introduced English-language tests for citizens who seek public office and have argued that English should become the official language of the United States, which would make it difficult for non-English-speaking citizens to participate in public life.[12]

Restrictionist movements have fought to revoke female citizens' right to abortion, which was given constitutional protection by the Supreme Court in 1974, introduced legislation to give "rights" to fetuses and make it more onerous for women to obtain contraception and abortions, deny funding for Planned Parenthood, which provides health care for millions of women, and demeaned the victims of rape.[13] Restrictionists have worked to undermine or revoke the right of citizen workers to organize unions, bargain collectively, and exercise their solidarity.[14] And they have denied or revoked the right of gay and lesbian citizens to marry or obtain civil unions and kept sodomy statutes on their books even though the Supreme Court has ruled that these laws are unconstitutional.[15]

Restrictionists announced plans to revoke the "birthright" status of citizens born in the United States to foreign parents and create a two-tier system of birth certificates, deny public school education to the children of illegal immigrants, access that is currently protected by a Supreme Court ruling, and question the legal status of citizens and denizens alike.[16]

Restrictionists have imposed curfews on denizen youths, limited their ability to drive their cars with other minors, and attached red stickers on their license plates "to make it easier for the police to enforce . . . curfew and passenger restrictions."[17] An editorial against underage drinkers expressed restrictionist sentiments with the headline: "Enforce the Laws Ruthlessly."[18]

Restrictionists encouraged parents to use corporal punishment to discipline their children. The authors of *To Train Up a Child*, which has been purchased by 650,000 Christian homeschoolers, instruct parents to use "a switch from as early as six months to discourage misbehavior and describe how to make use of implements for hitting [children] on the arms, legs or back, including a quarter-inch flexible plumbing line that [the author notes] 'can be rolled up and carried in your pocket.'"[19] The authors, Mr. and Mrs. Peal, argue that the practices they advocate in the book are "based on the same principles the Amish use to train their stubborn mules," and maintain, "To give up the rod is to give up our views of human nature, God, eternity."[20] Several sets of parents who adopted the practices outlined in the book have been charged with "homicide by abuse" of minors in their care.[21]

Restrictionists introduced "three-strike" and mandatory-sentencing laws for many crimes, restricted opportunities for parole, and disenfranchised felons who have completed their sentences and been released from jail. These measures have contributed to the expansion of the subject population in the United States and increased the social-legal distance between citizens and subjects.

LICENSED TO KILL

During the past two hundred years, state officials have slowly revoked the ability of male nonstate actors to use violence on their own authority, a development that has contributed to the monopolization of the legitimate use of physical force by the state, though the process that Weber described is by no means anywhere complete. But in recent years, restrictionists have fought to recover the authority of nonstate actors to use violence on their own initiative. They fought to weaken gun-control laws and advanced "stand-your-ground" and "concealed-carry" legislation, which gives legal protection to nonstate actors, most of them male, to use guns in "self-defense," on their own authority. They passed legislation barring doctors from asking their patients whether they own a gun, a question that gun owners view as "unnecessarily harassing."[22] As a result, police did not prosecute Brice Harper, who killed an unarmed man, Dan Friedenberg, the husband of a woman Harper was having an affair with, when Friedenberg approached Harper at his home; police did not initially prosecute George Zimmerman after he shot and killed Trayvon Martin, an unarmed black teenager in Florida. In both cases, the police believed that the killers had the legal authority to act as they did.[23] "Given [Mr. Harper's] reasonable belief that he was about to be assaulted, [Mr. Harper's] use of deadly force against [Mr. Friedenberg] was justified" under Montana's new stand-your-ground law, the county attorney explained.[24] Harper shot Friedenberg three times. "There is no justice," Mrs. Friedenberg complained.[25]

Of course, one can "use" a gun without firing a shot. The public display of guns can be used by individuals to threaten, provoke, or cow others, depending on the circumstances. When women in Dallas held a meeting in a restaurant for Moms Demand Action for Gun Sense in America, a group formed after the mass shooting at Sandy Hook Elementary School in Newtown, Connecticut, a heavily armed group of gun-rights activists belonging to Open Carry Texas gathered in the parking lot outside the restaurant and brandished assault rifles and shotguns in an intimidating display of force. "Sadly, these bullies are attempting to use guns to intimidate moms and children and to infringe on our constitutional right to free speech," Shannon Watts, the national founder of Moms Demand Action, observed.[26] As Stephen Stills and Buffalo Springfield observed in the 1967 song "For What It's Worth": "There's a man with a gun over there / Telling me I got to beware."

CAPABILITY, DIFFERENCE, AND INEQUALITY

In dynastic states, restrictionists rejected constitutional government based on popular sovereignty because they believed in social *in*equality, which was the basis of claims to power by dynastic rulers and aristocracies, and because they thought that the multitude were *in*capable of governing themselves. In the republics, restrictionists believed in social equality for *some* people, though not for all, and reserved citizenship and suffrage for themselves, whom they described in the Constitution as "the People." They did not believe in equality for *all* because they thought that the multitude was incapable of exercising popular sovereignty. Because the multitude, which were often described as "childlike," was incapable of exercising the rights and responsibilities associated with citizenship and suffrage, they should be treated differently, as denizens or subjects, not as citizens. Restrictionists simultaneously defended social equality for some but not all, as a matter of principle, arguing that it was based on the difference between the *capable* and the *incapable.*

During the past two hundred years, restrictionists have argued that people assigned to denizen and subject populations lacked the moral capacity, the economic autonomy, the social agency, and the self-discipline necessary to exercise popular sovereignty responsibly. Restrictionists have defended the resulting social inequalities because these inequalities are based on social *differences* that reflect different individual and social *capacities.*

Of course, denizens and subjects have argued that they, too, are capable of exercising popular sovereignty, that they are not so different as restrictionists imagine, and that they, too, should be allowed to claim citizenship and suffrage, liberty and equality. One way that they demostrated "capacity," agency, and autonomy was by organizing social movements to demand change. By organizing movements, they demonstrated an ability to *act* like citizens, even if citizens did not yet treat them as citizens, as equals. But subaltern groups have not always *challenged* the idea that *capacity* should be used as a criterion to determine who might exercise popular sovereignty, which is the rationale used to justify persistent social inequality and deny some "people" from being seen as members of "the People." Although many subaltern groups have objected to social inequality, they have not challenged the principle that underlies it. In fact, many aspiring and altruistic movements that fought to expand citizenship in the republics also embraced or adopted this principle as their own.

ARE WE ALL RESTRICTIONISTS?

Social movements have expanded citizenries in republics around the world. But social inequality persists, even in the most "advanced" republics, where citizenship has been extended to the vast majority of people, where denizen populations are modest (mostly young people and a small number of immigrants) and subject populations (convicts) are relatively small. Of course, restrictionist movements fought to limit the expansion of citizenries and keep social and economic inequalities intact, and they still do. But social inequality is not the product of their efforts alone. Inequality persists in part because many of the denizens and subjects who became citizens and obtained suffrage subsequently worked to *prevent* its extension to others, even to their own. Immigrants who became citizens joined restrictionist, anti-immigration groups, youths who became adults campaigned to restrict the rights of minors, white women who obtained suffrage denied it to black women in the South, male workers who obtained the right to bargain collectively denied women and minorities admission to their unions, and the Islamic demonstrators who struggled for democracy in Arab states then fought to exclude women from public and political life. Do the citizens of any republics now support the extension of citizenship to minors, immigrants, or convicts? Perhaps, but they are few in number.

Subaltern groups, who were once oppressed, participated in restrictionist social movements for different reasons. They may have done so because they wanted to secure their own interests, exercise their own liberty, or treat others as they were treated. This last practice has been a common response to hazing, abuse, and mistreatment by others. But while such reasons may have played a role, this behavior also has social explanations.

Immigrants who join anti-immigration groups do so not because they see themselves as having something in common with new immigrants, being immigrants themselves, but because they see new immigrants as *different*: "*We* came here legally, worked hard, and asked for nothing. *They* came here illegally, are lazy, and ask for resources and special treatment from the state." Adults who were, of course, once children imposed driving restrictions on youth because they think contemporary youth are *not* the children they once were. If people persuade themselves that others are *different*, if others lack the capacities that they possess, then it is easy to justify measures that would constrain others' liberty and rationalize the inequalities that result.

Of course, denizen and subject populations who aspired to citizenship often found it effective to argue that they were *not* different but the *same* as others. For example, gay and lesbian movements successfully argued that they were not different, not a threat to public health or safety, and should therefore be allowed to serve in the army, teach in a public school, or marry their partner, just *like* other citizens. As Mary Bernstein observes, "[T]he lesbian and gay movement seems largely to have abandoned its emphasis on *difference* from the straight majority in favor of a moderate politics that highlights *similarities* to the straight majority."[27] Of course, they were able to make this argument more easily than some other subaltern groups because they were already citizens, though in a precarious, second-class status, so they were less different, in some ways, than children, immigrants, or convicts.

Ironically, the postmodern scholars who insist on "difference" and exhort subaltern populations to exercise their "self-determination" and portray themselves as "different," one from another, make it easier for restrictionists to differentiate themselves from other people, rationalize differential treatment, and maintain social inequality.

The problems for the remainders—children, immigrants, and convicts—is that denizen and subject populations are now a minority of people in the republics, which means that their *capacity* to act, ascend, and change their condition is fairly weak, given the fact that a majority of people now belong to the citizenry. The citizen majority have displayed little interest in inviting or allowing the remainders to join them, largely because they view the remainders as different, as lacking the capacity, autonomy, or agency needed to act as citizens. In fact, this is a dubious assertion. Are children less capable than senior citizens with dementia? Are immigrants less capable than adult citizens with Down syndrome or any chronic and debilitating disease? Are convicts less capable than citizens taking mood-altering prescribed drugs? When children in Manhattan, Kansas, elementary schools were given the opportunity to participate in a mock election for presidential candidates in the 2012 election, 56 percent voted for President Obama, compared with only 41 percent of adults in the town and in the state, a fact that attests not only to the children's agency and autonomy (they voted quite differently from their parents) but also to their maturity and sagacity.[28] Age is no more a measure of capacity than ethnicity, class, gender, or place of birth. Yet so long as citizens use capacity as a criterion for admission to the citizenry, social inequality in the republics will persist. Citizens will insist on it.

Chapter Thirteen

Theories and Opportunities

Social movements reshaped the world. They established republics, democratized republics, and expanded citizenries within them. Their development curbed violence in the capitalist interstate system and in the republics. The rise of the republics reduced the interstate violence associated with competition between dynastic states, which fought rival states and indigenous peoples for control of colonial empires. The democratization of the republics disarmed the dictators who violated the rights and took the lives of civilian populations. The expansion of citizenries curbed violence by male nonstate actors, who had been licensed by the state to abuse wives, children, servants, workers, slaves, and animals.[1]

Of course, global social change has been complex, partial, and incomplete. Billions of people still live in authoritarian dynastic state and republican dictatorships. A billion more languish as denizens and subjects in democratic republics. Injustice, inequality, and violence endure. It is important, therefore, to keep both developments—growing liberty and persistent inequality—in mind at the same time. In *Capital*, Karl Marx urged readers to take a dialectical approach to understanding social change. He asked them to appreciate the contradictory character of unequal social relations, understand how people's struggle for equality might transform these relations, and recognize that social change would create relations characterized by new contradictions. In the United States, social movements abolished slavery and transformed unequal social relations, but these changes led to a new set of unequal relations under Jim Crow. People's efforts changed the meaning of inequality, but they did not eliminate it. By holding two contradictory ideas in mind at the same time, by recognizing that liberty and inequality advance together, one might view global social change during the past two hundred years with both optimism and a realistic appreciation that change has had real limits.

SOCIAL CHANGE *AND* SOCIAL MOVEMENTS

This book examines social change *and* social movements. This approach contrasts with much of the social movement literature. Many social movement scholars have complained that it is difficult to study both social movements and social change, to determine how social movements actually contributed to change. Sidney Tarrow observes that it has not been "particularly fruitful [for scholars] to examine the outcome of single social movements on their own.[2] Doug McAdam, John McCarthy, and Meyer Zald observe that "it is somewhat surprising that movement scholars were slow to devote systematic empirical attention to the crucial issue of 'outcomes and impacts.'"[3] Paul Burstein, Rachel Einwohner, and Jocelyn Hollander agree: "The field of social movements grew tremendously in the 1970s and 1980s, but the study of social movement outcomes did not. . . . [The result is] that we still know very little about the impact of social movements on social change."[4] William Gamson said simply: "Success is an elusive idea."[5]

"Overall, researchers have managed to demonstrate relatively few effects of social movements on their society,"[6] Goodwin and Jasper observe. Their colleagues McAdam, McCarthy and Zald agree, arguing that social movement scholars found it a "daunting methodological challenge" to determine the relation between social movements and social change because the connection between them may be "spurious" and because it is difficult for scholars to identify the causal mechanisms that link a particular movement activity to a specific policy change or social outcome to "the specific processes that account for the causal impact."[7] Goodwin and Jasper dismiss efforts to link social movements with social change, arguing that "scholars of social movements would like to believe that the mobilizations they study affect the course of history, but usually they have had to assert this without much good evidence."[8]

Suzanne Staggenborg agrees with McAdam, McCarthy, and Zald that "outcomes are the most difficult aspects to evaluate," though she says it was difficult to determine outcomes both because movements produced lots of outcomes and provoked "counter-movements," which produced different "rounds" of outcomes, and because causality was difficult to determine in a context of reciprocating change and struggle.[9]

These are fairly cynical views of change. If social movements did not make change or affect the course of history, who or what did? The market? Adam Smith's "invisible hand?" In many respects, social movement scholars have adopted a Hegelian perspective of history, insofar as they imagine history moving forward without the conscious participation of human beings.

Scholars who started with social movements and then tried to link them to specific outcomes and social changes have encountered many difficulties. Given the problems inherent in this approach, they might instead consider the alternative framework outlined here. By starting with social change, it is easier then to determine how social movements advanced, assisted, and resisted change.

This book takes a global, historical view of social change and social movements. It follows in the footsteps of Charles Tilly, Sidney Tarrow, E. P. Thompson, Eric Hobsbawm, and Immanuel Wallerstein, who examined the emergence of social movement organizations that contributed to what David Meyer and Sidney Tarrow describe as a "social movement society."[10] Tilly and Tarrow argue that social movement organizations and the social movement society first emerged in the late eighteenth century, while Wallerstein argues that the discovery of "organization" by social movements in 1848 was "the great innovation in the technology of rebellion," an invention that helped "prepare the ground politically for fundamental social change."[11]

The argument here is that the American, French, and Haitian revolutions invited citizens, denizens, and subjects to make change, not only by organizing political parties and social movement organizations but also by struggling, as individuals and as participants of social networks, often in disorganized or unorganized ways, to claim "liberty, equality, and solidarity" and so shape the direction and meaning of social change. By 1800, citizens, denizens, and subjects organized different kinds of social movements (aspiring, altruistic, and restrictionist) that engaged in a variety of actions or "repertoires" (among them lawsuits and hunger strikes, riots and rebellion, electoral campaigns and legislation) to obtain liberty, equality, and solidarity by creating democratic and republican institutions. Their determined and ongoing efforts shaped global social and political change.

Of course, other scholars have examined many of the social movements that "challenged authority," what I have called "aspiring movements." Ralph Turner and Lewis Killian in 1957 described collective behavior as "forms of social behavior in which . . . people collectively transcend, bypass, or subvert established institutional patterns and structures"; William Kornhauser argued that "mass movements mobilize people who . . . do not believe in the legitimacy of the established ruler, and who therefore are ready to engage in efforts to destroy it"; Tilly argued that challengers outside the policy resort to collective action to make their voices heard; and Tarrow defined movements "as collective challenges by people with common purpose and solidarity in sustained interaction with elites, opponents, and authorities."[12]

Although this was a useful starting point, these scholars defined social movements in narrow terms. They did not examine movements in relation to other movements, particularly those that defended "authority." They did not consider how these movements related to people with different social statuses as citizens, denizens, and subjects or to different kinds of "authority" in dynastic states, dictatorships, and democratic republics.

Other scholars, such as McAdam, McCarthy, and Zald, recognized that churches, foundations, and other "conscience constituents" have provided significant resources to social movements that challenge authority.[13] And some scholars, such as Tilly, recognized that "countermovements," the movements that mobilize "in response to the real or perceived loss of power" or in response to the actions of antiauthoritarian movements, should be studied more closely.[14]

But by defining "conscience constituents" and "countermovements" only in relation to social movements that *challenge* authority, scholars strip what I have called "altruistic" and "restrictionist" movements of any real agency, initiative, or autonomy. The view here is that they have displayed plenty of agency, initiative, and autonomy and shaped change in important ways. As such, they should be treated as social movements, not viewed with condescension or hostility. Of course, this means abandoning the definition of social movements adopted by many scholars who focus in the literature on groups that challenge authority.

Scholars who contributed to the social movement literature used the sociological theories of Emile Durkheim to study "collective behavior," used Max Weber's ideas to examine social movement "organizations," and used Robert Michels's theories to analyze bureaucratic organizations and political parties. This book suggests that scholars reassess their assumptions about, and reliance on, the theories provided by Durkheim, Weber, and Michels.

DURKHEIM

Before and after World War II, many scholars used Durkheim to study the "collective behavior" of mobs.[15] Drawing on Durkheim, they made three related arguments. First, they argued that riots and other kinds of demonstrative public behavior by mobs and social networks were the product either of the "strains" experienced by subordinate or disadvantaged groups or as a result of the "breakdown" or collapse of public order or "social control" on everyday, "quotidian" routines. "When the quotidian is disrupted then, routinized patterns of action are rendered problematic and the natural attitude is fractured," Snow and others have argued.[16]

Second, they argued that the response of mobs to "strain" or "breakdown" was typically irrational, a form of deviant or criminal behavior.[17] Gustave Le Bon argued that "when the crowd acts, it becomes a mob," and that mobs "reduce otherwise rational adults" to the "impulsiveness, irritability, incapacity to reason, the absence of judgment and the critical spirit, the exaggerations of sentiments one typically finds in *children*" (italics added).[18] (Note that Le Bon's depiction of people in mobs as "childlike" is an epithet, an expression of contempt. "Childlike" has long been used as a slur used to demean diverse subaltern groups.) Third, they argued that because riots were spontaneous and disorganized, it was difficult for mobs to make any significant or lasting change.[19] This view of riotous mobs was widely shared. As Wallerstein argues, many subordinated groups "were rambunctious in their various ways," but their riots and rebellions were short-lived and "served as safety valves for pent-up anger or . . . as mechanisms that . . . set minor limits to the exploitative process," and, as a result, "spontaneous violence had the effect of throwing paper on a fire. The fire flamed up but quickly went out. Such violence was not a very durable fuel."[20]

Charles and Louise Tilly challenged this perspective. They argued that because "strain" was a constant feature of capitalist society, it could not be used to explain why and when riots erupted when they did. They also challenged the idea that mobs were irrational, arguing that mobs had rational motives and purposeful goals.[21] Still, the Tillys and Wallerstein agreed that riotous mobs did not contribute much to social change. As a result, Tilly famously rejected Durkheim and embraced Marx and Weber, describing himself as "doggedly anti-Durkheim, resolutely pro-Marxian, but sometimes indulgent to Weber and sometimes reliant on [John Stuart] Mill."[22] Tilly and many other scholars then abandoned Durkheim and the study of "collective behavior" and embraced Weber (and sometimes Marx) and the study of social movement *organizations*, which had the ability to make rational choices and the capacity to make lasting and significant social change.[23] Most social movement scholars heeded Tilly's advice and joined a paradigm shift from Durkheim and collective behavior to Weber and social movement organizations.[24]

But scholars might revisit Durkheim for several reasons. First, individuals, social networks, and mobs have engaged in spontaneous and planned demonstrative public behavior that shaped social change. Although many scholars dismissed the capacity of individual and informal social networks to make change and asserted that real change was made only by durable social movement organizations, there is considerable evidence that individuals and informal groups were effective at advancing, assisting, and resisting change: mobs in Cairo transformed the political landscape in Egypt; white lynch mobs in the Jim Crow South enforced the subordination of black denizens.

The fact that individuals, alone or as part of social networks, conducted hunger strikes, self-immolations, and other kinds of risky, suicidal behavior to protest inequality and demand liberty suggests that Durkheim's theory about suicide might usefully apply to an examination of Mohandas Gandhi, Bobby Sands and IRA hunger strikers, Tunisians and Tibetan monks who burned themselves to protest dictatorship, or Black Panther cofounder Huey P. Newton, who wrote a book called *Revolutionary Suicide*. Of course, Durkheim's ideas are not the only ones that might be used to understand how and why individuals and social groups make change or why their activity takes different forms (lawsuits or hunger strikes, migrations or riots).

Second, individuals and social groups act not only in response to social inequality or the "strains" they experience as citizens, denizens, and subjects and as a way to seize the political opportunities associated with the breakdown of authority, but also in response to the crackdowns mounted by state authorities and nonstate actors, to situations such as the police brutality that triggered the Watts and Rodney King riots in Los Angeles. The scholars who used Durkheim to study collective behavior treated strain as relatively uniform and constant, which made it difficult for them to explain why people who experienced strain might suddenly riot. But if they recognized that people experience very different kinds of social inequality, which might intensify or suddenly become transparent, it might become easier to explain why protest erupts in some circumstances and not others, for instance, why gay youths resisted the police raid at Stonewall. They also need to recognize that dominant groups also riot, not because they experience strain but because they want to assert their authority and use violence to put subaltern people in their place. Durkheim did not appreciate the "police riots" waged by state authorities or the "white riots" conducted by nonstate citizenries.

WEBER

During the 1970s, social movement scholars abandoned Durkheim and adopted Weber, arguing that social movement organizations were rational actors that could make effective social change. Tilly and Wallerstein argued that organization was an important strategic innovation that allowed movements to challenge authority on a permanent basis and seek substantive, even "revolutionary" change. Other scholars used Weber's approach to analyze how social movement organizations "mobilized resources," seized "political opportunities," and "framed" issues to their advantage.[25] These scholars made important contributions to the study of *social movements*, though perhaps less to an understanding of *social change*, for reasons that we have discussed.

Although Weber's ideas informed much of the social movement literature, scholars might reconsider two assertions that are central to his approach. First, Weber argued that the state was an institution that possessed a monopoly on the legitimate use of physical force. Plainly, this has *never* been true. It has not been true even in dictatorships that possess an overwhelming superiority over domestic populations. In China, for example, the regime, strong as it is, nonetheless licenses nonstate actors to arrest and detain dissident petitioners in unofficial "black jails" and forcibly return or "deport" them to their hometowns.[26] Moreover, the Chinese regime, like most states around the world, gives male nonstate actors the authority to use physical force against household members.

As we have seen, social movements fought to restrict and restrain the kind of physical force that state officials might legitimately use, for example, demanding an end to the use of the death penalty and corporal punishment. Their efforts have redefined the meaning of what Weber called the legitimate use of force.

Social movements also demanded that state officials revoke the authority they routinely gave to male nonstate actors to use violence against intimates and strangers on their own initiative. In a sense, social movements have urged state officials to *monopolize* or consolidate the legitimate use of physical force in their hands, an effort that was initiated by social movements, *not* by state officials. Social movements demanded that the state act *like* the state that Weber imagined. Although no state has yet monopolized the legitimate use of force, states have gradually restricted and reduced the scope of legal violence by nonstate actors.

These developments suggest that scholars reconsider their assumptions about the relation between violence and the state. They might also reevaluate their assumptions about the relation between violence and social movements, which too often champion violence. Charles Tilly argued that "the participants in European collective violence knew what they were doing" and that the fit between grievances, actions, and demands "is far too good to justify thinking of participation in collective violence as impulsive, unreflective, spur-of-the-moment."[27] Many scholars justify the use of violence by social movements as "effective and rational" by citing Gamson, who argued that violence "should be viewed as an instrumental act aimed at furthering the purposes of the group that uses it when they have some reason to think it will help their cause. . . . Unruly groups that use violence . . . have better than average success. . . . With respect to violence and success, it appears better to give than to receive."[28]

But Gamson's argument that violence is a rational and effective strategy is an extremely dubious assertion based on faulty assumptions and methods. He drew these conclusions from a small, biased sample. Much of the violence included in his data set was deployed by white male citizens who, during the nineteenth century in the United States, were effectively licensed or deputized by state officials to organize lynch mobs, break strikes, or attack immigrants. Because they were deputized and their violence legitimated either by the state or by juries of their peers, who allowed them to commit violent crimes without penalty, it should not be surprising that Gamson found that violence was a "successful" and "effective" strategy for social movements. Unfortunately, this egregiously flawed study, which was the product of a misguided methodology, ignored both the social standing of the actors and victims and the historical context in which the violence occurred. Its findings blinded many scholars to the social character of violence in the United States and in other republics and persuaded them to endorse, uncritically, the use of violence by social movements and ignore the male character of violence.

Scholars might also reexamine a second assumption by Weber, who argued that bureaucracy was a "superior" form of organization. "The decisive reason for the advance of bureaucratic organization has always been its purely *technical* superiority over any other form of organization," Weber asserted.[29] Many social movement scholars have agreed, arguing that organization was an important strategic innovation that allowed social movements to challenge authority on an ongoing basis and make revolutionary social change.

Some scholars demurred from this view. In *Poor People's Movements*, Frances Fox Piven and Richard Cloward challenged the assumption that change was best made by bureaucratic social movement organizations and argued instead that real power was "mobilized, not organized."[30] They argued that factory workers "had their greatest influence . . . *before* they were organized into unions. This power was not rooted in organization, but in their capacity to disrupt the economy."[31] As soon as unions entered the factory, they became "collaborators in the process that emasculated the movement."[32]

Although Piven and Cloward gave a telling critique of many Weberian social movement organizations, such as unions, and offered a stout defense of *un*organized forms of protest, scholars might recognize that the efficacy of social movements (organized and unorganized) may depend on the kind of authorities that aspiring movements challenge. For example, the poor people's movements heralded by Piven and Cloward—local and autonomous grassroots labor, civil rights, and welfare movements—were effective when they campaigned against *local* public officials and *private* employers. This has often been the case. The grassroots environmental groups that organized against toxic chemicals and nuclear power were successful because they could pressure local public officials, public utility companies, and private employers to change their practices and policies.[33] But environmental movements that relied on grassroots forms of mobilization foundered when they confronted *central* government authorities. For example, while grassroots anti–nuclear power activists successfully forced public utility companies to abandon nuclear power, grassroots activists who opposed the development of nuclear weapons and the arms race failed to persuade federal authorities to abandon nuclear weapons.[34] When they confronted central government authorities, grassroots groups of the sort that Piven and Cloward champion have often been *in*effective, while the large bureaucratic organizations celebrated by Weberian scholars—Solidarity in Poland, the African National Congress in South Africa—successfully challenged centralized authority. The ability of social movements to make change depends both on their objectives and on the kind of social structures they challenge or defend. Instead of asserting theoretically that one form of mobilization is superior to another (grassroots mobilizations v. bureaucratic organizations), scholars might consider the historical context and social relations and then demonstrate empirically which one might be more appropriate.

MICHELS

Piven and Cloward criticized Weberian social movement organizations because they believed that disruptive grassroots mobilizations made change more effectively and because they agreed with the argument made by political scientist Robert Michels that bureaucratic organization leads inevitably to "oligarchy," or the rule by a few, which then co-opts movements and stifles or obstructs real change.[35]

Many Weberian scholars agree that while organization is an effective instrument of change, it also leads to oligarchy, or at least to the "professionalization" of movement organizations. Because oligarchic organizations may be effective, many scholars insist that oligarchy is not necessarily a bad thing. Vladimir Lenin argued that oligarchic forms of social movement organization, such as a "vanguard" party led by a small, disciplined cadre of professional revolutionaries, were a more effective instrument of change than their more democratic counterparts.

While scholars have disagreed about the consequences of oligarchy—Piven and Cloward argued that it *inhibited* change, Lenin and others maintained that it *facilitated* change—they both agreed that bureaucratic forms of organization inevitably led to oligarchy, a pattern so common that Michels described it as an "iron law."

Of course, social movements often changed their character during the course of struggle. Spontaneous grassroots mobilizations created organizations that came to be dominated by professional elites. Aspiring movements that fought to obtain citizenship and suffrage later worked to prevent others from becoming citizens. But these developments were not inevitable, the product of some iron law, as Michels and others have argued.

Proof of this is simple. If Michels were correct, then dynastic states, which were run by powerful oligarchies and disciplined bureaucracies, would never have surrendered power to colonial subjects, the factions that established dictatorships and created monstrous oligarchic bureaucracies would never have been overthrown, and the global corporate bureaucracies that once bestrode the planet, such as Standard Oil, would have survived intact. But these bureaucratic oligarchies all fell, both because factions within them pressed for change from the inside and because dissident groups and competitors challenged them from the outside.

Activists in social movements read Michels. They became aware that oligarchy is an organizational problem. So they took two steps to prevent its emergence. First, they created organizational forms designed to prevent the emergence of oligarchy. Anarchist groups initiated wildcat strikes, riots, and flash mobs. Feminists organized consciousness-raising groups. Grassroots environmental groups practiced participatory democracy and consensus-based decision making. The participants in the "Occupy" movement mobilized people around the world using strategies that they consciously designed to prevent the emergence of organization, bureaucracy, and oligarchy.

Second, social movement activists purposely created diverse and multiple social movement organizations. Organizational diversity created a friendly and sometimes fiercely contentious rivalry among social movement organizations. This often prevented any one group from establishing a monopoly on power and discouraged associated organizations from promoting oligarchy, in part because activists who were denied the ability to participate meaningfully in organizational decision making could exit and join another organization that might be more democratic and accommodating. The economist Albert Hirschman provided an excellent account of this kind of behavior in his book *Exit, Voice, and Loyalty*.[36]

Organizational competition and diversity in the environmental, feminist, and civil rights movements curbed organizational tendencies toward oligarchy.[37] When SDS and NOW were taken over by oligarchies, activists departed. The exit of the Weatherman faction destroyed SDS as an organization. The exit of lesbian and other feminists from NOW created a host of diverse, competitive organizations outside of NOW. The women's movement is both stronger and less oligarchic than it was. These developments suggest that scholars reevaluate Michels's characterization of change in social movement organizations.

They might also rethink the artificial disciplinary distinction between social movements, which are typically studied by sociologists, and political parties, which are typically studied by political scientists. As Buechler observes, "Sociology largely ceded questions of politics to its sister discipline of political science. The latter, in turn, defined its subject matter as the organized and institutionalized dimensions of state, governments, elections, and parties. Because social movements involve extra-institutional elements, they were off the radar screens of political scientists."[38]

OPTIMISM

This book takes an optimistic view of social movements and social change, though its optimism is tempered by a realistic appreciation of its limits. It differs from the pessimistic views of many social movements scholars, who have expressed frustration with the inability of social movements to make change. William G. Martin has argued that "for at least several hundred years . . . successive waves of movements . . . have attacked and destabilized the capitalist world-economy, its hegemonic power, and dominant geo-cultures, and yet, . . . have come to provide legitimacy and the foundation for a new ordering of accumulation and political rule on a world scale."[39] This is a gloomy view of social movements' ability to make change.

This kind of pessimism, which is common in a literature that finds it difficult even to assess whether social movements have *contributed* to appreciable social change, stems from two sources. The first is methodological. Many scholars set a high standard for change. They argue that unless a movement makes a "revolution" or changes *everything* or transforms the capitalist world-system as a *whole*, then it changes *nothing*. Moreover, movements that make minor changes or "reforms" may actually strengthen the system and make things worse.

But scholars need not set the bar so high. They might recognize that the slow, partial, and incremental changes made by social movements may be significant nonetheless. By all accounts, the individuals and small groups that fought to end the laws against interracial marriage or make contraceptives widely available to married and unmarried couples, heterosexuals and homosexuals, made modest change. It might be easy to dismiss them as reformists who made no real change. But one might also argue that they did much more: they transformed race and gender relations, changed the meaning of marriage, the reproductive decisions made by women, and the demographic contours of people living in the United States and countries around the world.

Cynicism too often rationalizes *in*action. The perspective here is that action by social movements is better than inaction because action, even when it is misguided, has at least *some* chance of making change, while inaction has *no* chance of making change.

The optimism advocated here does not require people to blind themselves to persistent inequality or harrowing violence. It asks only that people recognize that the changes they advance will likely be partial, complex, and subject to reverse. As Martin Luther King Jr. observed, "Let us realize the arc of the moral universe is long but it bends toward justice."[40]

Pessimism also stems from a second source: recent experience. The recent failure of many "revolutionary" nationalist, socialist, and religious movements to promote democracy or economic development in many post-colonial republics, the collapse of the labor movement, the inability of civil rights, feminist, youth, immigrant, and gay and lesbian movements to secure social equality, and the rise of restrictionist movements and violent male groups that attack women and girls has persuaded many scholars to adopt a pessimistic view of social movements and their ability to make constructive change. Of course, inequality persists. But social movements face *different* challenges today than they did in the past. Gone are the dynastic empires that sent Cortez to the Americas and slave traders to Africa; the fascist regimes that committed genocide and waged worldwide wars to establish slave-based empires; the dictatorships that conducted dirty wars and throttled liberty in southern and eastern Europe, Latin America, East Asia, and North Africa; the segregated social systems imposed by Jim Crow states and apartheid governments in South Africa; and much of the violence that male authorities routinely inflicted on women, children, students, servants, workers, conscripts, convicts, and slaves. Social movements fought to extinguish these evils. By any measure, the dynastic states, dictatorships, and restrictionist movements that threaten liberty, promote inequality, and relish violence today are *lesser* evils.

If one takes a long view, there is considerable evidence that social movements have transformed social relations and produced a rising tide of global social change. Of course, change, like the tide, advances and retreats. But just as global warming, which is a product of human agency, has lifted the seas, social movements have raised the waterline and lifted the sands, so we now stand, between waves, on higher ground.

Notes

1. SOCIAL MOVEMENTS AND GLOBAL SOCIAL CHANGE

1. In Europe, there were a few small city-state republics. See George Athan Billias, *American Constitutionalism around the World, 1776–1989: A Global Perspective* (New York: New York University Press, 2009), 26. After the French conquered the Netherlands, they established the "Batavian Republic" in 1795, but the area was merely occupied by France and was not a sovereign state or a republic. In 1806, Napoleon Bonaparte unilaterally turned it into the Kingdom of Holland and placed his brother Louis on the throne.

2. Robert K. Schaeffer, *Red Inc.: Dictatorship and the Development of Capitalism in China, 1949 to the Present* (Boulder, CO: Paradigm, 2012).

3. "Today more than half of the countries in the world have followed America's lead by making . . . declarations of independence, thereby changing the course of global history from a world of empires in 1776 to the modern world of [republican] nation-states." Billias, *American Constitutionalism*, 4, 14.

4. As Charles Tilly noted, "Even today's democratic states exclude children, prisoners and certified incompetents from some citizenship rights." However, this list is suggestive, not exhaustive. Charles Tilly, "Where Do Rights Come From?" in *Democracy, Revolution and History*, ed. Theda Skocpol (Ithaca, NY: Cornell University Press, 1998), 58.

5. As Wallerstein has argued, "Inside the states, attempts by groups to achieve inclusion as citizens became a central focus of the anti-systemic movements, that is, organizations which seek to bring about fundamental changes in social organization." *World-System Analysis: An Introduction* (Durham: Duke University Press, 2004), 67.

6. "The American states . . . represented a form of government all but forgotten at the time," Charles Bright argued. Charles Bright, "The State in the United States during the Nineteenth Century," in *Statemaking and Social Movements: Essays in History and Theory*, ed. Charles Bright and Susan Harding (Ann Arbor: University of Michigan Press, 1984), 126. The motto on the Great Seal of the United States lays claim to a novel form of government: "*Novus ordo seclorum*: 'A New Order of the Ages.'" Billias, *American Constitutionalism*, 5.

7. Bright, "The State in the United States," 128.

8. Thomas O. Ott, *The Haitian Revolution, 1798–1804* (Knoxville: University of Tennessee Press, 1973).

9. Of course, this is subject to reversal. The government in Hungary recently announced that it had dropped "Republic" from its name, a step that opposition parties argued was a sign that the ruling party had repudiated constitutional government. Palko Karasz and Melissa Eddy, "Opposition Protests Constitution in Hungary," *New York Times*, January 3, 2012.

10. See Robert Schaeffer, *Warpaths: The Politics of Partition* (New York: Hill and Wang, 1990); Robert Schaeffer, *Severed States: Dilemmas of Democracy in a Divided World* (Lanham, MD: Rowman and Littlefield, 1999).

11. See Robert Schaeffer, *Power to the People: Democratization around the World* (Boulder, CO: Westview, 1997).

12. Jeffree Gettleman, "Accounts Emerge in South Sudan of 3,000 Deaths in Ethnic Violence," *New York Times*, January 6, 2012.

13. Jeffrey Gettleman, "Born in Unity, South Sudan Is Torn Again," *New York Times*, January 13, 2012.

14. Robert Schaeffer, "Dilemmas of Sovereignty and Citizenship in the Republican Interstate System," in *The Constitutional and Political Regulation of Ethnic Relations and Conflicts*, ed. Mitja Zagar, Boris Jesih, and Romana Bester (Ljubljana: Institute for Ethnic Studies, 1999), 11–12.

Of course, individuals have multiple identities, which are based on their age, gender, ethnicity, class, religion, and mental or physical health, among other things. Each identity is assigned a different place in the social hierarchy. As a result, people with multiple social identities often simultaneously inhabit different places in the social hierarchy and experience what feminist scholars describe as a set of "intersecting and overlapping hierarchies." The place or identity that is most salient for an individual at any given time depends on whether it is mobilized by institutions in the state or civil society or by social networks and social movements, or whether people develop a self-conscious recognition of that place based on their personal experience or "situated knowledge," as Donna Haraway calls it. See Torry Dickinson and Robert Schaeffer, *Transformations: Feminist Pathways to Global Change* (Boulder, CO: Paradigm, 2009), 3–4.

15. "Today, virtually every country claims that its citizens are all equal, and exercise their sovereignty through a system of universal suffrage. Except we know in reality this is not really so. Only part of the population exercise the full rights of citizens in most countries. . . . The 'people,' which began as a concept of inclusion, rather quickly turned into a concept of exclusion," Wallerstein argues. *World-System Analysis*, 51.

16. Sidney Tarrow, *Power in Movement: Social Movements and Contentious Politics* (New York: Cambridge University Press, 1998), 4.

17. Julie Bosman, "The Case of Loving v. Bigotry," *New York Times Magazine*, January 1, 2012, 39; Jessica Cumberbatch Anderson, "'The Loving Story' Takes Intimate Look at Virginia's First Legal Interracial Marriage," *Huffington Post* (blog), January 18, 2012, http://www.huffingtonpost.com/2012/01/18/the-loving-story-takes-intimate-look-at-first-legal-interracial-marriage_n_1213451.html.

18. James Joll, *The Second International* (New York: Harper Colophon, 1966), 56.

19. This issue is the subject of considerable debate. Chinese authorities argue that the protests are "orchestrated" by Tibetan organizations (the Dalai Lama) and Buddhist monks and have closed monasteries and arrested monks. But some writers have argued that the protests are the work of individuals who are joined by shared ideas, *not* linked by any affiliation with a social network or membership in an organization. If the latter is true, it may be difficult for Chinese authorities to suppress the protests, precisely because they are not "organized." See

Sharon LaFraniere, "More Monks Die by Fire in Protest of Beijing," *New York Times*, January 10, 2012; Jeffrey Bartholet, "Aflame: A Wave of Self-Immolation Sweeps Tibet," *New Yorker*, July 8 and 15, 2013.

20. Nada Bakri, "Self-Immolation Is on the Rise in the Arab World," *New York Times*, January 21, 2010.

21. Robert K. Schaeffer, "The Chains of Bondage Broke: The Proletarianization of Seafaring Labor, 1600–1800," PhD diss., State University of New York, Binghamton, 1984.

22. William G. Martin, *Making Waves: Worldwide Social Movements, 1750–2005* (Boulder, CO: Paradigm, 2008), 6.

23. Tarrow, *Power in Movement*, 25. McAdam and Snow argued that "it is somewhat surprising that movement scholars were slow to devote systematic empirical attention to the crucial issues of 'outcomes and impacts.'" Doug McAdam and David A Snow, eds., *Readings on Social Movements: Origins, Dynamics, and Outcomes* (New York: Oxford University Press, 2010), 659.

2. THE NEW REPUBLIC

1. George Athan Billias, *American Constitutionalism around the World, 1776–1989: A Global Perspective* (New York: New York University Press, 2009), 18.

2. See Billias, *American Constitutionalism*, 9–10.

3. See Immanuel Wallerstein, *The Modern World-System: Capitalist Agriculture and the Origins of the European World-Economy in the Sixteenth Century* (New York: Academic, 1974).

4. Wallerstein, *Modern World-System*, 349.

5. Immanuel Wallerstein, *Historical Capitalism with Capitalist Civilization* (London: Verso, 1996), 132.

6. Wallerstein, *Modern World-System*, 242. "In both countries, the feudal aristocracies had largely converted themselves into capitalist farmers and were playing a large role in non-agricultural activities. In both countries, those who were not aristocrats also played significant roles as capitalist entrepreneurs in agriculture, commerce, and industry, and the non-aristocratic bourgeoisie was sooner or later rewarded with access to higher status." Immanuel Wallerstein, *The Modern World-System II: Mercantilism and the Consolidation of the European World-Economy, 1600–1750* (New York: Academic, 1980), 119.

7. "This last element, the politics of the class struggle, is the key to the others," Wallerstein argues. Wallerstein, *Modern World-System II*, 113, 115, 120. See also Wallerstein, *Historical Capitalism*, 50–55, 57, 63; Immanuel Wallerstein, *World-Systems Analysis: An Introduction* (Durham: Duke University Press, 2004), 46–51.

8. Wallerstein, *Modern World-System*, 195.

9. Wallerstein, *Modern World-System*, 196.

10. Wallerstein, *Modern World-System*, 191. Wallerstein argues that much the same was true in France, where the "state machinery was at once too strong and too weak" (263).

11. Wallerstein, *Modern World-System*, 184.

12. Although states recognized one another as "sovereign," Wallerstein argues that "their degree of autonomy [was] strictly limited." Immanuel Wallerstein, *Unthinking Social Science: The Limits of Nineteenth-Century Paradigms* (Cambridge: Polity, 1991), 35. "The modern state has never been a completely autonomous entity. The states developed and were shaped as

integral parts of the interstate system, which was a set of rules within which the states had to operate and a set of legitimations without which states could not survive. From the point of view of the state machineries of any given state, the interstate system represents constraints on its will." Wallerstein, *Historical Capitalism*, 56–57.

13. Wallerstein, *Historical Capitalism*, 48.

14. Charles Tilly, "Where Do Rights Come From?" in *Democracy, Revolution and History*, ed. Theda Skocpol (Ithaca, NY: Cornell University Press, 1998), 63.

15. When American settlers in the British colonies demanded representation in Parliament so that they would not be subjected to taxes without their consent, a British official said that while they could not expect to represent *themselves* in Parliament, they would nonetheless be "virtually represented" there. As Edmund S. Morgan explains, "Parliament could tax the colonists because they [already] *were* represented there; and he invented a term for his argument that has been with us ever since, 'virtual representation': the colonists might not vote for representatives in the Commons, but neither did most Englishmen. They were not actually but 'virtually' represented. Every member of the House of Commons represented, not only the constituents who chose him, but all the king's subjects, not only in Great Britain but in the colonies too." Edmund S. Morgan, *Inventing the People: The Rise of Popular Sovereignty in England and America* (New York: Norton, 1988), 240.

16. As Sellers explains, "States that actually [protect the common good of the people as a whole] are 'republics,' because they protect the (*"res publica"*) or common good of the people." M. N. S. Sellers, *Republican Legal Theory: The History, Constitution and Purposes of Law in a Free State* (Houndmills, UK: Palgrave Macmillan, 2003), 64.

17. Gordon S. Wood, *The Radicalism of the American Revolution* (New York: Knopf, 1992), 169.

18. Sellers, *Republican Legal Theory*, 21.

19. John Markoff, *Waves of Democracy: Social Movements and Political Change* (Thousand Oaks, CA: Pine Forge, 1996), 41.

20. Wood, *Radicalism of the American Revolution*, 162.

21. Morgan, *Inventing the People*, 123. See also the contractual legacy of the Mayflower Compact in Richard D. Brown, "The Ideal of the Written Constitution: A Political Legacy of the Revolution," in *Legacies of the American Revolution*, ed. Larry R. Gerlach (Provo: Utah State University Press, 1978), 86.

22. Alexander Hamilton, James Madison, and John Jay, *The Federalist: A Commentary on the Constitution of the United States* (New York: Tudor, 1937), 161–64.

23. During the proceedings of the Continental Congress, Judge Drayton argued, "It is therefore undeniable that George the Third had also broken the original contract between king and people." James H. Kettner, *The Development of American Citizenship, 1608–1870* (Chapel Hill: University of North Carolina Press, 1978), 169.

24. Kettner, *American Citizenship*, 171.

25. Billias, *American Constitutionalism*, xi, 9–10.

26. Billias, *American Constitutionalism*, 9.

27. The Scottish philosopher David Hume noted, with irony, that the only person who actually gets to choose, on a voluntary basis, whether to subscribe to the social contract is the *immigrant*. The native-born citizen has no such opportunity. David Hume, "Of the Original Contract," in *Social Contract: Essays By Locke, Hume, and Rousseau*, introduction by Ernest Barker (New York: Oxford University Press, 1962), 156–57.

28. Adam Liptak, "'We the People' Loses Followers," *New York Times*, February 7, 2012.

29. Billias, *American Constitutionalism*, 62.

30. Hamilton, Madison, and Jay, *Federalist*, 62.

31. Hamilton, Madison, and Jay, *Federalist*, 63. Rousseau also expressed a fear of faction, "by which he meant any group, large or small, acting in its own private interests." Sellers, *Republican Legal Theory*, 21; Sung Bok Kim, "The American Revolution and the Modern World," in *Legacies of the American Revolution*, ed. Larry R. Gerlach (Provo: Utah State University Press, 1978), 225.

32. Cecelia Kenyon, "Originality Underestimated," in *Men of Little Faith: Selected Writings of Cecelia Kenyon*, ed. Stanley Elkins, Eric McKitrick, and Leo Weinstein (Boston: University of Massachusetts Press, 2002), 94.

33. Sellers, *Republican Legal Theory*, 9.

34. Sellers, *Republican Legal Theory*, 88. As Kenyon argues, "The chief improvement in government, in modern times, has been the complete separation of the great distractions of power, placing the *legislature* in different hands from those which hold the *executive*; and again severing the *judicial* part from the ordinary *administrative*. 'When the legislative and executive powers . . . are united in the same person, or in the same body of magistrates, there can be no liberty.'" Kenyon, "Originality Underestimated," 45, 46.

35. Pennsylvania, Vermont, and Georgia were the only states with unicameral legislatures. Alfred F. Young, *Liberty Tree: Ordinary People and the American Revolution* (New York: New York University Press, 2006), 188.

36. Young, *Liberty Tree*, 193.

37. Hamilton, Madison, and Jay, *Federalist*, 380. "Had every Athenian citizen been a Socrates, every Athenian assembly would still have been a mob," Madison complained.

38. Charles Bright, "The State in the United States during the Nineteenth Century," in *Statemaking and Social Movements: Essays in History and Theory*, ed. Charles Bright and Susan Harding (Ann Arbor: University of Michigan Press, 1984), 124–25. Kenyon, "Originality Underestimated," 34, 110.

39. Bright, "The State in the United States," 125–26; Young, *Liberty Tree*, 200–201.

40. Kenyon, "Originality Underestimated," 53.

41. Young, *Liberty Tree*, 194.

42. Young, *Liberty Tree*, 235.

43. Kenyon, "Originality Underestimated," 55.

44. Frances Fox Piven, *Challenging Authority: How Ordinary People Change America* (Lanham, MD: Rowman and Littlefield, 2006), 62, 64; Morgan, *Inventing the People*, 274.

45. Piven, *Challenging Authority*, 70.

46. Brown, "The Ideal of the Written Constitution," 90.

47. Brown, "The Ideal of the Written Constitution," 90, 91.

48. Liptak, "'We the People.'"

49. Gerbach, *Legacies*, 12; Alexander Keyssar, *The Right to Vote: The Contested History of Democracy in the United States* (New York: Basic, 2009), 2, 20–21.

50. Hamilton, Madison, and Jay, *Federalist*, 68. Madison urged his peers to expand the boundaries of the state and encourage immigration of diverse people to "make it less probable that a majority of the whole will have a common motive to invade the rights of other citizens; or if such a common motive exists, it will be more difficult for all who feel it to *discover* their own strength and to act in unison with each other" (italics added) (69, 339–40, 357–58; Morgan, *Inventing the People*, 268–69, 273).

51. Max Weber, "Politics as a Vocation," available at http://anthropos-lab.net/wp/wp-content/uploads/2011/12/Weber-Politics-as-a-Vocation.pdf.

52. Wood, *Radicalism of the American Revolution*, 49, 54–55, 72–73, 89.

53. Kenneth Finegold and Theda Skocpol, "State, Party, and Industry: From Business Recovery to the Wagner Act in America's New Deal," in *Statemaking and Social Movements:*

Essays in History and Theory, ed. Charles Bright and Susan Harding (Ann Arbor: University of Michigan Press, 1984), 162.

54. Martin Carnoy, *The State and Political Theory* (Princeton, NJ: Princeton University Press, 1984), 218.

55. Carnoy, *State and Political Theory*, 6.

56. Carnoy, *State and Political Theory*, 219–20.

57. Carnoy, *State and Political Theory*, 5–6.

58. Fred Block pretty much agrees with this formulation: "In order to serve the *general* interests of capital, the state must have some autonomy from *direct* ruling-class control" (italics added). Fred Block, *Revising State Theory: Essays in Politics and Post-Industrialism* (Philadelphia: Temple University Press, 1987), 53. However, Block goes on to urge theorists to "reject the idea of a class-conscious ruling class" (53–54).

59. Bright, "The State in the United States," 136.

60. Bright, "The State in the United States," 144.

61. Block, *Revising State Theory*, 84; Bob Jessop, *State Power: A Strategic-Relational Approach* (Cambridge: Polity, 2008), 9.

62. Robert K. Schaeffer, *Red Inc.: Dictatorship and the Development of Capitalism in China, 1949 to the Present* (Boulder: Paradigm, 2011), 37–62.

63. Although the founders thought that parties would be temporary, they soon established themselves as permanent political institutions. "The mass franchise inevitably [gave] rise to mass political parties," which became "*the* central intermediate and intermediary structure between society and government," Frances Fox Piven observed (Piven, *Challenging Authority*, 58).

64. Barbara Clark Smith, "Social Visions of the American Resistance Movement," in *The Transforming Hand of Revolution: Reconsidering the American Revolution as a Social Movement*, ed. Ronald Hoffman and Peter T. Albert (Charlottesville: US Capitol Historical Society and University Press of Virginia, 1995), 27–28.

65. Political scientists such as Joseph Schumpeter and Robert Dahl have argued that citizens responded to the architects' invitation by organizing "an unspecified number of multiple, voluntary, competitive, non-hierarchically ordered and self-determined . . . categories which are not specifically licensed, recognized, subsidized, created, or otherwise controlled by the state" to express their separate interests and persuade the state to address them, a strategy they described as "pluralism." Carnoy, *State and Political Theory*, 37. This is a useful characterization, though its proponents see the state as a "neutral" arbiter of separate and competing interests. The argument here is that the state is not a neutral arbiter. The state invites factions or "interest groups," in the language of Robert Dahl, to express their views but, by dividing power, prevents any one of them from capturing the state and using it to advance their "special interest" in order to protect the state as the representative of the "collective interest" of the capitalist ruling class.

66. David S. Meyer and Sidney Tarrow, eds., *The Social Movement Society: Contentious Politics for a New Century* (Lanham, MD: Rowman and Littlefield, 1998), 4. Tarrow defines a social movement society fairly narrowly, arguing that social movements consist only of permanent and bureaucratic organizations aimed at challenging state authority. But if social movements are more broadly defined to include political parties, mobs, interest groups, social networks, and some individuals, then it could be argued that the social movement society emerged not in the late twentieth century, as Tarrow insists, but in the *eighteenth* century.

67. Young, *Liberty Tree*, 224.

68. Theda Skocpol, "Did the Civil War Further American Democracy? A Reflection on the Expansion of Benefits for Union Veterans," in *Democracy, Revolution and History*, ed. Theda

Skocpol (Ithaca, NY: Cornell University Press, 1998), 73; Allan Kulikoff, "Was the American Revolution a Bourgeois Revolution?" in *The Transforming Hand of Revolution: Reconsidering the American Revolution as a Social Movement*, ed. Ronald Hoffman and Peter T. Albert (Charlottesville: US Capitol Historical Society and University Press of Virginia, 1995), 61.

69. Alfred F. Young, "American Historians Confront 'The Transforming Hand of Revolution,'" in *The Transforming Hand of Revolution: Reconsidering the American Revolution as a Social Movement*, ed. Ronald Hoffman and Peter T. Albert (Charlottesville: US Capitol Historical Society and University Press of Virginia, 1995), 347–48.

70. Young, *Liberty Tree*, 14, 231–32.

71. Wood, *Radicalism of the American Revolution*, 5.

72. Immanuel Wallerstein, *The Modern World-System IV: Centrist Liberalism Triumphant, 1789–1914* (Berkeley: University of California Press, 2011), 145.

73. Billias, *American Constitutionalism*, 88.

74. Wallerstein, *Modern World-System IV*, 145n2, 147n3.

3. THE RISE OF THE REPUBLICS

1. Robert Schaeffer, *Warpaths: The Politics of Partition* (New York: Hill and Wang, 1990), 73–86.

2. In 2011, the United Nations counted 193 members, though there are other states that have not been counted as members or that do not belong. For example, Switzerland does not belong to the United Nations. Steve Coll, "Membership Dues," *New Yorker*, September 26, 2011, 51.

3. Economic development in all three countries and political democracy in Japan was underwritten by US military, economic, and political aid during the first two decades after World War II. See Robert K. Schaeffer, *Power to the People: Democratization around the World* (Boulder, CO: Westview, 1997), 132–58.

4. Immanuel Wallerstein, *The Modern World-System III: The Second Era of Great Expansion of the Capitalist World-Economy, 1730–1840s* (New York: Academic, 1989), 193. The republics they created were ruled either by citizen minorities (see chapter 2) or by dictators who made citizens their subjects. It would not be until 1920, when citizenship was extended to adult women, that citizens represented a majority of inhabitants in first-generation republics in America and in second-generation republics in Europe.

5. Eric J. Hobsbawm, *Primitive Rebels: Studies in Archaic Forms of Social Movements in the 19th and 20th Centuries* (New York: Norton, 1959).

6. Paul A. Gilje, *The Road to Mobocracy: Popular Disorder in New York City, 1763–1834* (Chapel Hill: Institute for Early American History and Culture, University of North Carolina Press, 1987); Paul A. Gilje, *Rioting in America* (Bloomington: Indiana University Press, 1996).

7. Peter Linebaugh and Marcus Rediker, *The Many-Headed Hydra: Sailors, Slaves, Commoners, and the Hidden History of the Revolutionary Atlantic* (Boston: Beacon, 2000).

8. Wallerstein, *World-System III*, 204–6, 207.

9. Wallerstein, *World-System III*, 217–18.

10. Great Britain lost the thirteen colonies but retained possession of all its other colonies in Canada and the Caribbean, decisively defeated the French fleet at the Battle of the Saints in the West Indies, and repulsed the Spanish-French attack on Gibraltar. "These British successes against her European enemies outweighed the defeat at Yorktown," Wallerstein argues. Waller-

stein, *World-System III*, 227. As Arthur Young observed, "it was 'a most extraordinary event in world politics' for [the British] to lose an empire [in North America] 'and to gain by the loss'" (229).

11. Wallerstein, *World-System III*, 240. There were about 24,000 whites, 20,000 mulattoes, and 408,000 black slaves on the French part of the island. Thomas O. Ott, *The Haitian Revolution, 1789–1804* (Knoxville: University of Tennessee Press, 1973), 9; Wallerstein, *World-System III*, 241. The three-sided civil war consisted of three stages: "the Fronde of the important whites; the mulatto revolt, and the Negro revolution" (241).

12. Ott, *Haitian Revolution*, 81. The French lost ten thousand to disease before Napoleon decided to withdraw (170).

13. Ott, *Haitian Revolution*, 93; Wallerstein, *World-System III*, 242.

14. Ott, *Haitian Revolution*, 49, 112, 175, 178, 179.

15. Ott, *Haitian Revolution*, 190. When Dessalines took power in 1804, "he announced that 'the bones of the dead [blacks] would not rest until their blood was avenged,'" and he organized large-scale reprisals, in one case "executing 400 whites in front of [his] headquarters" (190). Ott has argued that Dessalines believed that "extermination . . . was the only way to rid Haiti of the white man" (190). According to John Lynch, "The new regime systematically exterminated the remaining whites," in what might be described as an early form of ethnic cleansing. John Lynch, "The Origins of Spanish American Independence," in *The Independence of Latin America*, ed. Leslie Bethell (Cambridge: Cambridge University Press, 1987), 45.

16. Ott, *Haitian Revolution*, 180.

17. Ott, *Haitian Revolution*, 182.

18. Ott, *Haitian Revolution*, 194–95.

19. Lynch, "Origins," 29. "To Spanish America, Haiti was an example and a warning, observed by rulers and ruled [creoles] alike with growing horror" (45). Wallerstein observed, "The effect of [Haiti] was to instill a great deal of prudence not only in the European powers but above all, among the white settlers of the Americas," many of whom held slaves. Wallerstein, *World-System III*, 244.

20. Wallerstein, *World-System III*, 219–22; Lynch, "Origins," 11, 34, 36–37, 46.

21. Wallerstein, *World-System III*, 249–50.

22. Lynch, "Origins," 48. In Portugal, "the decision to transfer the court to Brazil was regarded by the local population as a cowardly desertion, and ignominious and disorderly flight." David Bushnell, "The Independence of Spanish South America," in *The Independence of Latin America*, ed. Leslie Bethell (Cambridge: Cambridge University Press, 1987), 167.

23. Wallerstein, *World-System III*, 250.

24. D. A. G. Waddell, "International Politics and Latin American Independence," in *The Independence of Latin America*, ed. Leslie Bethell (Cambridge: Cambridge University Press, 1987), 197.

25. Bushnell, "Independence," 108, 137.

26. Bushnell, "Independence," 144; Lynch, "Origins," 6.

27. Bushnell, "Independence," 144.

28. As Wallerstein argued, these republicans were driven both by "the grievance of Creole against the peninsular and the fear that both had of the non-white strata." Wallerstein, *World-System III*, 224.

29. There was also a rebellion by Indians in Peru from 1814 to 1815. Timothy Anna, "The Independence of Mexico and Central America," in *The Independence of Latin America*, ed. Leslie Bethell (Cambridge: Cambridge University Press, 1987), 59–64; Wallerstein, *World-System III*, 250.

30. Anna, "Independence," 63–64.

31. Anna, "Independence," 64.

32. Wallerstein, *World-System III*, 251.

33. Wallerstein, *World-System III*, 252.

34. Wallerstein, *World-System III*, 253.

35. Wallerstein, *World-System III*, 254.

36. Wallerstein, *World-System III*, 254.

37. George Athan Billias, *American Constitutionalism around the World, 1776–1989: A Global Perspective* (New York: New York University Press, 2009), 176; Immanuel Wallerstein, *The Modern World-System IV: Centrist Liberalism Triumphant, 1789–1914* (Berkeley: University of California Press, 2011), 157.

38. Billias, *American Constitutionalism*, 192.

39. Peter N. Stearns, *1848: The Revolutionary Tide in Europe* (New York: Norton, 1974), 33–34; 71–72.

40. Billias, *American Constitutionalism*, 184. For some, the republic they demanded would be a state that was *smaller* than the empire they inhabited, an independent Sicily or Italy. For others, it meant a state *larger* than the one they inhabited, a Germany, not a Saxony.

41. Billias, *American Constitutionalism*, 195; Stearns, *1848*, 107.

42. Stearns, *1848*, 239.

43. Billias, *American Constitutionalism*, 199.

44. Stearns, *1848*, 169.

45. Stearns, *1848*, 155.

46. Stearns, *1848*, 188.

47. Stearns, *1848*, 92.

48. Billias, *American Constitutionalism*, 198; Eric Hobsbawm, *The Age of Revolution: 1789–1848* (New York: New American Library, 1962), 159–60; Stearns, *1848*, 27; Schaeffer, *Warpaths*, 39–40.

49. Schaeffer, *Warpaths*, 40.

50. Wallerstein, *World-System IV*, 161; Wallerstein, *World-System III*, 256.

51. Wallerstein, *World-System IV*, 159.

52. Schaeffer, *Warpaths*, 32–33.

53. Schaeffer, *Warpaths*, 32–33.

54. Schaeffer, *Warpaths*, 33. See James Joll, *The Second International* (New York: Harper Colophon, 1966).

55. B. N. Pandey, *The Breakup of British India* (New York: St. Martin's, 1969), 42.

56. Amos Perlmutter, *Israel: The Partitioned State* (New York: Scribner, 1985), 21.

57. After a civil war, Ireland was divided north and south. In 1922 the southern part became the Irish Free State, which retained some ties with Great Britain. Ireland became a republic only in 1949. The northern part remained part of Great Britain, though with its own parliament and considerable autonomy. Schaeffer, *Warpaths*, 43.

58. Billias, *American Constitutionalism*, 250.

59. Billias, *American Constitutionalism*, 253–67.

60. Lee Burcheit, *Secession: The Legitimacy of Self-Determination* (New Haven, CT: Yale University Press, 1978), 115.

61. V. I. Lenin, *National Liberation, Socialism and Imperialism* (New York: International, 1968), 80; W. Ofautey-Kodjoe, *The Principle of Self-Determination in International Law* (New York: Nellen, 1977), 79.

62. Branko Lazitch and M. Drachkovitch, *Lenin and the Comintern* (Stanford, CA: Hoover Institution, 1972), 369; Burcheit, *Secession*, 100.

63. Schaeffer, *Warpaths*, 47.

64. Jean-Baptiste Duroselle, *From Wilson to Roosevelt: Foreign Policy of the United States* (New York: Harper and Row, 1963), 37.

65. Schaeffer, *Warpaths*, 47–48.

66. Schaeffer, *Warpaths*, 55–57.

67. Schaeffer, *Warpaths*, 58–59.

68. This is a representative list of major actions; it does not include all the various campaigns, counterinsurgencies, and emergencies imposed on colonial peoples by dynastic empires.

69. Anna, "Independence," 71–72.

70. Stearns, *1848*, 170, 197.

71. Britain upgraded the status of its colonies, rebranding them as "Commonwealth nations" instead of "dominions." Schaeffer, *Warpaths*, 62.

72. Reginald Coupland, *The Indian Problem: Report on the Constitutional Problem in India* (London: Oxford University Press, 1944), 1:52–53.

73. Rudolf Von Albertini, *Decolonization* (Garden City, NY: Doubleday, 1971), 85.

74. Coupland, *Indian Problem*, 132.

75. Hugh Kay, *Salazar and Modern Portugal* (New York: Hawthorn, 1970), 68, 70.

76. Raymond Carr and Juan Pablo Fusi Aizpurua, *Spain: Dictatorship to Democracy* (London: George Allen and Unwin, 1979), 17.

77. Paul Preston, *The Politics of Revenge: Fascism and the Military in Twentieth-Century Spain* (London: Unwin Hyman, 1990), 41–42.

78. Iris Chang, *The Rape of Nanking: The Forgotten Holocaust of World War II* (New York: Basic, 1997); John D. Dower, *War without Mercy: Race and Power in the Pacific War* (New York: Pantheon, 1986).

79. John Keegan, *The Second World War* (New York, Viking, 1989), 284, 289.

80. Michael Howard, "The Historical Development of the U.N.'s Role in International Security," in *United Nations, Divided World: The U.N.'s Role in International Relations*, ed. Adam Robert and Benedict Kinsbury (Oxford: Clarendon, 1993), 63.

81. Roger W. Louis, *Imperialism at Bay* (New York: Oxford University Press, 1978), 226.

82. Peter W. Rodman, *More Precious Than Peace: The Cold War and the Struggle for the Third World* (New York: Scribner, 1991), 42.

83. Ruth B. Russell, *A History of the United Nations Charter: The Role of the United States, 1940–1945* (Washington, DC: Brookings Institution, 1958), 83.

84. Robert K. Schaeffer, *Severed States: Dilemmas of Democracy in a Divided World* (Lanham, MD: Rowman and Littlefield, 1999), 14.

85. Schaeffer, *Warpaths*, 76.

86. Schaeffer, *Severed States*, 14–15.

87. Schaeffer, *Power*, 12–13. When they signed the UN Charter, the European colonial powers agreed in article 73 to promise only eventual self-government. But the anticolonial block in the United Nations soon revised the language and insisted on independence, not simply self-government. Schaeffer, *Severed States*, 15.

88. I. Brownlie, "An Essay in the History of the Principle of Self-Determination," in *Grotian Society Papers 1968*, ed. C. H. Alexandrowicz (The Hague: Nijoff, 1970), 98.

89. Arnold Whitridge, *Men in Crisis: The Revolutions of 1848* (New York: Scribner, 1949), 14.

90. Schaeffer, *Severed States*, 16.

91. Schaeffer, *Power*, 17.

92. Schaeffer, *Severed States*, 16.

93. Shigeto Tsuru, *Japan's Capitalism: Creative Defeat and Beyond* (Cambridge: Cambridge University Press, 1993), 68.

94. John Markoff, *Waves of Democracy: Social Movements and Political Change* (Thousand Oaks, CA: Pine Forge, 1996), 78.

95. Richard M. Nixon, *RN: The Memoirs of Richard Nixon* (New York: Warner, 1978), 461. One British member of Parliament complained, "We are sitting here today as the representatives of a victorious people. . . . [But] if a visitor were to come . . . he might well be pardoned for thinking he was listening to the representatives of a vanquished people discussing the . . . penalties of defeat." Malcolm Chalmers, *Paying for Defense* (London: Pluto, 1985), 37.

96. B. N. Pandey, *The Breakup of British India* (New York: St. Martin's, 1969), 160.

97. Schaeffer, *Severed States*, 17.

4. DICTATORSHIP AND DIVISION

1. Factions often claim to make revolution on behalf of the multitude. But this is an erroneous claim. On closer inspection, most of the "revolutionary" republics actually represented only a minority faction of the multitude, such as the Bolsheviks or the Chinese communists, not the majority of the inhabitants. They never obtained the consent of the multitude they claimed to represent.

2. John Lynch, *Caudillos in Spanish America, 1800–1850* (Oxford: Clarendon, 1992), passim.

3. George Athan Billias, *American Constitutionalism around the World, 1776–1989: A Global Perspective* (New York: New York University Press, 2009), 108; Lynch, *Caudillos*; Frank Safford, "Politics, Ideology and Society in Post-independence Spanish America," in *The Cambridge History of Latin America*, vol. 3, *From Independence to c. 1870*, ed. Leslie Bethell (Cambridge: Cambridge University Press, 1985), 381.

4. Lynch, *Caudillos*, 130.

5. The United States is not immune from the efforts of families to establish political dynasties: the Adamses, Roosevelts, Rockefellers, Kennedys, Bushes, Browns, Romneys, Clintons, and Daleys.

6. Safford, "Politics, Ideology and Society," 350.

7. Lynch, *Caudillos*, 426–28.

8. Lynch, *Caudillos*, 8–9.

9. Robert K. Schaeffer, *Warpaths: The Politics of Partition* (New York: Hill and Wang, 1990), 1–45.

10. Schaeffer, *Warpaths*, 41–44.

11. Robert K. Schaeffer, *Power to the People: Democratization around the World* (Boulder, CO: Westview, 1997), 209.

12. Robert K. Schaeffer, *Red Inc.: Dictatorship and the Development of Capitalism in China, 1949 to the Present* (Boulder, CO: Paradigm, 2012), 167–69.

13. Adolf Hitler organized a fairly wide base of support, perhaps about one-third of the electorate, in the elections that brought the Nazi Party to power. See David Schoenbaum, *Hitler's Social Revolution: Class and Status in Nazi Germany 1933–1939* (New York: Doubleday, 1966).

14. Keith S. Rosenn, "The Success of Constitutionalism in the United States and Its Failure in Latin America," in *The U.S. Constitution and the Constitutions of Latin America*, ed. Kenneth W. Thompson (Lanham, MD: University Press of America, 1991), 24–25.

15. Billias, *American Constitutionalism*, 106. Billias has argued that in Latin America, the North American "pattern of presidentialism proved to be a disaster" (105, 106).

16. Safford, "Politics, Ideology and Society," 349–50.

17. Billias, *American Constitutionalism*, 112.

18. Schaeffer, *Power*, 195–99.

19. John Lynch, *Argentine Caudillo: Juan Manuel de Rosas*, 2nd ed. (Wilmington, DE: Scholarly Resources, 2001), 90.

20. T. E. Vadney, *The World since 1945* (London: Penguin, 1992), 98.

21. David Barboza, "Seeking to Tap Olympic Pride, Western Ads Cheerlead for China," *New York Times*, July 20, 2008.

22. Richard W. Lombardi, *Debt Trap: Rethinking the Logic of Development* (New York: Praeger, 1985), 86; Robert K. Schaeffer, *Understanding Globalization: The Social Consequences of Political, Economic, and Environmental Change*, 4th ed. (Lanham, MD: Rowman and Littlefield, 2009), 85.

23. Torry D. Dickinson and Robert K. Schaeffer, *Fast Forward: Work, Gender and Protest in a Changing World* (Lanham, MD: Rowman and Littlefield, 2001), 140–41.

24. Safford, "Politics, Ideology and Society," 370.

25. C. M. Woodhouse, *The Rise and Fall of the Greek Colonels* (London: Granada, 1985), 134–40.

26. Christopher Hitchens, *Cyprus* (London: Quartet, 1984), 93–94. Some years earlier, Ionnidis had approached Makarios with a plan to exterminate the entire Turkish population in Cyprus (Woodhouse, *Rise and Fall*, 7).

27. Sue Branford and Bernardo Kucinski, *The Debt Squads: The U.S., the Banks and Latin America* (London: Zed, 1988), 24.

28. Schaeffer, *Red Inc.*, 8, 27, 60, 117, 177.

29. Schaeffer, *Red Inc.*, 27, 90–93.

30. Billias, *American Constitutionalism*, 124.

31. Vadney, *World since 1945*, 198.

32. Billias, *American Constitutionalism*, 397. See Madison's reply, 44.

33. Immanuel Wallerstein, *The Modern World-System III: The Second Era of Great Expansion of the Capitalist World-Economy, 1730–1840s* (New York: Academic, 1989), 213, 231.

34. "While the federalists gave us the Constitution, the legacy of the anti-federalists was the Bill of Rights," Herbert Storing observes. Quoted in Billias, *American Constitutionalism*, 49.

35. Lynch, *Caudillos*, 150.

36. Lynch, *Caudillos*, 40.

37. Schaeffer, *Warpaths*, 172, 184–85.

38. Italy's colonies in Ethiopia and Eritrea were transferred, in stages, to the kingdom of Haile Selassie.

39. Schaeffer, *Warpaths*, 87–152.

40. Schaeffer, *Warpaths*, 100–115.

41. Carl Sandburg, *Abraham Lincoln: The War Years* (New York: Harcourt, Brace and Company, 1939), 1:131.

42. Sandburg, *Lincoln*, 131.

43. Sandburg, *Lincoln*, 131.

44. Quoted in Schaeffer, *Warpaths*, 256–57.

45. Quoted in Schaeffer, *Warpaths*, 257.

46. Schaeffer, *Warpaths*, 100–152.

47. John Sullivan, *Two Koreas—One Future?* (Lanham, MD: University of America Press, 1987), 100; Gregory Henderson, R. N. Lebow, and J. G. Stroessinger, *Divided Nations in a Divided World* (New York: David McKay, 1974), 60–61.

48. Henderson, Lebow, and Stroessinger, *Divided Nations*, 61.

49. Benny Morris, *The Birth of the Palestinian Refugee Problem, 1947–1949* (Cambridge: Cambridge University Press, 1988), 297–98; Milton J. Esman and Itamar Rabinovich, *Ethnicity, Pluralism and the State in the Middle East* (Ithaca, NY: Cornell University Press, 1988), 97.

50. R. F. Holland, *European Decolonization, 1918–1981* (New York: St. Martin's, 1985), 80.

51. Holland, *European Decolonization*, 80.

52. Schaeffer, *Warpaths*, 160.

53. Edward Said and Christopher Hitchens, *Blaming the Victims* (London: Verso, 1988), 252, 268.

54. Schaeffer, *Warpaths*, 186–201.

55. Schaeffer, *Warpaths*, 191, 193.

56. Schaeffer, *Warpaths*, 202–31.

57. Schaeffer, *Warpaths*, 218–20.

58. Mitchell Reiss, *Without the Bomb* (New York: Columbia University Press, 1987), 103.

59. Schaeffer, *Warpaths*, 226–27.

60. Schaeffer, *Warpaths*, 217–31.

61. Robert K. Schaeffer, *Severed States: Dilemmas of Democracy in a Divided World* (Lanham, MD: Rowman and Littlefield, 1999), 177–89.

62. Schaeffer, *Severed States*, 195–229.

63. Schaeffer, *Severed States*, 195–229.

64. Robert K. Schaeffer, "Democratization and Division in Czechoslovakia: Economics and Ethnic Politics," in *Ethnicity and Democratisation in the New Europe*, ed. Karl Cordell (London: Routledge, 1999), 157–68.

65. Jon Lee Anderson, "A History of Violence: A Year Ago, Sudan Broke into Two Countries. Will That End Its Long Civil War?" *New Yorker*, July 23, 2012, 49–59.

5. THE DEMOCRATIZATION OF THE REPUBLICS

1. Samuel P. Huntington, *The Third Wave: Democratization in the Late Twentieth Century* (Norman: University of Oklahoma Press, 1991), xiii.

2. Huntington, *Third Wave*, 25.

3. Gaddis Smith, *The Last Years of the Monroe Doctrine, 1945–1993* (Hill and Wang, 1994), 130; Robert K. Schaeffer, *Power to the People: Democratization around the World* (Boulder, CO: Westview, 1997), 18–20.

4. Smith, *Monroe Doctrine*, 55.

5. Robert K. Schaeffer, *Severed States: Dilemmas of Democracy in a Divided World* (Lanham, MD: Rowman and Littlefield, 1999), 20; Schaeffer, *Power*, 30–31.

6. Smith, *Monroe Doctrine*, 70–71. US treasury secretary George Humphrey argued, "The United States should back strong men in Latin American governments [because] whenever a dictator was replaced, communists gained ground" (Smith, *Monroe Doctrine*, 191). US offi-

cials took this advice and mounted coups that led to the installment of new dictators around the world: Honduras in 1963, Brazil and Bolivia in 1964, Peru in 1968, Panama in 1969, Chile in 1973, and Argentina in 1976.

7. Peter W. Rodman, *More Precious Than Peace: The Cold War and the Struggle for the Third World* (New York: Scribner, 1994), 47.

8. Schaeffer, *Power*, 33–35.

9. Peter Willetts, *The Non-aligned Movement: The Origins of a Third World Alliance* (London: Frances Pinter, 1978), 6.

10. Schaeffer, *Power*, 35. The 1955 Afro-Asian Conference in Bandung, Indonesia, which brought together twenty-nine states from Africa and Asia, was the first institutional expression of the nonaligned movement (35–36).

11. Rodman, *More Precious Than Peace*, 68.

12. John Lewis Gaddis, *The Long Peace: Inquiries into the History of the Cold War* (New York: Oxford University Press, 1987), 171.

13. Robert K. Schaeffer, *Red Inc.: Dictatorship and the Development of Capitalism in China, 1949 to the Present* (Boulder, CO: Paradigm, 2012), 68–70.

14. Schaeffer, *Power*, 172.

15. Schaeffer, *Power*, 55.

16. Schaeffer, *Power*, 84–97.

17. John Walton and David Seddon, *Free Markets and Food Riots: The Politics of Global Adjustment* (Cambridge, MA: Blackwell, 1994).

18. Raymond Carr and Juan Pablo Fusi Aizpurua, *Spain: Dictatorship to Democracy* (London: George Allen and Unwin, 1979), 57; Robert K. Schaeffer, *Understanding Globalization: The Social Consequences of Political, Economic, and Environmental Change*, 4th ed. (Lanham, MD: Rowman and Littlefield, 2009), 149.

19. Schaeffer, *Understanding Globalization*, 150–51.

20. Huntington, *Third Wave*, 3.

21. Schaeffer, *Power*, 73–74.

22. Schaeffer, *Understanding Globalization*, 152.

23. Schaeffer, *Understanding Globalization*, 152–55.

24. Schaeffer, *Understanding Globalization*, 154. In social, economic, and political terms, the dictatorship in the Philippines had more in common with regimes in Latin America than it did with regimes in East Asia.

25. Schaeffer, *Understanding Globalization*, 153–54.

26. Walton and Seddon, *Free Markets and Food Riots*, 119. Demonstrators who broke into the legislative palace in Panama painted this slogan on the walls: "Let the ones who stole the money pay" (107).

27. Schaeffer, *Understanding Globalization*, 155–56; Schaeffer, *Power*, 108–9.

28. Schaeffer, *Power*, 109.

29. Schaeffer, *Power*, 102–3, 120–22.

30. Robert A. Pastor, *Democracy in the Americas: Stopping the Pendulum* (New York: Holmes and Meier, 1989), xi.

31. Schaeffer, *Understanding Globalization*, 158.

32. Schaeffer, *Understanding Globalization*, 157.

33. Schaeffer, *Power*, 143–44.

34. Walden Bello and Stephanie Rosenfeld, *Dragons in Distress: Asia's Miracle Economies in Crisis* (San Francisco: Food First, 1990), 43.

35. Clyde Haberman, "Korean Declares 'Sweeping' Change Is the 'Only' Way," *New York Times*, July 5, 1987.

36. Schaeffer, *Understanding Globalization*, 160–61.

37. Schaeffer, *Red Inc.*, 101–20.

38. Schaeffer, *Red Inc.*, 121–35.

39. David F. Epstein, "The Economic Cost of Soviet Security and Empire," in *The Impoverished Superpower*, ed. Henry S. Rowen and Charles Wolf Jr. (San Francisco: Institute for Contemporary Studies, 1990), 153.

40. For a discussion of the poor performance of Soviet arms, see Schaeffer, *Understanding Globalization*, 164.

41. Schaeffer, *Understanding Globalization*, 163.

42. Schaeffer, *Understanding Globalization*, 163–64.

43. Marshall I. Goldman, "The Future of Soviet Economic Reform," *Current History* (October 1989): 329.

44. Serge Schmemann, "The Sun Has Trouble Setting on the Soviet Empire," *New York Times*, March 10, 1991.

45. Grigorii Khanin, "Economic Growth in the 1980s," in *The Disintegration of the Soviet Economic System*, ed. Michael Ellman and Vladimir Kontorovich (London: Routledge, 1992), 29.

46. Schaeffer, *Understanding Globalization*, 165.

47. Ralf Dahrendorf, *Reflections on the Revolution in Europe* (New York: Times, 1990), 16.

48. Schaeffer, *Power*, 194.

49. Schaeffer, *Power*, 194–201.

50. Schaeffer, *Power*, 189–94.

51. "A Dismantler's Guide to Apartheid," *The Economist*, February 10, 1990, 38; Jacques Derrida, "Racism's Last Word," *Harper's*, February 1986, 22.

52. Schaeffer, *Power*, 209–10.

53. Stephen R. Lewis Jr., *The Economics of Apartheid* (New York: Council on Foreign Relations, 1990), 28.

54. Schaeffer, *Power*, 211.

55. Schaeffer, *Power*, 212.

56. Martin J. Murray, *Revolution Deferred: The Painful Birth of Post-Apartheid South Africa* (London: Verso, 1994), 100.

57. Guy Arnold, *South Africa: Crossing the Rubicon* (New York: St. Martin's, 1992), 1.

58. Schaeffer, *Power*, 214.

59. Jamie Mackie, "Indonesia: Economic Growth and Depoliticization," in *Driven by Growth: Political change in the Asia Pacific Region*, ed. James W. Morley (Armonk, NY: M. E. Sharpe, 1999), 129–30.

60. Mackie, "Indonesia," 133.

61. Schaeffer, *Red Inc.*, 128–30.

62. Robert W. Hefner, *Civil Islam: Muslims and Democratization in Indonesia* (Princeton, NJ: Princeton University Press, 2000), 198.

63. Bob S. Hadiwinata and Christopher Schuck, "Mapping Indonesia's Way toward Democracy: In Search of a Theoretical Frame," in *Democracy in Indonesia: The Challenge of Consolidation*, ed. Bob S. Hadiwinata and Christopher Schuck (Baden-Baden: Nomos, 2007), 9.

64. Hadiwinata and Schuck, "Mapping Indonesia's Way," 9.

65. Hadiwinata and Schuck, "Mapping Indonesia's Way," 18.

66. Birol A. Yesilada, "Some Expected and Some Not-So-Expected Benefits of Turkey's EU Membership for Both Parties." Paper presented at the European Union Studies Conference in Montreal, Canada, May 17–20, 2007, 2; Schaeffer, *Power*, 239–40.

67. Yesilada, "Benefits," 23.

68. Kenneth M. Pollack, "Iraq: The Roller-Coaster of Democracy," in *The Arab Awakening: America and the Transformation of the Middle East* (Washington, DC: Brookings Institution Press, 2011), 94; Yousef K. Baker, "Building a Neo-liberal State: Investigating the Legacy of the American Occupation of Iraq," paper presented at the American Sociology Association annual meeting in Denver, Colorado, August 13, 2012.

69. David I. Steinberg, "Burma/Myanmar: Under the Military," in *Driven by Growth: Political Change in the Asia Pacific Region*, ed. James W. Morley (Armonk, NY: M. E. Sharpe, 1999), 41.

70. Steinberg, "Burma/Myanmar," 42–45, 48.

71. Evan Osnos, "The Burmese Spring," *New Yorker*, August 6, 2012, 56–57.

72. Lin Noueihed and Alex Warren, *The Battle for the Arab Spring: Revolution, Counter-Revolution, and the Making of a New Era* (New Haven, CT: Yale University Press, 2012), 33.

73. Noueihed and Warren, *Battle*, 3, 27–31, 36–38; Jack A. Goldstone, "Understanding the Revolutions of 2011," in *The New Arab Revolt* (New York: Council of Foreign Relations, 2011), 336; Magdi Amin et al., *After the Spring: Economic Transitions in the Arab World* (New York: Oxford University Press, 2012), 54–57, 60.

74. Noueihed and Warren, *Battle*, 40.

75. Noueihed and Warren, *Battle*, 25, 34–35.

76. Noueihed and Warren, *Battle*, 12; Goldstone, "Understanding the Revolutions," 335; Amin, *After the Spring*, 42–43.

77. Akram Al-Turk, "Libya: From Revolt to State Building," in *The Arab Awakening: America and the Transformation of the Middle East* (Washington, DC: Brookings Institution Press, 2011), 119.

78. Noueihed and Warren, *Battle*, 74.

79. Noueihed and Warren, *Battle*, 76–77.

80. Shadi Hamid, "Tunisia: Birthplace of the Revolution," in *The Arab Awakening: America and the Transformation of the Middle East* (Washington, DC: Brookings Institution Press, 2011), 112.

81. Noueihed and Warren, *Battle*, 107–8.

82. Eric Trager, "Letter from Cairo: The People's Military in Egypt," in *The New Arab Revolt* (New York: Council of Foreign Relations, 2011), 81.

83. Shadi Hamid, "Egypt: The Prize," in *The Arab Awakening: America and the Transformation of the Middle East* (Washington, DC: Brookings Institution Press, 2011), 102–4.

84. Michael W. Doyle, "The Folly of Protection: Is Intervention against Qaddafi's Regime Legal or Legitimate?" in *The New Arab Revolt* (New York: Council of Foreign Relations, 2011), 263; Al-Turk, "Libya," 117.

85. Noueihed and Warren, *Battle*, 187.

86. Schaeffer, *Power*, 236–38.

87. Nathan J. Brown, "Egypt's Constitutional Ghosts," in *The New Arab Revolt* (New York: Council of Foreign Relations, 2011), 129.

6. THE EXPANSION OF CITIZENSHIP IN THE UNITED STATES

1. Frances Fox Piven, *Challenging Authority: How Ordinary People Change America* (Lanham, MD: Rowman and Littlefield, 2006), 7, 22. Alexander Keyssar estimates that only about 30 percent of the adult male population could vote in 1820. Alexander Keyssar, *The*

Right to Vote: The Contested History of Democracy in the United States (New York: Basic, 2009), 42. In 1800, the total US population was about four million (*Right to Vote*, 22). If slaves and immigrants made up 20 percent of the population and children another 20 percent, and the remaining 60 percent were divided equally between men and women, then adult white men would have made up 30 percent of the population. If 30 percent of these men were eligible to vote, then the men who could claim citizenship in the new republic amounted to less than 10 percent of the population, or about four hundred thousand of the country's four million inhabitants, excluding American Indians.

2. Linda Kerber, *No Constitutional Right to Be Ladies: Women and the Obligations of Citizenship* (New York: Hill and Wang, 1998), 93. "The Thirteenth Amendment of 1865 made slavery illegal, but . . . the former states of the Confederacy struggled hard to carve out an intermediate and secondary form of citizenship for black people—limiting or denying their right to serve on juries, to control their own labor, and to marry whites. . . . Against these efforts, liberals employed a rhetoric that denied that there could be an intermediate category between 'slave' and 'citizen.'"

But that category already existed. As Linda Kerber notes, "Before the Civil War, there had been ample conceptual space . . . to accommodate a wide variety of discriminations; free white women were located in this intermediate space" (*No Constitutional Right*, 97, 305). This "intermediate" space for "second-class" citizens describes what I call the denizen population, a category that women shared with immigrant aliens, children, and free black men and women in the South after the Civil War.

3. Immanuel Wallerstein, *The Modern World-System IV: Centrist Liberalism Triumphant, 1789–1914* (Berkeley: University of California Press, 2011), 47.

4. The term "fraternity" has an archaic character, given the fact that it described the bonds between men. I think it more appropriate to describe this as the "solidarity" provided by community, of whatever sort.

5. Torry D. Dickinson and Robert K. Schaeffer, *Transformations: Feminist Pathways to Global Change* (Boulder, CO: Paradigm, 2008), 274–75.

6. Keyssar, *Right to Vote*, 5.

7. Keyssar, *Right to Vote*, 9.

8. Keyssar, *Right to Vote*, 25.

9. Keyssar, *Right to Vote*, 24.

10. Keyssar, *Right to Vote*, 27.

11. Keyssar, *Right to Vote*, 27–28. The pro-immigrant stance taken by Republican legislators in the 1840s contrasts sharply with the anti-immigrant legislation introduced by Republican legislators in many of these same states in the 2000s. In Kansas and other states, Republican legislators adopted "voter ID" laws to prevent immigrants from voting, though there was little evidence that immigrants engaged in "voter fraud" or voted before they became naturalized citizens.

12. Keyssar, *Right to Vote*, 28.

13. Keyssar, *Right to Vote*, 321–23, table A.6.

14. Keyssar, *Right to Vote*, 42.

15. Keyssar, *Right to Vote*, 44–45; Kenneth Karst, *Belonging to America: Equal Citizenship and the Constitution* (New Haven, CT: Yale University Press, 1989), 43–44.

16. Keyssar, *Right to Vote*, 90.

17. Keyssar, *Right to Vote*, 91.

18. Keyssar, *Right to Vote*, 92–93.

19. Keyssar, *Right to Vote*, 86.

20. Keyssar, *Right to Vote*, 89; Kerber, *No Constitutional Right*, 69.

21. Kerber, *No Constitutional Right*, 56; Keyssar, *Right to Vote*, 84.

22. Kerber, *No Constitutional Right*, 59.

23. Kerber, *No Constitutional Right*, 69. "Broadly defined vagrancy laws . . . enabled police to round up idle blacks in times of labor scarcity and also give employers a coercive tool . . . to keep workers on the job."

24. Kerber, *No Constitutional Right*, 64–65.

25. Theda Skocpol, "Did the Civil War Further American Democracy? A Reflection on the Expansion of Benefits for Union Veterans," in *Democracy, Revolution, and History* (Ithaca, NY: Cornell University Press, 1998), 74.

26. The meeting in Seneca Falls "was only one of the numerous conventions called to promote women's rights in the late 1840s and early 1850s; its special place . . . stems partially from [Elizabeth Cady] Stanton's subsequent role as the preeminent leader and chronicler of the movement." Keyssar, *Right to Vote*, 142.

27. "Declaration of Sentiments," in *A History of Woman Suffrage*, ed. Elizabeth Cady Stanton, Susan B. Anthony, and Matilda Joslyn Gage (Rochester, NY: Fowler and Wells, 1899), 1:70–71.

28. Stanton, Anthony, and Gage, *Woman Suffrage*, 71.

29. Keyssar, *Right to Vote*, 143.

30. Keyssar, *Right to Vote*, 146.

31. Keyssar, *Right to Vote*, 146.

32. Keyssar, *Right to Vote*, 149.

33. Keyssar, *Right to Vote*, 150.

34. Warren B. Smith, *White Servitude in Colonial South Carolina* (Columbia: University of South Carolina Press, 1961), 159–64; Keyssar, *Right to Vote*, 166.

35. Kerber, *No Constitutional Right*, 134, 137.

36. Kerber, *No Constitutional Right*, 227–28, 252.

37. Keyssar, *Right to Vote*, 12.

38. Keyssar, *Right to Vote*, 69.

39. Keyssar, *Right to Vote*, 174, 178. "Whose life is imperiled when the soldier is born?" the feminist Lucy Stone asked. Although she was stretching a point, she wanted politicians to recognize that women's service to the country, even if not done in uniform, should be rewarded with suffrage. Kerber, *No Constitutional Right*, 244.

40. Kerber, *No Constitutional Right*, 103.

41. Kerber, *No Constitutional Right*, 81.

42. Keyssar, *Right to Vote*, 31.

43. Keyssar, *Right to Vote*, 31.

44. Keyssar, *Right to Vote*, 38.

45. Keyssar, *Right to Vote*, 160. Some feminists objected to the "ill-advised" movement that "enfranchised the foreigner, the negro, and the Indian" (Keyssar, *Right to Vote*, 154, 163).

46. Keyssar, *Right to Vote*, 34.

47. Keyssar, *Right to Vote*, 32, 41, 72.

48. Keyssar, *Right to Vote*, 141; Kerber, *No Constitutional Right*, 94. For example, in the wake of the 2012 election, some Republicans have urged leaders to rethink their anti-immigration policies after Hispanic voters expressed their disapproval. This would deprive Democrats from using immigration as an issue and allow Republicans to enlist some Hispanic voters.

49. Keyssar, *Right to Vote*, 172, 176.

50. Keyssar, *Right to Vote*, 173.

7. PERSISTENT INEQUALITIES

1. Richard D. Brown, "The Ideal of the Written Constitution: A Political Legacy of the Revolution," in *The Radicalism of the American Revolution*, ed. Gordon S. Wood (New York: Knopf, 1992), 288.

2. James H. Kettner, *The Development of American Citizenship, 1608–1870* (Chapel Hill: University of North Carolina Press, 1978), 290.

3. Russel Lawrence Barsh and James Youngblood Henderson, *The Road: Indian Tribes and Political Liberty* (Berkeley: University of California Press, 1980), 32.

4. Kettner, *American Citizenship*, 290.

5. "Except for the Oneidas and Tuscaroras among the Iroquois and factions among the Cherokees and Creeks, the Indians joined the British." Bernard W. Sheehan, "Ignoble Savagism and the American Revolution," in *The Radicalism of the American Revolution*, ed. Gordon S. Wood (New York: Knopf, 1992), 152.

6. John W. Shy, "The Legacy of the American Revolutionary War," in *The Radicalism of the American Revolution*, ed. Gordon S. Wood (New York: Knopf, 1992), 7–8.

7. Sheehan, "Ignoble Savagism," 151.

8. Shy, "The Legacy," 332.

9. Barsh and Henderson, *The Road*, 40.

10. Barsh and Henderson, *The Road*, 41–54.

11. Alexander Keyssar, *The Right to Vote: The Contested History of Democracy in the United States* (New York: Basic, 2009), 48.

12. Kettner, *American Citizenship*, 295, 296.

13. Barsh and Henderson, *The Road*, 53. Chief Justice Marshall's "use of the words 'tutelage' and 'pupilage' suggests he was thinking of guardianship in the Roman . . . sense [where it described] small, often noncitizen households patronized by politically powerful citizens" (55–56, 90).

14. William G. Martin, *Making Waves: Worldwide Social Movements, 1750–2005* (Boulder, CO: Paradigm, 2008), 18.

15. Francis Paul Prucha, *Indian Policy in the United States: Historical Essays* (Lincoln: University of Nebraska Press, 1981), 100, 105; Martin, *Making Waves*, 18; Barsh and Henderson, *The Road*, 61; Eric R. Wold, *Europe and the People without History* (Berkeley: University of California Press, 1982), 284–85.

16. Martin, *Making Waves*, 18. Estimates about the size of the Indian population differ. "In 1783, 150,000 Indians lived east of the Mississippi; by 1844, less than one-fourth remained." Alfred F. Young, *Liberty Tree: Ordinary People and the American Revolution* (New York: New York University Press, 2006), 243.

17. Barsh and Henderson, *The Road*, 62–63, 86.

18. Keyssar, *Right to Vote*, 133.

19. Keyssar, *Right to Vote*, 48; Sharon V. Salinger, *To Serve Well and Faithfully: Labor and Indentured Servants in Pennsylvania, 1682–1800* (Cambridge: Cambridge University Press, 1987), 133–34.

20. Kettner, *American Citizenship*, 179.

21. Kettner, *American Citizenship*, 177–79, 191.

22. Jim Piecuch, *Three Peoples, One King: Loyalists, Indians, and Slaves in the Revolutionary South, 1775–1782* (Columbia: University of South Carolina Press, 2008), 334; Kettner, *American Citizenship*, 183.

23. In 1802, the republic reluctantly agreed to pay six hundred thousand pounds to the British government, which it used to compensate some royalists for lost assets. Kettner, *American Citizenship*, 186–87. See US government compensation to Japanese Americans below.

24. Hans L. Trefousse, *Reconstruction: America's First Effort at Racial Democracy* (New York: Van Nostrand, 1971), 12–13; John Hope Franklin, *Reconstruction after the Civil War* (Chicago: University of Chicago Press, 1994), 30. By 1867, only three hundred ex-Confederates were still disenfranchised. And in 1868, most of the remaining number were pardoned, including General Robert E. Lee, even though he had broken his military oath to protect and defend the United States, committed treason, waged war against the Republic, and refused to swear an oath of allegiance to it (Franklin, *Reconstruction after the Civil War*, 33, 82).

25. Trefousse, *Reconstruction*, 14–15; Franklin, *Reconstruction after the Civil War*, 47–48.

26. Franklin, *Reconstruction after the Civil War*, 43; Trefousse, *Reconstruction*, 15.

27. Trefousse, *Reconstruction*, 35; Franklin, *Reconstruction after the Civil War*, 57–58.

28. Kenneth M. Stampp, *The Era of Reconstruction, 1865–1877* (New York: Knopf, 1966), 200; Trefousse, *Reconstruction*, 41–43, 63–64.

29. Franklin, *Reconstruction after the Civil War*, 70–71.

30. Southern historians have described this group as "scalawags," a derogatory term used by ex-Confederates to denigrate their opponents. It might be better to call them "loyalists" and for Confederates, who described themselves as "redeemers," to be described as "reprobates." Franklin, *Reconstruction after the Civil War*, 79, 101.

31. Trefousse, *Reconstruction*, 56–59.

32. One white militia member "claimed that his group [Heggie's Scouts] had killed 116 blacks and threw their bodies into the Tallahatchie River." Franklin, *Reconstruction after the Civil War*, 154–55. Others organized processions in which "coffins were paraded through the streets marked with the names of prominent [black and white reconstructionists] and labeled with such inscriptions as 'Dead, damned, and delivered'" (156). Trefousse, *Reconstruction*, 70; Stampp, *Era of Reconstruction*, 201–2.

33. Stampp, *Era of Reconstruction*, 210; Trefousse, *Reconstruction*, 76.

34. Trefousse, *Reconstruction*, 76–80.

35. Franklin, *Reconstruction after the Civil War*, 224.

36. Franklin, *Reconstruction after the Civil War*, 198.

37. Congress repealed the Reconstruction period enforcement acts in 1894. Franklin, *Reconstruction after the Civil War*, 202; Trefousse, *Reconstruction*, 73–74, 80; Stampp, *Era of Reconstruction*, 214.

38. Regin Schmidt, *Red Scare: FBI and the Origins of Anti-Communism in the United States, 1919–1943* (Copenhagen: Museum Tusculanum Press/University of Copenhagen, 2000), 55–56; Keyssar, *Right to Vote*, 112. Some states also denied suffrage to anarchist citizens (136).

39. Robert K. Murray, *Red Scare: A Study in National Hysteria, 1919–1920* (Minneapolis: University of Minnesota Press, 1955), 13–14.

40. Schmidt, *Red Scare*, 72.

41. Murray, *Red Scare*, 25.

42. Murray, *Red Scare*, 25–26.

43. Frances H. Early, *A World without War: How U.S. Feminists and Pacifists Resisted World War I* (Syracuse, NY: Syracuse University Press, 1997), 97, 99; Schmidt, *Red Scare*, 84. The Selective Service Act allowed the members of some peace churches—Quakers, Mennonites, Dukhobors—to claim conscientious objector status, but the law "did not recognize conscientious objector status on any other basis" (Early, *World without War*, 93–94).

44. Early, *World without War*, 97.

45. Schmidt, *Red Scare*, 105–6, 109–10, 115.

46. Early, *World without War*, 82, 97; Schmidt, *Red Scare*, 84.

47. Schmidt, *Red Scare*, 65.

48. Schmidt, *Red Scare*, 67.

49. Schmidt, *Red Scare*, 148; Murray, *Red Scare*, 70–71, 78.

50. Murray, *Red Scare*, 62.

51. Murray, *Red Scare*, 132.

52. Schmidt, *Red Scare*, 74.

53. Murray, *Red Scare*, 193.

54. Schmidt, *Red Scare*, 246–62; Murray, *Red Scare*, 207. "I do not consider it a punishment to be sent back to Soviet Russia. I consider it an honor to be chosen as the first political agitator to be deported from the United States," Goldman said (Murray, *Red Scare*, 208).

55. Murray, *Red Scare*, 233.

56. Murray, *Red Scare*, 235.

57. Murray, *Red Scare*, 269.

58. Murray, *Red Scare*, 226–29.

59. Murray, *Red Scare*, 211. In 1893, the Supreme Court in *Fong Yue Ting v. United States* ruled that the "act of deportation did not constitute punishment in a legal sense but was simply an administrative process since, according to the court, 'it is but a method of enforcing the return to his own country of an alien who has not complied with the conditions upon the performance of which the Government . . . has determined that his continuing to reside here shall depend'" (Schmidt, *Red Scare*, 57).

The policies that deprived dissident citizens and immigrant denizens of their rights and status during World War I would subsequently be adopted, in part, during and after World War II and again after 9/11.

60. Schmidt, *Red Scare*, 56.

61. Roger Daniels, *The Decision to Relocate the Japanese Americans* (Philadelphia: Lippincott, 1975), 39.

62. Daniels, *The Decision to Relocate*, 8, 12. Legislators meeting with California attorney general Ed Warren said they did not trust the federal government to proceed against aliens and favored "shooting on sight all Japanese residents of the state" (Daniels, *The Decision to Relocate*, 40); Roger Daniels, *Prisoners without Trial: Japanese Americans in World War II* (New York: Hill and Wang, 1993), 56–57. John McCloy, assistant secretary of war, agreed: "If it is a question of the safety of the country and the Constitution . . . why the Constitution is just a scrap of paper to me" (Daniels, *The Decision to Relocate*, 35; Daniels, *Prisoners without Trial*, 45).

63. Daniels, *Prisoners without Trial*, 46. "Internment" is not an accurate legal term to describe events because "in law, internment can only apply to aliens," whereas during World War II, *citizens* were also imprisoned. Citizens were denied access to the courts and were imprisoned, without trial, on a collective basis: "The mass incarceration that took place was based simply on ethnic origin and geography" (46).

64. Daniels, *The Decision to Relocate*, 113–14.

65. Daniels, *Prisoners without Trial*, 46.

66. Daniels, *Prisoners without Trial*, 59–60.

67. Daniels, *Prisoners without Trial*, 61–62. Justice William O. Douglas agreed: "We cannot sit in judgment of the military requirements of the war" (Daniels, *The Decision to Relocate*, 57).

68. Daniels, *The Decision to Relocate*, 9–10.

69. Daniels, *Prisoners without Trial*, 26.

70. Daniels, *Prisoners without Trial*, 3–4.

71. Daniels, *Prisoners without Trial*, 63–64. "During the war . . . 5,766 Americans of Japanese ancestry formally renounced their citizenship" and after the war, 4,724 were deported to Japan. Years later, the Justice Department "ruled that acts of renunciation signed behind bars were, in essence, made under duress and were therefore null and void. A majority of the renunciants . . . have probably regained their American citizenship," largely as a result of the efforts of Wayne Collins, a civil rights attorney in San Francisco (85).

72. Daniels, *Prisoners without Trial*, 27, 47, 305.

73. Daniels, *The Decision to Relocate*, 4; Daniels, *Prisoners without Trial*, 15, 16.

74. Daniels, *The Decision to Relocate*, 39.

75. Daniels, *The Decision to Relocate*, 56.

76. Daniels, *Prisoners without Trial*, 52.

77. Daniels, *The Decision to Relocate*, 27–28.

78. Daniels, *Prisoners without Trial*, 72–77.

79. Daniels, *Prisoners without Trial*, 63.

80. Keyssar, *Right to Vote*, 51.

81. Philip M. Ferguson, *Abandoned to Their Fate: Social Policy and Practice toward Severely Retarded People in America, 1820–1920* (Philadelphia: Lippincott, 1975), 76; David J. Rothman, *The Discovery of the Asylum: Social Order and Disorder in the New Republic* (Boston: Little, Brown, 1971), 43.

82. Rothman, *Discovery of the Asylum*, 1, 130–31.

83. Rothman, *Discovery of the Asylum*, 143–44.

84. Rothman, *Discovery of the Asylum*, 144.

85. Rothman, *Discovery of the Asylum*, 144.

86. Rothman, *Discovery of the Asylum*, 277.

87. Ferguson, *Abandoned to Their Fate*, 36.

88. Scott Christianson, *With Liberty for Some: 500 Years of Imprisonment in America* (Boston: Northeastern University Press, 1998), 195–96.

89. Nell Irvin Painter, "When Poverty Was White," *New York Times*, March 25, 2012.

90. Painter, "Poverty."

91. Painter, "Poverty."

92. Judith Walzer Leavitt, *Typhoid Mary: Captive to the Public's Health* (Boston: Beacon, 1996), 8, 246.

93. Leavitt, *Typhoid Mary*, 42, 71, 77.

94. In 1905, the Supreme Court ruled in *Jacobson v. Massachusetts* that "the liberty secured by the Constitution of the United States to every person . . . does not impart an absolute right to each person to be, in all times and in all circumstances, wholly free from restraint. There are manifold restraints to which every person is necessarily subject for the common good." Leavitt, *Typhoid Mary*, 78.

95. Leavitt, *Typhoid Mary*, xvii–xviii.

96. Leavitt, *Typhoid Mary*, 49, 55, 57.

97. Leavitt, *Typhoid Mary*, 20–21. Mallon said of her confinement without trial: "I never had typhoid in my life and have always been healthy. Why should I be banished like a leper and compelled to live in solitary confinement with only a dog for a companion. My own doctors say that I have no typhoid germs. I am an innocent human being. I have committed no crime and I am treated like an outcast, a criminal. It is unjust, outrageous, uncivilized. It seems incredible that in a Christian community a defenseless woman can be treated in this manner" (180).

98. Margot Canaday, *The Straight State: Sexuality and Citizenship in Twentieth-Century America* (Princeton, NJ: Princeton University Press, 2009), 4.

99. Canaday, *Straight State*, 11, 22.

100. Canaday, *Straight State*, 20.

101. Canaday, *Straight State*, 2. In 1952, the McCarran-Walter Act made an "explicit assurance of homosexual exclusion." Moreover, the act enlisted nonstate actors to screen potential immigrants with homosexual characteristics: "The [act] authorized fines for any person who knowingly brought a psychopathic [homosexual] personality into the country; the ship captain and airline stewardess served as another [informal] checkpoint" (217, 222).

102. Canaday, *Straight State*, 58.

103. Canaday, *Straight State*, 58.

104. Canaday, *Straight State*, 88.

105. Canaday, *Straight State*, 148.

106. Canaday, *Straight State*, 161.

107. Canaday, *Straight State*, 264.

108. In 1953, Alfred Kinsey wrote, "There appears to be no other culture in the world" in which homosexual relations were "so severely penalized." Canaday, *Straight State*, 1–2.

109. Mary Ann Mason, *From Father's Property to Children's Rights: The History of Child Custody in the United States* (New York: Columbia University Press, 1994), 46.

110. Mason, *Children's Rights*, 46, 85–86.

111. Mason, *Children's Rights*, 74.

112. Mason, *Children's Rights*, 79–80.

113. Mason, *Children's Rights*, 31.

114. Mason, *Children's Rights*, 39.

115. Mason, *Children's Rights*, 2, 24.

116. Mason, *Children's Rights*, 26–27, 29.

117. Christianson, *Liberty for Some*, 44.

118. Mason, *Children's Rights*, 33, 73, 68–69.

119. Joseph M. Hawes, *The Children's Rights Movement: A History of Advocacy and Protection, Social Movements Past and Present* (Boston: Twayne, 1991), 51, 18, 42.

120. Hawes, *Children's Rights Movement*, 49–50.

121. Torry D. Dickinson, *CommonWealth: Self-Sufficiency and Work in American Communities, 1830–1993* (Lanham, MD: University Press of America, 1995).

122. Davis S. Tanenhaus, "Creating the Child, Constructing the State: People v. Turner, 1870," in *Children as Equals: Exploring the Rights of the Child*, ed. Kathleen Alaimo and Brian Klug (Lanham, MD: University Press of America, 2002), 142.

123. Mason, *Children's Rights*, 103.

124. Lewis Pitts, "The Right to Be Heard: The Child as a Legal Person," in *Children as Equals: Exploring the Rights of the Child*, ed. Kathleen Alaimo and Brian Klug (Lanham, MD: University Press of America, 2002), 128–34.

125. Pitts, "Right to be Heard," 137.

126. Kettner, *American Citizenship*, 246. Between 1798 and 1802, Congress insisted that immigrants wait fourteen years before they could be naturalized. Prior to this, Congress allowed immigrants to naturalize after two years (1790) and then five years (1795) (236–46).

127. Keyssar, *Right to Vote*, 114.

128. Robert K. Schaeffer, *Understanding Globalization: The Social Consequences of Political, Economic, and Environmental Change*, 4th ed. (Lanham, MD: Rowman and Littlefield, 2009), 105.

129. Small groups of people remain as the subjects of private or state authorities. Orphans in foster care remain in a kind of indenture to private authorities who are licensed by the state; people with mental disabilities remain as the subjects of public and private authorities in various kinds of health-care facilities and asylums.

130. See list. Keyssar, *Right to Vote*, 131.

131. In 1901, the sponsor of a disenfranchisement law in Alabama boasted that "the crime of wife-beating alone would disqualify sixty percent of the Negroes." Jeff Manza and Christopher Uggen, *Locked Out: Felon Disenfranchisement and American Democracy* (New York: Oxford University Press, 2008), 49–51, 57–58.

132. Manza and Uggen, *Locked Out*, 73, 75–78.

133. Christianson, *Liberty for Some*, 253, 181–83.

134. Christianson, *Liberty for Some*, 130, 190, 228–29.

135. John Tierney, "For Lesser Crimes, Rethinking Life behind Bars," *New York Times*, December 12, 2012. Of course, many of the people living in jail are not convicts but prisoners awaiting trial who are unable to make bail.

136. Although the multitude did not exercise a tyranny over a citizen minority, they did, in some ways, exercise a kind of tyranny over the denizen and subject minority by preventing them from claiming citizenship and suffrage.

137. Jill Lepore, "Benched: The Supreme Court and the Struggle for Judicial Independence," *New Yorker*, June 18, 2012, 81–82.

138. Status anxiety may also have motivated some citizens to support the status quo. Citizens from immigrant or incorporated groups such as Hispanics may have recognized that their status was contingent and might be revoked and consequently felt vulnerable as minorities. They may have worked hard to demonstrate their loyalty to the system so that their new status would not be questioned by others, an understandable response.

139. George Ryley Scott, *The History of Corporal Punishment: A Survey of Flagellation in Its Historical, Anthropological, and Sociological Aspects* (Detroit: Gale Research, 1974), 76.

140. Scott, *Corporal Punishment*, 75.

141. Myra C. Glenn, *Campaigns against Corporal Punishment: Prisoners, Sailors, Women, and Children in Antebellum America* (Albany: SUNY Press, 1984).

142. Five million African men, women, and children died during their first year of captivity. Marcus Rediker, *The Slave Ship: A Human History* (New York: Viking, 2007), 5.

143. Scott, *Corporal Punishment*, 78.

144. David M. Oshinsky, *"Worse Than Slavery": Parchman Farm and the Ordeal of Jim Crow Justice* (New York: Free Press, 1996), passim.

145. J. Thorsten Sellin, *Slavery and the Penal System* (New York: Elsevier, 1976), 145–46.

146. "We are not afraid to maul a black man on the head if he dares to vote," one Mississippi senator explained, "but we can't treat women, even black women, that way." Keyssar, *Right to Vote*, 169.

147. Scott, *Corporal Punishment*, 93; Glenn, *Campaigns against Corporal Punishment*, 57, 129. The ban on flogging in the navy provided for the use of other kinds of punishment: gagging, bucking, and tricking up (130).

148. Glenn, *Campaigns against Corporal Punishment*, 114.

149. Glenn, *Campaigns against Corporal Punishment*, 116.

150. Glenn, *Campaigns against Corporal Punishment*, 133.

151. Glenn, *Campaigns against Corporal Punishment*, 134.

152. In Boston, corporal punishment immediately declined by 25 percent. Glenn, *Campaigns against Corporal Punishment*, 136.

153. Glenn, *Campaigns against Corporal Punishment*, 32.

154. Glenn, *Campaigns against Corporal Punishment*, 128.

155. Glenn, *Campaigns against Corporal Punishment*, 79.

156. Glenn, *Campaigns against Corporal Punishment*, 71.

157. Glenn, *Campaigns against Corporal Punishment*, 68.

158. Glenn, *Campaigns against Corporal Punishment*, 65.

159. Linda K. Kerber, *No Constitutional Right to Be Ladies: Women and the Obligations of Citizenship* (New York: Hill and Wang, 1998), xxiii, 307.

8. THE FURTHER EXPANSION OF CITIZENSHIP

1. Leon F. Litwack, *Trouble in Mind: Black Southerners in the Age of Jim Crow* (New York: Vintage, 1998), 484. The number of migrants is difficult to determine. Litwack says that 40,000 blacks settled in Kansas, though estimates of "the actual number who moved vary from 6,000 to 82,000" (52, 53–54, 484).

2. Richard Wormser, *The Rise and Fall of Jim Crow* (New York: St. Martin's, 2003).

3. Daniel M. Johnson and Rex R. Campbell, *Black Migration in America: A Social Demographic History* (Durham, NC: Duke University Press, 1981), 56.

4. Johnson and Campbell, *Black Migration*, 55.

5. Johnson and Campbell, *Black Migration*, 71–72.

6. Johnson and Campbell, *Black Migration*, 74.

7. Litwack, *Trouble in Mind*, 487; Michael J. Klarman, *"Brown v. Board of Education*: Law or Politics?" in *From the Grassroots to the Supreme Court:* Brown v. Board of Education *and American Democracy*, ed. Peter F. Lau (Durham, NC: Duke University Press, 2004), 198; Johnson and Campbell, *Black Migration*, 104.

8. Johnson and Campbell, *Black Migration*, 80, 95, 101. One observer argued that "the fundamental and immediate cause of this Negro exodus is economic," a conclusion that needs to be reexamined (80–81).

9. Johnson and Campbell, *Black Migration*, 84–85.

10. Johnson and Campbell, *Black Migration*, 85–86.

11. Isabel Wilkerson, *The Warmth of Other Suns: The Epic Story of America's Great Migration* (New York: Random House, 2010), 11.

12. Litwack, *Trouble in Mind*, 490.

13. Florette Henri, *Black Migration: Movement North, 1900–1920* (Garden City, NY: Anchor, 1976), 60.

14. Litwack, *Trouble in Mind*, 492.

15. Johnson and Campbell, *Black Migration*, 112.

16. Eric Foner, "The Emancipation of Abe Lincoln," *New York Times*, January 1, 2013. The Emancipation Proclamation in 1863 freed about 3.1 million black slaves in the South but did not immediately free about 750,000 black slaves in slaveholding Union states, according to the historian Eric Foner.

17. Richard M. Dalfiume, *Desegregation of the U.S. Armed Forces: Fighting on Two Fronts, 1939–1953* (Columbia: University of Missouri Press, 1969), 26, 44.

18. Dalfiume, *Desegregation*, 52; Jack D. Foner, *Blacks and the Military in American History: A New Perspective* (New York: Praeger, 1974), 140, 143.

19. Foner, *Blacks and the Military*, 142.

20. Foner, *Blacks and the Military*, 145; Frances Fox Piven and Richard A. Cloward, *Poor People's Movements: Why They Succeed, How They Fail* (New York: Vintage, 1979), 206. During the war, "the percentage of blacks registered to vote quadrupled from 3 to 12 percent, and the numbers continued to rise thereafter." Alexander Keyssar, *The Right to Vote: The Contested History of Democracy in the United States* (New York: Basic, 2009), 199.

21. Foner, *Blacks and the Military*, 181.

22. Dalfiume, *Desegregation*, 169; Foner, *Blacks in the Military*, 180–81; Keyssar, *Right to Vote*, 196–97.

23. Dalfiume, *Desegregation*, 169; Foner, *Blacks in the Military*, 182.

24. Foner, *Blacks in the Military*, 173–74. Dalfiume, *Desegregation*, 134.

25. He had earlier issued an order banning discrimination in federal employment. Dalfiume, *Desegregation*, 157, 170–71.

26. Foner, *Blacks in the Military*, 185.

27. Foner, *Blacks in the Military*, 189.

28. Foner, *Blacks in the Military*, 198.

29. The NAACP grew from 50,000 members in 1940 to 350,000 members by 1945. Robert Frederick Burk, *The Eisenhower Administration and Black Civil Rights* (Knoxville: University of Tennessee Press, 1984), 7.

30. Larissa M. Smith, "A Civil Rights Vanguard: Black Attorneys and the NAACP in Virginia," in *From the Grassroots to the Supreme Court: Brown v. Board of Education and American Democracy*, ed. Peter F. Lau (Durham, NC: Duke University Press, 2004), 146–47.

31. Peter F. Lau, "From the Periphery to the Center: Clarendon County, South Carolina, *Brown*, and the Struggle for Democracy and Equality in America," in *From the Grassroots to the Supreme Court: Brown v. Board of Education and American Democracy*, ed. Peter F. Lau (Durham, NC: Duke University Press, 2004), 103; Johnson and Campbell, *Black Migration*, 14.

32. Klarman, "*Brown v. Board*," 207–8.

33. Klarman, "*Brown v. Board*," 208–9.

34. Klarman, "*Brown v. Board*," 209.

35. Legal social movements are often assembled around a single legal issue or lawsuit, and the participants disband as soon as it is adjudicated. In some respects, it resembles the kind of temporary organizations created in contemporary Hollywood to make a single movie—the writers, actors, directors, and crew work together, make the film, and, when it is completed, disband. The studio plays a role in assembling the cast and crew and raising the money, but it does not retain them on long-term contracts, as the studios of old used to do. In this case, the NAACP assembled the plaintiffs and argued the case, but the team that was assembled quickly disbanded.

36. Wormser, *Rise and Fall*, 181; Lau, "From the Periphery," 117–19.

37. Lau, "From the Periphery," 120.

38. Piven and Cloward, *Poor People's Movements*, 208–9.

39. Piven and Cloward, *Poor People's Movements*, 209.

40. Piven and Cloward, *Poor People's Movements*, 145.

41. Piven and Cloward, *Poor People's Movements*, 211; Robert A. Goldberg, *Grassroots Resistance: Social Movements in Twentieth Century America* (Belmont, CA: Wadsworth, 1991), 146.

42. Robert K. Schaeffer, *Severed States: Dilemmas of Democracy in a Divided World* (Lanham, MD: Rowman and Littlefield, 1999), 184.

43. Piven and Cloward, *Poor People's Movements*, 222–24; Goldberg, *Grassroots Resistance*, 148.

44. Wormser, *Rise and Fall*, 114.

45. "The Voting Rights Act of 1965 was . . . simply an effort to enforce the 15th Amendment, which had been law for almost a century," Keyssar observes. Keyssar, *Right to Vote*, 212; Piven and Cloward, *Poor People's Movements*, 242–43; Goldberg, *Grassroots Resistance*, 151, 158.

46. "Between 1964 and 1968, the number of the South's black voters had increased from one million to over three million," Goldberg argues. Goldberg, *Grassroots Resistance*, 160. Piven and Cloward argue that "the provisions extending the franchise to five million potential black voters in the South (over two million had been registered by the election of 1964) created a substantial bloc whose allegiance to the Democratic Party could be counted on . . . to offset permanent defections among . . . southern whites . . . and to offset the trend toward Republicans." Piven and Cloward, *Poor People's Movements*, 252.

47. Keyssar, *Right to Vote*, 200–204.

48. Alice Echols, *Shaky Ground: The '60s and Its Aftershocks* (New York: Columbia University Press, 2002), 54.

49. Malcolm G. Scully, "Who Are/Were the Youth in Revolt," in *American Youth in a Changing Culture*, ed. Grant S. McClellan (New York: H. W. Wilson, 1972), 14–15.

50. John H. Schaar and Sheldon S. Wolin, "Youth in Politics," in *American Youth in a Changing Culture*, ed. Grant S. McClellan (New York: H. W. Wilson, 1972), 145.

51. Henry Steele Commager, "Why Student Rebellion?" in *American Youth in a Changing Culture*, ed. Grant S. McClellan (New York: H. W. Wilson, 1972), 88–89.

52. Herbert A. Otto, "Communes: The Alternative Lifestyle," in *American Youth in a Changing Culture*, ed. Grant S. McClellan (New York: H. W. Wilson, 1972), 81–82.

53. Echols, *Shaky Ground*, 70.

54. Massimo Teodori, ed., *The New Left: A Documentary History* (New York: Bobbs-Merrill, 1969), 68; Kevin Mattson, *Engaging Youth: Combatting the Apathy of Young Americans toward Politics* (New York: Century Foundation Press, 2003), 8.

55. Teodori, *The New Left*, 14–15.

56. Teodori, *The New Left*, 61.

57. "Between 1946 and 1964, 76 million Americans were born and launched on a society where institutions proved inadequate to acculturate them without serious social problems," one author complains. Klaus P. Fischer, *America in White, Black and Gray: The Stormy 1960s* (New York: Continuum, 2006), 53; Peter F. Drucker, "The Youth Culture and the Economy," in *American Youth in a Changing Culture*, ed. Grant S. McClellan (New York: H. W. Wilson, 1972), 190–91; Mattson, *Engaging Youth*, 7–8.

58. Drucker, "Youth Culture," 192.

59. Teodori, *The New Left*, 73; Otto, "The Communes," 82.

60. American Council on Education, "A Declaration on Campus Unrest," in *American Youth in a Changing Culture*, ed. Grant S. McClellan (New York: H. W. Wilson, 1972), 113–14; Jonathan Eisen and David Steinberg, "The Student Revolt against Liberalism," in *Seasons of Rebellion: Protest and Radicalism in Recent America*, ed. Joseph Boskin and Robert A. Rosenstone (New York: Holt, Rinehart and Winston, 1972), 188.

61. Edgar Z. Friedenberg, "The Oppression of Youth," in *Seasons of Rebellion: Protest and Radicalism in Recent America*, ed. Joseph Boskin and Robert A. Rosenstone (New York: Holt, Rinehart and Winston, 1972), 229.

62. Teodori, *The New Left*, 31–32.

63. Mario Savio, "An End to History," in *The New Left: A Documentary History*, ed. Massimo Teodori (New York: Bobbs-Merrill, 1969), 159; Teodori, *The New Left*, 31; Bradley Cleveland, "Free Speech," in *The New Left: A Documentary History*, ed. Massimo Teodori (New York: Bobbs-Merrill, 1969), 150–51.

64. Teodori, *The New Left*, 55, 57.

65. Keyssar, *Right to Vote*, 225.

66. Teodori, *The New Left*, 34, 64–66.

67. Teodori, *The New Left*, 57.

68. John and Margaret Rowntree, "Youth as a Class," in *The New Left: A Documentary History*, ed. Massimo Teodori (New York: Bobbs-Merrill, 1969), 419; Echols, *Shaky Ground*, 24, 27.

69. *Berkeley Barb*, "From the Haight," in *The New Left: A Documentary History*, ed. Massimo Teodori (New York: Bobbs-Merrill, 1969), 363–64.

70. Schaar and Wolin, "Youth in Politics," 150.

71. Teodori, *The New Left*, 76–77.

72. Echols, *Shaky Ground*, 18, 21. Echols argues that "most histories of the period make only passing mention of the counterculture" (17). Rock star Janis Joplin observed that you can "destroy your now by worrying about tomorrow. We look back on our parents and see how they grew up and compromised and wound up with very little. So the kids now want a lot of something now rather than a little of hardly anything spread over seventy years" (23).

73. Bob Dylan, "The Times They Are a-Changin'," quoted in Linda Hirshman, *Victory: The Triumphant Gay Revolution* (New York: HarperCollins, 2012), 62.

74. Linda Gordon and Ann Popkin, "Women's Liberation: 'Let Us Now Emulate Each Other,'" in *Seasons of Rebellion: Protest and Radicalism in Recent America*, ed. Joseph Boskin and Robert A. Rosenstone (New York: Holt, Rinehart and Winston, 1972), 287.

75. Gordon and Popkin, "Women's Liberation," 287.

76. Echols, *Shaky Ground*, 34.

77. Echols, *Shaky Ground*, 69.

78. Gordon and Popkin, "Women's Liberation," 287.

79. *Rat* staff, "Cock Rock: Men Always Seem to End Up on Top," in *Seasons of Rebellion: Protest and Radicalism in Recent America*, ed. Joseph Boskin and Robert A. Rosenstone (New York: Holt, Rinehart and Winston, 1972), 97.

80. *Rat* staff, "Cock Rock," 99.

81. SNCC, "The Basis of Black Power," in *The New Left: A Documentary History*, ed. Massimo Teodori (New York: Bobbs-Merrill, 1969), 273, 279.

82. Keyssar, *Right to Vote*, 225–28.

83. Mary Goddard Zon, "The Youth Vote," in *American Youth in a Changing Culture*, ed. Grant S. McClellan (New York: H. W. Wilson, 1972), 170, 174.

84. Flora Davis, *Moving the Mountain: The American Women's Movement since 1960* (New York: Simon and Schuster, 1991), 491.

85. Davis, *Moving the Mountain*, 18.

86. Davis, *Moving the Mountain*, 491.

87. Davis, *Moving the Mountain*, 45.

88. Taylor Branch, *Pillar of Fire: America in the King Years, 1963–65* (New York: Simon and Schuster, 1998), 231–34; Davis, *Moving the Mountain*, 39–45.

89. Davis, *Moving the Mountain*, 78, 87–90, 100–102, 167–68.

90. The ERA "fell three states short of the thirty-eight needed to pass." Davis, *Moving the Mountain*, 135, 172–79, 212. The feminist historian Flora Davis argues that "feminists achieved half a revolution" (16).

91. Hirshman, *Victory*, 17, 131–39; Patricia A. Cain, *Rainbow Rights: The Role of Lawyers and Courts in the Lesbian and Gay Civil Rights Movement* (Boulder, CO: Westview, 2000), 93.

92. Davis, *Moving the Mountain*, 260; Hirshman, *Victory*, 40–42, 50–51; Cain, *Rainbow Rights*, 52–55.

93. Hirshman, *Victory*, 1–94; Cain, *Rainbow Rights*, 88–90.

94. Davis, *Moving the Mountain*, 260.

95. Echols, *Shaky Ground*, 145.

96. Davis, *Moving the Mountain*, 263.

97. Davis, *Moving the Mountain*, 264–72; Hirshman, *Victory*, 112.

98. Davis, *Moving the Mountain*, 261; Hirshman, *Victory*, 96–99, 127.

99. Davis, *Moving the Mountain*, 273–74.

100. Hirshman, *Victory*, xiii.

101. Julia Preston, "National Push by a Local Immigration Activist: No G.O.P. Retreat," *New York Times*, August 7, 2013.

102. Ashley Parker, "Bushes Look to Immigration Debate to Reclaim Their Influence," *New York Times*, September 4, 2013; Ashley Parker and Michael D. Shear, "Catholic Push to Overhaul Immigration Goes to the Pews," *New York Times*, August 22, 2013.

103. Piven and Cloward, *Poor People's Movements*, 182. Of course, this does not mean that violence and imprisonment are no longer used as means of social control. Antidrug legislation and the incarceration of black men and youths are still used not only as means of social control but also as ways to disenfranchise blacks and force them into denizen and subject populations.

9. SOCIAL MOVEMENTS AND GLOBAL SOCIAL CHANGE

1. Julie Bosman, "The Case of Loving v. Bigotry," *New York Times Magazine*, January 1, 2012, 39.

2. Adam Liptak, "Justices Weigh Diversity Issue at Universities," *New York Times*, October 11, 2012.

3. Jim Yardley, "Leader of Corruption Protest Arrested," *New York Times*, August 17, 2011; Jim Yardley, "Deal Would End Standoff with Protest Leader in India," *New York Times*, August 18, 2011.

4. Jim Yardley, "Thousands Back Anti-graft Hunger Striker in New Delhi," *New York Times*, August 22, 2011.

5. Jason DeParle, "The Anti-immigration Crusader," *New York Times*, April 17, 2011; Julia Preston, "With Drive (and without a Law Degree), a Texan Fights for Immigrants," *New York Times*, March 6, 2011.

6. Douglas Dalby, "Half of Irish Homeowners Join Boycott of New Tax That Has Symbolized Fiscal Woes," *New York Times*, April 3, 2012; Douglas Dalby, "Growing Antitax Movement Shows Irish Stoicism Wearing Thin," *New York Times*, March 20, 2012.

7. Dalby, "Irish Homeowners Join Boycott."

8. Kareen Fahim, "Slap to a Man's Pride Set Off Tumult in Tunisia," *New York Times*, January 22, 2011.

9. Andrew Jacobs, "Another Tibetan Nun Dies by Self-Immolation in China," *New York Times*, November 4, 2011; Sharon LaFraniere, "Three Tibetan Herders Self-Immolate in Protest," *New York Times*, February 6, 2012; Isabel Kershner, "Israeli's Act of Despair Disheartens a Movement," *New York Times*, July 17, 2012.

10. Robert Schaeffer, *Warpaths: The Politics of Partition* (New York: Hill and Wang, 1990), 39–40.

11. Roni Caryn Rabin, "Nearly 1 in 5 Women in U.S. Survey Say They Have Been Sexually Assaulted," *New York Times*, December 15, 2011; Jenny Anderson, "National Study Finds

Widespread Sexual Assault of Students in Grade 7 to 12," *New York Times*, November 7, 2011; Damien Cave, "Wave of Violence Swallows More Women in Juarez," *New York Times*, June 24, 2012.

12. Megan Davidson Ladly, "Defying Parents, Some Pakistani Women Risk All to Marry Whom They Chose," *New York Times*, September 9, 2012; Tim Arango, "Where Arranged Marriages Are Customary, Suicides Grow More Common," *New York Times*, June 7, 2012; Graham Bowley, "Afghan Kin Are Accused of Killing Woman for Not Bearing a Son," *New York Times*, January 31, 2012; Jack Healy, "Afghans Rage at Young Lovers; A Father Says Kill Them Both," *New York Times*, July 31, 2011; Declan Walsh, "Taliban Gun Down a Girl Who Spoke Up for Rights," *New York Times*, October 10, 2012; Isabel Kershner, "Israeli Girl, 8, Finds Herself at Center of Tension over Religious Extremism," *New York Times*, December 28, 2011.

13. Neil MacFarquhar and Dina Salah Amer, "In Scattered Protest, Saudi Women Take the Wheel," *New York Times*, June 18, 2011.

14. Anahad O'Connor, "Using 'Pox Parties' as Alternative to Vaccinations," *New York Times*, November 17, 2011; Michael Specter, "Resistant: Why a Century-Old Battle over Vaccination Continues to Rage," *New Yorker*, May 30, 2011.

15. Alexei Barrionuevo, "With Kiss-Ins and Dances, Young Chileans Push for Reform," *New York Times*, August 5, 2011; Ethan Bronner, "Where Politics Are Complex, Simple Joys at the Beach: Israelis and Palestinians Dare to Swim Together," *New York Times*, July 27, 2011; Neil MacFarquhar, "In Protests, Syrians Find the Spark of Creativity: Shaking Free of Cultural Constraints with Dancing, Singing, and Laughter," *New York Times*, December 20, 2011.

16. Paul A. Gilje, *Rioting in America* (Bloomington: Indiana University Press, 1996), 2–3.

17. Gilje, *Rioting in America*, 180–81.

18. See Robert K. Schaeffer, "The Chains of Bondage Broke: The Proletarianization of Seafaring Labor" (PhD diss., State Univesity of New York, Binghamton, 1984).

19. Giovanni Arrighi, Terence K. Hopkins, and Immanuel Wallerstein, *Antisystemic Movements* (London: Verso, 1989); Immanuel Wallerstein, *The Modern World-System III: The Second Era of Great Expansion of the Capitalist World-Economy, 1730–1840s* (New York: Academic, 1989), 30; Immanuel Wallerstein, *Historical Capitalism with Capitalist Civilization* (London: Verso, 1996), 66; Immanuel Wallerstein, *World-System Analysis: An Introduction* (Durham, NC: Duke University Press, 2004), 65; Immanuel Wallerstein, *Unthinking Social Science: The Limits of Nineteenth-Century Paradigms* (Cambridge: Polity, 1991), 20–21.

20. Elizabeth A. Armstrong, *Forging Gay Identities: Organizing Sexuality in San Francisco, 1950–1994* (Chicago: University of Chicago Press, 2002), 36.

21. We organized the first union at an environmental organization, Friends of the Earth, in the United States.

22. Kevin Roose, "Nuns Who Won't Stop Nudging," *New York Times*, November 13, 2011; Laurie Goodstein, "American Nuns Vow to Fight Vatican Criticism," *New York Times*, June 2, 2012; Laurie Goodstein, "Bishops Open 'Religious Liberty' Drive," *New York Times*, November 15, 2011.

23. John B. Judis, *William F. Buckley, Jr.: Patron Saint of the Conservatives* (New York: Simon and Schuster, 1988), 193.

24. Frances Fox Piven, *Challenging Authority: How Ordinary People Change America* (Lanham, MD: Rowman and Littlefield, 2006), 58.

25. Piven, *Challenging Authority*, 59.

26. The terminology is a little confusing because many social movement organizations call themselves "parties"—the Communist Party, the Black Panther Party—even though they play

no role in government. And when they obtain power, communist parties do not permit participation in government by other political parties.

27. Wallerstein, *Modern World-System III*, 57.

28. Wallerstein, *Unthinking Social Science*, 36.

29. Wallerstein, *Modern World-System III*, 102.

30. Alice Echols, *Shaky Ground: The '60s and Its Aftershocks* (New York: Columbia University Press, 2002); Armstrong, *Forging Gay Identities*.

31. James Dao, "In Beer and Brotherhood, Marines Remember," *New York Times*, May 29, 2012; Patricia Leigh Brown, "When the Uprooted Put Down Roots: For Income and a Taste of Home, Refugees Turn to Farming," *New York Times*, October 10, 2011; Nicholas Kulish, "Where History Casts a Fearsome Shadow, Murmurings about the Far Right," *New York Times*, August 23, 2011; James Dao and Serge F. Kovaleski, "Music Style Is Called Supremacist Recruiting Tool," *New York Times*, August 8, 2012; Robert Futrell and Pete Simi, "The Sound of Hate: How Music Nurtures the White-Power Movement," *New York Times*, August 9, 2012; Sophia Kishkovsky and David M. Herszenhorn, "In Moscow, Religious Protesters Burn Feminist Punk Band's Poster," *New York Times*, August 9, 2012; Simon Romero, "An Indigenous Language with Unique Staying Power," *New York Times*, March 12, 2012; "Don't Miss the Tiki Bar at Burning Man," *New York Times*, August 5, 2012; David M. Herszenhorn and Andrew Roth, "Trial Begins over an Anti-Putin Song," *New York Times*, July 31, 2012; Campbell Robertson, "Making a Stand for the Confederacy, 150 Years Later," *New York Times*, February 21, 2011; Nicholas Kulish, "Germany Permits Itself to Celebrate Prussian King," *New York Times*, January 25, 2012.

32. This is a selection drawn from Putnam's much longer list. Robert D. Putnam, *Bowling Alone: The Collapse and Revival of American Community* (New York: Simon and Schuster, 2000), 386–87.

33. Benedict Anderson, *Imagined Communities: Reflections on the Origins and Spread of Nationalism* (London: Verso, 1983).

34. For Putnam, all sorts of developments contribute to anomie: time pressures, suburbanization, television, generational change. All of them might be described as changes associated with the development of capitalism. Putnam, *Bowling Alone*.

35. Putnam goes on to say that there are two kinds of social capital: "bonding" social capital, a kind of "superglue" that binds people together; and "bridging" social capital, a "sociological WD-40" that makes it possible for people to reach out to others and work together on collective interests. Putnam, *Bowling Alone*, 23.

36. Putnam, *Bowling Alone*, 351. Unfortunately, social capital is a poor substitute for "fraternity" in the slogan: "Liberty, Equality, and *Social Capital*." I think "solidarity" is a better fit.

10. ASPIRING SOCIAL MOVEMENTS

1. Wallerstein argues that some movements rallied around "status group" identities rooted in ethnicity and religion while others organized around secular, class-based identities. Immanuel Wallerstein, *World-System Analysis: An Introduction* (Durham, NC: Duke University Press, 2004), 73. I think it is important to note that some movements organized around religious identities.

2. Robert Schaeffer, *Warpaths: The Politics of Partition* (New York: Hill and Wang, 1990), 19–45.

3. Schaeffer, *Warpaths*.

4. Ravi Somaiya, "Girl, 9, Gives a School Lunch Failing Grade," *New York Times*, June 16, 2012; Al Baker, "Baring Shoulders and Knees, Students Protest a Dress Code," *New York Times*, June 7, 2012; Manny Fernandez, "Vying for Campus President, Illegal Immigrant Gets a Gamut of Responses," *New York Times*, March 10, 2012.

5. Ian Lovett, "California Prison's Strike Resumes as Sides Dig In," *New York Times*, October 8, 2011; Adam Liptak and Lisa Faye Petak, "Juvenile Killers in Jail for Life Seek a Reprieve," *New York Times*, April 21, 2011.

6. Adam Gopnik, "The Caging of America," *New Yorker*, January 30, 2012, 72.

7. Schaeffer, *Warpaths*, 26–28.

8. Mary C. Bromage, *De Valera and the March of a Nation* (New York: Noonday, 1956), 38.

9. See Douglas C. Waller, *Congress and the Freeze: An Inside Look at the Politics of a Mass Movement* (Amherst: University of Massachusetts Press, 1987).

10. James Joll, *The Second International* (New York: Harper Colophon, 1966), 56.

11. Joll, *The Second International*, 56.

12. Elizabeth A. Armstrong, *Forging Gay Identities: Organizing Sexuality in San Francisco, 1950–1994* (Chicago: University of Chicago Press, 2002), 35–37.

13. Schaeffer, *Warpaths*, 94.

14. Schaeffer, *Warpaths*, 92.

15. Suzanne Daly, "After Assassinations, Basque Killers Explain," *New York Times*, July 16, 2012.

16. Daly, "Basque Killers Explain."

17. Steven M. Buechler, *Understanding Social Movements: Theories from the Classical Era to the Present* (Boulder, CO: Paradigm, 2011), 87.

18. William Gamson, *The Strategy of Social Protest* (Belmont, CA: Wadsworth, 1990), 72, 79, 87.

19. Gamson, *Strategy of Social Protest*, 19.

20. Gamson, *Strategy of Social Protest*, 19, 110.

21. Gamson, *Strategy of Social Protest*, 81.

22. Gamson, *Strategy of Social Protest*, 81–82.

23. Military service by conscript youths during the Vietnam War may also have helped youth secure citizenship and suffrage during the 1970s. It is less clear what role youth violence on the streets during the 1960s played in these developments.

24. "Colonial resistance movements, a romantic term, are not going to help us through our problems. We need have no truck with the view that the downfall of [the British Empire] was brought about by colonial freedom-fighters because, except in some Pickwickian sense, these processes involved next to no fighting. . . . [There were] no Dublin Post Offices [in most colonial settings]." John Gallagher, *The Decline, Revival and Fall of the British Empire: The Ford Lectures and Other Essays* (Cambridge: Cambridge University Press, 1982), 73–74.

11. ALTRUISTIC SOCIAL MOVEMENTS

1. Torry D. Dickinson and Robert K. Schaeffer, *Transformations: Feminist Pathways to Global Change* (Boulder, CO: Paradigm, 2008), 282–83.

2. Herbert Aptheker, *Abolitionism: A Revolutionary Movement* (Boston: Twayne, 1989); Larry E. Sullivan, *The Prison Reform Movement: Forlorn Hope* (Boston: Twayne, 1990); Hyung-chan Kim, *A Legal History of Asian Americans, 1790–1990* (Westport, CT: Greenwood, 1994). For example, the San Francisco Drug Users Union advocates on behalf of chronic drug users, a much-despised group with poor legal standing. Jesse McKinley, "Familiarity with Drugs Helps a Group Speak for Users," *New York Times*, March 12, 2012.

3. Dickinson and Schaeffer, *Transformations*, 254, 255; Campbell Robinson, "Alabama Law Criminalizes Samaritans, Bishops Say," *New York Times*, August 14, 2011.

4. Dickinson and Schaeffer, *Transformations*, 60; J. David Goodman, "Backlash Aside, Charities See Lessons in a Web Video," *New York Times*, March 16, 2012.

5. Dickinson and Schaeffer, *Transformations*, 283.

6. Michael Schwirtz, "Teddy Bears Fall from Sky, and Heads Roll in Minsk," *New York Times*, August 2, 2012.

7. Sheryl Gay Stolberg, "Shy U.S. Intellectual Created Playbook Used in a Revolution," *New York Times*, February 17, 2011.

8. Stephanie Strom, "Web Sites Shine Light on Petty Bribery Worldwide," *New York Times*, March 16, 2012.

9. Ethan Bronner, "Israeli Government Backs Limits on Financing for Nonprofit Groups," *New York Times*, November 14, 2011.

10. Scott Shane, "Groups to Help Online Activists in Authoritarian Countries," *New York Times*, June 12, 2012; Seth Mydans, "Monitoring Rights in Chechen Region, a Month at a Time," *New York Times*, September 25, 2011.

11. Jim Dwyer, "A Billionaire Philanthropist Struggles to Go Broke," *New York Times*, August 8, 2012; Nicholas Confessore, "Policy-Making Billionaires," *New York Times*, November 27, 2011; Carnegie Corporation, "Preserving the Past, Investing in the Future," advertisement in *New York Times*, November 10, 2011; Olivier Zunz, "Philanthropy by the Rest of Us," *New York Times*, December 23, 2011; Torry D. Dickinson and Robert K. Schaeffer, *Fast Forward: Work, Gender, and Protest in a Changing World* (Lanham, MD: Rowman and Littlefield, 2001), 256, 264.

12. Hans L. Trefousse, *Reconstruction: America's First Effort at Racial Democracy* (New York: Van Nostrand, 1971), 60.

13. Jill Lepore, "Birthright: What's Next for Planned Parenthood?" *New Yorker*, November 14, 2011, 48–50.

14. Lepore, "Birthright," 46.

15. Wallerstein argues that this shift began earlier, in the 1860s, in Great Britain, and Theda Skocpol says that the origins of social security can be traced back to the Civil War in the United States. I think that efforts were made, early on, to shift responsibility but that it did not generally occur until later, in part because women's suffrage made it possible for a majority of voters to support this development.

16. See Flora Davis, *Moving the Mountain: The Women's Movement in America since 1960* (New York: Simon and Schuster, 1991). Flora Davis, like many other feminist scholars, complains that women did not *do* very much with their newfound opportunity to vote. I think this view is mistaken. I think they did quite a lot but got very little credit for what they achieved.

17. Adam Gopnik, "Market Man," *New Yorker*, October 18, 2010, 83.

18. Natalie Angier, "Thirst for Fairness May Have Helped Us Survive," *New York Times*, July 5, 2011.

19. Alexander Keyssar, *The Right to Vote: The Contested History of Democracy in the United States* (New York: Basic, 2009), 31.

20. David Brooks, "The Rugged Altruists," *New York Times*, August 23, 2011.

21. Karl Marx, *The Communist Manifesto* (Chicago: Charles Kerr, 1998), 53.

22. Marx, *Communist Manifesto*, 27.

23. C. R. Fay, *Life and Labour in the Nineteenth Century* (Cambridge: Cambridge University Press, 1920), 33–34.

24. Immanuel Wallerstein, *The Modern World-System IV: Centrist Liberalism Triumphant, 1789–1914* (Berkeley: University of California Press, 2011), 132. "Reform by the state . . . would simultaneously advance economic growth (or rather the accumulation of capital) and tame the dangerous classes (by incorporating them into the citizenry and offering them a part, albeit a small part . . . of the imperial economic pie" (137).

25. US officials provide tax exemptions to charitable 501(c)(3) organizations on the condition that they engage only in "good works," providing services that the state refuses to provide so long as they promise not to engage in political activity aimed at social change. Of course, many religious organizations ignore this requirement and encourage their members to participate in social and political change: black churches in the civil rights movement; Catholic churches in support of farmworkers and against abortion and gay marriage; and evangelical churches in support of Republican candidates and against gay rights, evolution, and global warming.

26. SNCC, "The Basis of Black Power," in *American Youth in a Changing Culture*, ed. Grant S. McClellan (New York: H. W. Wilson, 1972), 271–73.

27. SNCC, "The Basis of Black Power," 273.

28. Stokely Carmichael, "A Declaration of War," in *The New Left: A Documentary History*, ed. Massimo Teodori (New York: Bobbs-Merrill, 1969), 276–78.

29. Carmichael, "A Declaration of War," 279, 282.

30. Philip Gourevitch, "Alms Dealers," *New Yorker*, October 11, 2010.

31. Alex de Waal, *Famine Crimes: Politics and the Disaster Relief Industry in Africa* (Bloomington: Indiana University Press, 1997), xvi; Michael Maren, *The Road to Hell: The Ravaging Effects of Foreign Aid and International Charity* (New York: Free Press, 1997).

32. Maren, *Road to Hell*, 161, 135.

33. De Waal, *Famine Crimes*, 212.

34. Wallerstein, *World-System Analysis*, 71.

35. Wallerstein, *World-System Analysis*, 71–72; Giovanni Arrighi, Terence K. Hopkins, and Immanuel Wallerstein, *Antisystemic Movements* (London: Verso, 1989), 34.

36. Immanuel Wallerstein, *Unthinking Social Science: The Limits of Nineteenth-Century Paradigms* (Cambridge: Polity, 1991), 36. Wallerstein suggests that social movements should be prepared to relinquish power and maneuver politically, "since it is in the process of movement, of mobilization, that the really constructive power of movements lies" (36).

12. RESTRICTIONIST SOCIAL MOVEMENTS

1. Sidney Tarrow, *Power in Movement: Social Movements and Contentious Politics* (Cambridge: Cambridge University Press, 1998), 8.

2. Tarrow, *Power in Movement*, 203. Still, he argues, "if our theories are any good, they ought to provide hints about the causal dynamics of different types of movements," presumably the ugly ones among them (204).

3. Alberto Melucci, "Ten Hypotheses in the Analysis of New Movements," in *Contemporary Italian Sociology*, ed. Diana Pinto (Cambridge: Cambridge University Press, 1981), 173.

4. William Gamson, *The Strategy of Social Protest* (Belmont, CA: Wasdsorth, 1990), 14.

5. Doug McAdam, John D. McCarthy, and Meyer Zald, "Introduction," in *Comparative Perspectives on Social Movements*, ed. Doug McAdam, John D. McCarthy, and Meyer Zald (Cambridge: Cambridge University Press, 2008), 2; Doug McAdam, "Conceptural Origins, Problems, Future Directions," in *Comparative Perspectives on Social Movements*, ed. Doug McAdam, John D. McCarthy, and Meyer Zald (Cambridge: Cambridge University Press, 2008), 29.

6. Tarrow, *Power in Movement*, 4; Suzanne Staggenborg, *Social Movements* (Oxford: Oxford University Press, 2011), 5.

7. Staggenborg, *Social Movements*, 6.

8. Staggenborg, *Social Movements*, 6; Steven M. Buechler, *Understanding Social Movements: Theories from the Classical Era to the Present* (Boulder, CO: Paradigm, 2011), 1.

9. Paul Street and Anthony Di Maggio, *Crashing the Tea Party: Mass Media and the Campaign to Remake American Politics* (Boulder, CO: Paradigm, 2011), 10.

10. Theda Skocpol and Vanessa Williams, *The Tea Party and the Remaking of Republican Conservatism* (Oxford: Oxford University Press, 2012), 6–7, 12, 22, 48–51.

11. "Editorial: Lots of Voting Limits, Little Evidence of Fraud," *USA Today*, March 19, 2012; Charlie Savage, "Holder Signals Tough Review of New State Laws on Voting," *New York Times*, December 14, 2011; Michael Cooper and Jo Craven McGinty, "Florida's New Election Law Blunts Voter Drives," *New York Times*, March 28, 2012.

12. Marc Lacey, "Arizona Candidate Challenged over English Skills," *New York Times*, January 26, 2012; Katharine Q. Seelye and Ashley Parker, "For Santorum, Trying to Tamp Down a Firestorm over Puerto Rico Remarks," *New York Times*, March 16, 2012.

13. Campbell Brown, "Planned Parenthood's Self-Destructive Behavior," *New York Times*, June 24, 2012; Robert Pear, "Senate Nears Showdown on Contraception Policy," *New York Times*, February 29, 2012; Jonathan Weisman, "Obama Backs Student in Furor with Limbaugh on Birth Control," *New York Times*, March 3, 2012; Erik Eckholm and Kim Severson, "Other States Take Notice of Measure on Abortion," *New York Times*, February 29, 2012; Robert Pear, "Senate Rejects Step Targeting Contraception," *New York Times*, March 2, 2012; Denise Grady, "Medical Nuances Drove 'No' Vote in Mississippi," *New York Times*, November 15, 2011; Erik Eckholm, "Voting on Contraception as the Legal Start to Life," *New York Times*, October 26, 2011; Sabrina Tavernise, "Shift in Virginia on Abortion Bill," *New York Times*, February 23, 2012; John Eligon and Michael Schwirtz, "In Rapes, Candidate Says, Body Can Block Pregnancy," *New York Times*, August 20, 2012.

14. Monica Davey, "The House in Indiana Passes a Bill on Unions," *New York Times*, January 26, 2012; Steven Greenhouse, "More Lockouts as Companies Battle Unions," *New York Times*, January 23, 2012.

15. A. G. Sulzberger, "Kansas Law on Sodomy Stays on Books Despite a Cull," *New York Times*, January 21, 2012.

16. Julia Preston, "State Lawmakers Outline Plans to End Birthright Citizenship, Drawing Outcry," *New York Times*, January 6, 2011; Marc Lacey, "On Immigration, Birthright Fight in U.S. Is Looming," *New York Times*, January 5, 2011; "Alabama's Bitter Harvest Was Predictable," *Manhattan Mercury*, October 20, 2011; Campbell Robertson, "Critics See Chilling Effect in Alabama Immigration Law," *New York Times*, October 28, 2011; Richard A. Oppel Jr., "Arizona, Bowing to Business, Softens Stand on Immigration," *New York Times*, March 19, 2011; Marc Lacey, "U.S. Says Arizona Sheriff Shows Pervasive Bias against Latinos," *New York Times*, December 16, 2011. One Kansas legislator suggested that gunmen in helicopters shoot illegal immigrants crossing into the United States: "If shooting these immigrating feral hogs works, maybe we have found a [solution] to the illegal immigration problem." Associated

Press, "Kansas Lawmaker Apologizes for Immigration Remark," *New York Times*, March 16, 2011.

17. Kate Zernike, "Youth Driver Limits Curb Even the Double Date," *New York Times*, August 14, 2012; Mike Males, "Ease Off on Pointless Juvenile Curfews," *Manhattan Mercury*, September 2, 2011.

18. "Enforce the Laws Ruthlessly," *Manhattan Mercury*, March 11, 2011.

19. Erik Eckholm, "Preaching Virtue of Spanking, Even as Deaths Fuel Debate," *New York Times*, November 7, 2011.

20. Eckholm, "Virtue of Spanking."

21. Eckholm "Virtue of Spanking."

22. Manny Fernandez, "Oklahomans Prepare for New Law That Will Make Guns a Common Sight," *New York Times*, October 31, 2012; Erin N. Marcus, "Gun Query Off Limits for Doctors in Florida," *New York Times*, August 9, 2011.

23. Serge Kovaleski and Campbell Robertson, "New Details Are Released in Shooting of Teenager," *New York Times*, May 18, 2012.

24. Jack Healy, "Unarmed and Gunned Down by Homeowner in His 'Castle,'" *New York Times*, October 23, 2012.

25. Healy, "Unarmed and Gunned Down."

26. Manny Fernandez, "A Face-Off outside Dallas in the Escalating Battle over Texas' Gun Culture," *New York Times*, November 11, 2013.

27. Mary Bernstein, "The Strategic Uses of Identity by the Lesbian and Gay Movement," in *The Social Movements Reader: Cases and Concepts*, ed. Jeff Goodwin and James M. Jasper (Malden, MA: Blackwell, 2003), 234.

28. Megan Moser, "Obama Is Kids' Choice Here," *Manhattan Mercury*, November 9, 2012.

13. THEORIES AND OPPORTUNITIES

1. Although democratization and the expansion of citizenries curbed "legitimate," state-sanctioned violence, did it also curb "illegitimate" violence? Perhaps. Both developments need further exploration.

2. Sidney Tarrow, *Power in Movement: Social Movements and Contentious Politics* (Cambridge: Cambridge University Press, 1998), 25. I agree. The argument here is that one has to begin with an appreciation of social change and then look at all of the social movements that shaped change.

3. Doug McAdam, John D. McCarthy, and Meyer Zald, eds., *Comparative Perspectives on Social Movements* (Cambridge: Cambridge Univeristy Press, 2008), 659.

4. Paul Burstein, Rachel Einwohner, and Jocellyn Hollander, "The Success of Social Movement Organizations on Public Policy: Some Recent Evidence and Theoretical Concerns," *Social Forces* 81 (2002): 276.

5. William Gamson, "Defining Social Movement 'Success,'" in *The Social Movements Reader: Cases and Concepts*, ed. Jeff Goodwin and James M. Jasper (Malden, MA: Blackwell, 2003), 350.

6. Jeff Goodwin and James M. Jasper, eds., *The Social Movements Reader: Cases and Concepts* (Malden, MA: Blackwell, 2003), 348.

7. McAdam, McCarthy, and Zald, *Comparative Perspectives*, 659–60; Goodwin and Jasper, *Social Movements Reader*, 347–48.

8. Goodwin and Jasper, *Social Movements Reader*, 348. However, they also assert that "social movements are one central source of social change" (4).

9. Suzanne Staggenborg, *Social Movements* (Oxford: Oxford University Press, 2011), 42–43. Elisabeth Clemens argues that because scholars relied on Michels's claim that efforts to make social change led to oligarchy, which inhibited "real" change, and because they relied on Michels and Weber's claims that "organization is the weapon of the weak in the struggle with the strong," they discounted "social movements as sources of change," particularly if they took nonbureaucratic or grassroots, democratic (nonoligarchic) organizational forms. Elisabeth S. Clemens, "Organizational Repertoires," in *The Social Movements Reader: Cases and Concepts*, ed. Jeff Goodwin and James M. Jasper (Malden, MA: Blackwell, 2003), 187–88, 191.

10. David S. Meyer and Sidney Tarrow, "A Movement Society: Contentious Politics for a New Century," in *The Social Movement Society: Contentious Politics for a New Century,* eds. David S. Meyer and Sidney Tarrow (Lanham, MD: Rowman and Littlefield, 1998), 4.

11. Giovanni Arrighi, Terence K. Hopkins, and Immanuel Wallerstein, *Antisystemic Movements* (London: Verso, 1989), 30; Immanuel Wallerstein, *Historical Capitalism with Capitalist Civilization* (London: Verso, 1991), 66; Immanuel Wallerstein, *World-System Analysis: An Introduction* (Durham, NC: Duke University Press, 2004), 65; Immanuel Wallerstein, *Unthinking Social Science: The Limits of Nineteenth-Century Paradigms* (Cambridge: Polity, 1991), 20–21.

12. Ralph Turner and Lewis Killian, *Collective Behavior*, 3rd ed. (Englewood Cliffs, NJ: Prentice-Hall, 1987), 3; William Kornhauser, *The Politics of Mass Society* (New York: Free Press, 2008), 212; Steven M. Buechler, *Understanding Social Movements: Theories from the Classical Era to the Present* (Boulder, CO: Paradigm, 2011), 128; Sidney Tarrow, *Power in Movement* (Cambridge: Cambridge University Press, 1994), 3–4.

13. Buechler, *Understanding Social Movements*, 113; Staggenborg, *Social Movements*, 18.

14. Staggenborg, *Social Movements*, 19; John D. McCarthy and Meyer N. Zald, "Social Movement Organizations," in *Comparative Perspectives on Social Movements*, ed. Doug McAdam, John D. McCarthy, and Meyer Zald (Cambridge: Cambridge Univeristy Press, 2008), 172; Buechler, *Understanding Social Movements*, 121; Nella Van Dyke and Sarah A. Soule, "Structural Social Change and the Mobilizing Effect of Threat: Explaining Levels of Patriot and Milita Organizing in the United States," in *The Social Movements Reader: Cases and Concepts*, ed. Jeff Goodwin and James M. Jasper (Malden, MA: Blackwell, 2003), 38; Goodwin and Jasper, *Social Movements Reader*, 1.

15. Buechler, *Understanding Social Movements*, 59.

16. David A. Snow, Daniel M. Cress, Liam Downey, and Andrew W. Jones, "'Disrupting the Quotidian': Reconceptualizing the Relationship between Breakdown and the Emergence of Collective Action," *Mobilization* 3 (1998): 5.

17. Buechler, *Understanding Social Movements*, 61, 62.

18. Buechler, *Understanding Social Movements*, 53, 62.

19. As Steven Buechler observes, "Such energy may lack a clear focus and its imports and consequences may become difficult to predict." Buechler, *Understanding Social Movements*, 55.

20. Arrighi, Hopkins, and Wallerstein, *Antisystemic Movements*, 29; Immanuel Wallerstein, *The Modern World-System: Capitalist Agriculture and the Origins of the European World-Economy in the Sixteenth Century* (New York: Academic, 1974), 357; Wallerstein, *Historical Capitalism*, 65; Wallerstein, *World-Systems Analysis*, 64.

21. Buechler, *Understanding Social Movements*, 104–5.

22. Charles Tilly, *From Mobilization to Revolution* (Reading, MA: Addison-Wesley, 1978), 48; Buechler, *Understanding Social Movements*, 127.

23. Buechler, *Understanding Social Movements*, 111.

24. Buechler, *Understanding Social Movements*, 106. Not everyone climbed aboard this theoretical bandwagon, Piven and Cloward among them.

25. Buechler, *Understanding Social Movements*, 109–56; Staggenborg, *Social Movements*, 17–25.

26. Robert K. Schaeffer, *Red Inc.: Dictatorship and the Development of Capitalism in China, 1949 to the Present* (Boulder, CO: Paradigm, 2012), 174–75.

27. Buechler, *Understanding Social Movements*, 115.

28. William Gamson, *The Strategy of Social Protest*, 2nd ed. (Belmont, CA: Wadsworth, 1990), 8.

29. Max Weber, *Economy and Society: An Outline of Interpretive Sociology* (Berkeley: University of California Press, 1978), 973.

30. Frances Fox Piven and Richard A. Cloward, *Poor People's Movements: Why They Succeed, How They Fail* (New York: Vintage, 1979), 5, 284; Buechler, *Understanding Social Movements*, 39.

31. Piven and Cloward, *Poor People's Movements*, 97. "In [Piven and Cloward's] reading of poor people's movements, once organization appears, effective protest dies," Steven Buechler observes. Buechler, *Understanding Social Movements*, 39; Staggenborg, *Social Movements*, 35.

32. Piven and Cloward, *Poor People's Movements*, 77.

33. Robert K. Schaeffer, *Understanding Globalization: The Social Consequences of Political, Economic, and Environmental Change* (Lanham, MD: Rowman and Littlefield, 2003), 260–61, 263–65.

34. Schaeffer, *Understanding Globalization*, 268–69.

35. Buechler, *Understanding Social Movements*, 37, 179–80.

36. Albert O. Hirschman, *Exit, Voice, and Loyalty: Responses to Decline in Firms, Organizations, and States* (Cambridge, MA: Harvard University Press, 1970).

37. Schaeffer, *Understanding Globalization*, 269–70.

38. Buechler, *Understanding Social Movements*, 75–76.

39. William G. Martin, "Introduction: The Search for Antisystemic Movements," in *Making Waves: Worldwide Social Movements, 1750–2005*, ed. William G. Martin (Boulder, CO: Paradigm, 2008), 1.

40. Martin Luther King Jr., *Nonviolence and Racial Justice* (Philadelphia: Quaker Press of Friends General Conference, 2008), 9.

Index

Index

Vandenburg, Arthur, 76
Veterans of Foreign Wars, 173
Viet Minh, 55
Vietnam, 60, 67, 72, 148, 150, 163, 176, 178, 185, 202
Vietnamese Communist Party, 54
Virginia, 69
Voting Rights Act of 1965, 145, 152

Wallerstein, Immanuel, 24, 43, 46, 97, 168, 172, 193, 194, 197, 211, 213, 215
Walton, John, 80
War for Southern Independence, 173
War of 1812, 42, 111, 113, 114, 185
Warren, Earl, 143
Wartime Relocation Authority, 120
Washington, George, 29
Weatherman, 170, 219
Weber, Max, 9, 32, 33, 35, 204, 212, 213, 215–218
West Bank, 71
western Europe, 139
West Germany, 72, 80
West Virginia, 69
Whigs, 70, 192
White Citizens' Council, 144
Whitney, Anita, 117
Wilkerson, Isabel, 141
Wilson, David Sloan, 191
Wilson, Woodrow, 48, 49, 106, 107, 116, 117, 166

Winthrop, James, 31
Wolin, Sheldon, 146
Woman Suffrage Association, 104
Wood, Gordon S., 25, 37
World War I, 40, 48, 50, 51, 66, 70, 106, 112, 115, 117, 123, 129, 140, 164, 177, 195
World War II, 5, 17, 39, 51, 54, 55, 67, 70, 75, 105, 112, 119, 123, 124, 132, 140, 141, 166, 185, 201
World War Veterans, 116
World Zionist Congress, 47

Yeltsin, Boris, 151
Yorktown, 41
Young, Alfred, 37
Young Europe, 46
Young Italy, 46
Young Men's Christian Association, 173
Yousafzai, Malala, 164
Yugoslavia, 59, 61, 62, 73, 76, 77, 81, 86, 94, 176
Yunis, Muhammad, 188

Zaire, 61
Zald, Meyer, 210, 212
Zimmerman, George, 204
Zine al-Abidine, 91
Zionist movement, 54, 175, 182
Zionists, 47
zoot suit riots, 166

About the Author

Robert Schaeffer is professor of global sociology at Kansas State University. He worked for many years in labor, peace, and environmental movement organizations and now teaches classes on social movements, global social change, and ethnic conflict and war. He is the editor of *War in the World-System* (1990), author of *Warpaths: The Politics of Partition* (1990), *Power to the People: Democratization around the World* (1997), *Understanding Globalization: The Social Consequences of Political, Economic, and Environmental Change* (1997, 2003, 2005, 2009), *Severed States: Dilemmas of Democracy in a Divided World* (1999), and *Red Inc.: Dictatorship and the Development of Capitalism in China, 1949 to the Present* (2012), and coauthor, with Torry D. Dickinson, of *Fast Forward: Work, Gender and Protest in a Changing World* (2001) and *Transformations: Feminist Pathways to Global Change* (2008).